BRIDELESS IN WEMBLEY

IN SEARCH OF INDIAN ENGLAND

SANJAY SURI

summersdale

BRIDELESS IN WEMBLEY

First published by Penguin Books India in 2006

This edition published in 2007 by Summersdale Publishers Ltd.

Summersdale Publishers Ltd
46 West Street
Chichester
West Sussex
PO19 1RP
UK

www.summersdale.com

Printed and bound in Great Britain.

ISBN: 1-84024-609-X
ISBN 13: 978-1-84024-609-4

Aditi,

Just save these stories.

Sanjay

13/09/07

ABOUT THE AUTHOR

Sanjay Suri is Europe editor for the Inter Press Service news agency. He contributes to the CNN-IBN television channel and to *Outlook*, a weekly news magazine published in India. He studied at Stanford University, the University of Delhi and the London School of Economics.

ACKNOWLEDGEMENTS

I must thank everyone in this book whose stories I came to share. They would never have been written without Krishan Chopra who thought first at Penguin India that they could sit together in a book. And not least, my thanks to Jennifer Barclay and Lucy York at Summersdale who thought of offering these stories to readers in Britain, and then editing them so watchfully.

CONTENTS

INTRODUCTION

Along introduction is usually pre-chapter suicide, but before I hand this introduction over to the great Gurdev Singh Manku, a quick word or two about what this book is not. It does not offer dining-table wisdom of the 'caught between two worlds' variety, enough to get anyone to abandon a more than averagely decent dinner. Nor is it a history book; I do not have a first chapter called 'Early Arrivals' followed by another called 'Settling In'.

The way Indians were being Indian, someone had to take notes. So this is a book of stories. Stories arising from hanging around people living their idea of 'Indian' in Britain. My principal skill in putting these stories together has been a lack of imagination; I could never have thought up the people in them.

I leave the introduction to Manku, or Manku ji I should say, to give him that due Indian suffix for the respectable that stands somewhere between a mister and a title. My own introduction would be too prosaic before Manku ji's poetic expressions of migration. I ran into him at the Redbridge Indian Social Klub. My friend Mr Bhandari, retired from a long career in Ford where he rose to a managerial position, had invited me to a meeting of the Klub in Redbridge, east of east London.

'Why do you spell club with a "k",' I asked Mr Bhandari; as manager in an English company he'd be more a mister than a ji.

'Because when you spell with a "k", we can shorten the name to "RISK". We are elderly people in this Klub, you know, and they are always at risk.'

If Wodehouse could make the disgruntled 'gruntled', and in Bollywood a night can be a 'nite', Bhandari too can make a club a 'Klub'.

Bhandari, who chaired the meeting in his usual black blazer and red tie that announced his managerial past, quickly invited Mankuji to address about fifty of us, mostly RISK members. From under a bold turban Mankuji took the mike with a challenging glint in the eye, and began to read from a piece of paper:

Ik duniya nai vasavaange
Mitran de samne baith ke,
Te ik gal sabh nu samjhavange,
Yaro Punjab nu London nai ban-ana,
Asi London nu Punjab banavange.

(We will create a brave new world
We will sit with our friends
And make one thing loud and clear
Friends, we'll never let Punjab become London,
We will turn London into Punjab.)

The poem went down well, the applause was undiluted by politeness. Everyone wanted more, and Manku was ready.

Goreya maein nai jaana
Chhad ke tera desh,
Goreya maein nai jaana
Chhad ke tera desh.

(Listen, you white guys
I won't leave your country now

Listen, you white guys
I won't leave your country now.)

Veleyan nu ethay roti mildi,
Dil vich fikr nai koi,
Khao piyo mauj udao'
Is da jikr nai koi.
Rajai le lao,
Sarana le lao,
Ya pher le lao khes,
Goreya main nai jana
Chhad ke tera desh…

(The jobless find plenty to eat
And find little to worry about.
Just eat, drink and be merry,
Nobody bothers what you do.
Wake up carefree, sleep in peace,
Just rest easy, do as you like.
Listen, you white guys,
I won't leave your country now…)

Rang roop da vehm nai koi,
Paaven hove kaala.
Ethay jamna, ethay marna,
Jeeja hove ya sala.
Bai final gal tenu samjhavan,
Toon chal ja pardes goreya,
Main nai jana chhad ke tera desh.

(Nobody cares about your colour,
Whatever it may be.
We will live here, we will die here,
Brother, or brother-in-law

Let me say this once finally,
You leave and go if you like, white guys,
But listen to me,
I'll never leave your country now.)

What Manku's poems didn't say is that the country back there doesn't leave you either. But that's between the characters and these stories, and anyone who cares to read them.

LEICESTER

Bestard

'**N**od twice when you see Silva.' So Dhanjibhai Atwal told me he'd been instructed to say if he ever wanted to get to England. He repeated that command a little dramatically, like he'd never forget it. It had after all been his passport to Britain. In 1956 he might still have made it without that little book with his photograph on it. But he couldn't without nodding to Silva.

Dhanjibhai put on his glasses as he spoke, like he was looking through them at the past not at me. Dhanjibhai, I'd been told by a friend, was Leicester's memory, though Leicester was beginning to forget that, and him. Few people ever dropped in to ask him where he came from, or where Leicester had come from – Indian Leicester, that is. He knew, he was there at the start. But founding fathers, after they've done their founding and their fathering, usually retire into endless repetitions of their own story. Life and Leicester have moved on, and who cares that its Indian story could have begun with someone nodding to Silva en route from Bombay to Heathrow.

I'd driven to Leicester from London, as I'd planned not to. If I could have got out in time I'd have taken a Bharat Coaches bus from Southall, the sub-National Express that connects all the properly Indian parts of Britain – Southall, Slough, Luton,

Leicester, Birmingham, Wolverhampton, Leeds. And in a concession to Pakistanis, Bradford. Its timetable at its depot on Western Avenue in Southall is a fairly accurate map of the Indian immigration story in Britain. That Southall bus station has smartened up a little since I first used it; it's now lost that fragrance arising from urine on concrete that is mandatory at all small bus stations in Punjab. It now has breatheable-in toilets. The coaches take you where you really want to go. A good Southall Indian only works at Heathrow; by way of holidaying he sits on a bus and goes to another Indian. So much more to talk about this way, better food, and think of the savings. For seeing places, there's television.

Like all good Indians, I'm starting my story with what I did not do. Once upon a time I never...

So I drove up the M1, the Asian corridor as we brownies like to call it among ourselves, because it takes you past Watford, Luton, Bedford and into the Midlands where we came to park, multiply and settle. I've taken that drive often. If from Wembley I travel to Leicester for its Indian experience, that must give the National Front a firm sense of much work ahead in this English town whose white is wearing off quite rapidly. Partly because our brethren move in, and partly because seeing them, white English move out. The city council has devised all sorts of ways of putting that politely, but the translations required are really quite simple. 'Increasingly multicultural' is one favourite; sometimes you hear a voice trained in covering despair, when it's a white council woman saying it. Back in Wembley I'm in an India that's half an hour's drive from London, unlike friends in India who are eight flying hours away. But Wembley does not concentrate its Indianness as Leicester can around Belgrave Road. The homes here are smaller, closer, and they all lead onto that one big road. It's where Indians really are community. Perfect gossip conditions. London, even Wembley, can't offer anything comparable. Wembley Indians are not busybody enough, never mind those central London Indians, who are only differently coloured internationalists. For an insufficiently globalised Indian, Leicester's the place.

In Leicester, I turned off the ring road, since Leicester is town enough to have one, over the Belgrave flyover and down into Belgrave Road, where you can smell the bhajias, or pakoras as you must call them if you started out in north India, on those infrequent days when English weather is decent enough to let you lower your car window. The drive down that flyover always felt like a touchdown into this Indian extension. Straight past the sari stores and jewellery shops, and yes, the veggie eats since this is Gujarati land, I continued into Melton Road, and looped right into Doncaster Road where Dhanjibhai lived.

Doncaster Road is an English-looking street in the usual way. The long row of houses was joined under red tiled roofs that appeared to continue all the way. Invisible walls separated the little drawing rooms underneath. The one Dhanjibhai invited me into was an almost straight repeat of most Gujarati drawing rooms in the Belgrave area of Leicester. It was small – about ten feet by eight – with a sofa in the bay window and the regulation Gujarati paper flowers counting years on the sill above the site of what was intended by the original builders to be a fireplace. By the flowers sat a foothigh Ganesha, 'Ganesha the elephant-headed god' as the council no doubt explains in its multicultural mission. The faded sandalwood garland around the peeling gold paint on the clay made this a quite elderly Ganesha. In that little house the god had not brought the prosperity it was intended to. But stay there he must, because you never know. And, because it could always have been worse; what if you had never migrated, for instance. Above Ganesha the family pictures looked down into the room. All families are different, but for some reason their pictures all look the same, especially when you place them about that height on the wall.

Some of those picture frames presented a younger Dhanjibhai posing with other Atwal additions and multiplications. But Dhanjibhai himself was here; I had followed him in from the front door, and he now sat me down on the sofa by his side. He still looked young for an eighty-something. His small frame and squarish head would always give him a boyish look. Past a certain stage what counts is the 'pass-for' age. Dhanjibhai's pass-for age could be 58, particularly in those moments of relived happiness when smiles creased his face but erased the years.

It was with a smile that he began to tell me of his flight from Bombay to London.

'Do you know, I used to be one of Gandhi's soldiers of peace, a *satyagrahi*, but I am from Bombay, don't forget, and we know our way around. I paid 2,800 rupees for my ticket to London. That was in 1956, the days of the Suez crisis. The ticket was for 1,300 rupees but, you know, with agent and all it came to 2,800. Of course, now they take hundreds of thousands. Then you could still go to England easily compared to now. It was a free country. But the British government had written that too many illiterate people are coming there and they cannot find work, and so they should be stopped.

'We were a group of four. We had bought our tickets, you know, in the black market. We met at Santa Cruz airport to take a BOAC flight via Karachi, Cairo and Frankfurt to Heathrow. But my ticket was for Nairobi. The agent had told us he would take care of it and someone in Karachi would change the ticket to one for London.

'But when we landed at Karachi, we got into trouble. The customs people took our passports and kept our bags on one side. They opened my bags, they were looking for addresses in England.

'"You are going to England! We will throw you behind the bars!" an officer shouted at us. I argued with him. He cannot arrest us, I told him. We are just in transit for Nairobi.

'Then one old man came out of an office. He looked at me and began to walk slowly to one side. I ran after him and shouted "*Salaam waleikhum*". He seemed holy, like God's own man, *Khuda ka banda* to me, I told him that. I said to him, we are in trouble, we want help. I told him what happened. He said to me I cannot help you, you will have to go to jail. But then he looked around and said there is a chance. He said, talk to a customs man called Silva. He said, nod twice when you see Silva.

'I returned, and saw Silva. I nodded to him twice, then many times. Silva did not see me nodding, I think. He asked me, who are you? Again I nodded twice. He got very angry. I said to him, "I am from Bombay, don't you remember me? Why didn't you come to receive me?" I am from Bombay, so that is what I said. Silva didn't seem to like it. He threw me out of the queue, and he said to me, go and stand to one side.

'I waited all day. Then at six in the evening, after the duty changed, Silva came to me. He told me I can get my passport and ticket to London. He said that, and then he just waited. I said, I want the passport and ticket first. He said I would have to go to a hotel and take the flight next morning. The other three fellows and I were taken to a hotel. There the old man came to see us – you know, that *Khuda ka banda*. I fell at the old man's feet, I literally begged him to help us. He said, don't worry, reach the airport at five in the morning. I gave him ten pounds, and he said, no, that is too much. I told him it is for his grandchildren, I told him I love his grandchildren. He was very happy.

'The next day we went to the airport and we found Silva waiting for us. I took him to one side and offered him a pack of cigarettes. Have a smoke, I said. He opened the packet. Inside I had put one five-pound note and one ten-pound note. He was very happy. He took me to a counter and gave me my passport and the ticket. The ticket was not for Nairobi, the ticket was for London.

'We arrived at Heathrow via Cairo and Frankfurt. There the police officer told us to stand to one side. He said he will arrest us because we have come here to settle. Then he called one army officer who had served in India. The officer came and abused us in Hindi. He called me a dog, *"kutta ka bachha"*. I told him to calm down. You stayed in our country for two hundred and fifty years, I said, we did not abuse you. I said we were all going to Nairobi, we have just come to see London for one week. He did not know I am from Bombay.

'Then one senior officer came. I told him I am a cloth trader and my companions are also here on business. We will see the place, see if we can do business and then go away in one week. I was wearing a Gandhi cap, and he was very impressed. Then one lady came. They talked and after some time they let us go. My friend Kunwarjibhai was waiting for us outside. He had come from Wednesbury to take us to his house. We went to Victoria Station to take a train to Wednesbury. And do you know something? I have never seen Victoria Station again.'

Some time after moving to Leicester the Gandhian must have taken over from the man of the world, as trained in Bombay. It started, Dhanjibhai said, after he heard the story of Jenabhai. 'I remember that day,' he said, and again he seemed to look a long way back through his glasses, this time to the story he'd heard. 'There was heavy snow – foot and a half. Nobody was outside, nobody. That was the day on which Jenabhai appeared. When I heard what he had gone through, I knew I now have to do something.'

Jenabhai too had arrived at Heathrow on a BOAC flight. His ticket had been arranged by an agent in Bombay who had made sure Jenabhai was not carrying any evidence on him – not even an address in Britain – that could raise an immigration officer's suspicion that he had come to settle there. He was told that the only word he should speak was 'Leicester'.

'Jenabhai told us a stewardess took him to the BOAC counter at Heathrow. Then BOAC staff called a taxi to take him to St Pancras Station in London. He had some pounds and shillings with him. The driver took Jenabhai to the ticketmaster at St Pancras and asked him to put Jenabhai on a train to Leicester. The ticketmaster found a passenger who would help Jenabhai get off at Leicester. At the London Road Station in Leicester the man put him in the hands of the stationmaster, who called a taxi to take him to Stafford Road, you know, very near this house. And they were all English people, all English strangers who were helping Jenabhai.

'But after Jenabhai got to Stafford Road he did not know what to do. He had never seen snow, he had never felt so cold. After some time one white woman came. Jenabhai, who had taken shelter inside a telephone booth, ran out shouting, "I Indian, I Indian". The woman was frightened by this black man in the snow. She ran away, and she was screaming. She went to a laundry on Stafford Road where an Indian, Hirabhai, worked. So Hirabhai came to the telephone booth and found Jenabhai. And you know what he did? He slapped Jenabhai. Then Jenabhai had to explain he was not attacking the woman. So Hirabhai took him to 63 Loughborough Road, where a lot of us Indians lived. There Jenabhai met Jeevanbhai, who was from the same village in Gujarat. They gave him hot food, and brandy and a bed in a room with fireplace.

'But, you see, the question was this: how many Jenabhais are there? And what are we going to do about them? There are Jenabhais coming in every day. We decided to do something that very week. We went to the stationmaster in Leicester and gave him 63 Loughborough Road as an address for all lost Indians. Then we took a train to St Pancras and left the same address with the stationmaster's office there. Then we went to

Heathrow airport to give the address as a sort of help centre for any Indian who needs it. Many people came to us after that.'

To an Indian arriving in England without an address, the usually recommended way, just Leicester became an address. Then destination, and then home.

Dhanjibhai Atwal had managed to get to Heathrow and, past it, to Leicester. Jenabhai had followed, and then more Jenabhais. But you couldn't just get to Britain and be. The 'what next' question wasn't easy, and it rose early. Dhanjibhai was with me and wasn't; he had slid back half a century. That was when he had lived, the rest was just an extension of the man who had lived then.

'The British people, they used to think we are a bunch of dark coolies from the Raj days,' Dhanjibhai said. 'They used to think we are mad, we have no brains, we cannot do proper work.' The first Indians were only given work that the British were too spoilt to touch, and it was as coolies that many worked, Dhanjibhai with them. Like other early Indians at 63 Loughborough Road, he negotiated long years searching for better work, and found mostly abuse. Until rescue came in the shape of the engineering company J.W. Bastard & Co. That unfortunately named company proved more than fortunate for Indians. It would make workers out of coolies.

'You must know how we managed to get a foothold in this city,' Dhanjibhai said. 'Otherwise all this history will die with me.' His wife had brought us some tea as he talked. It had rapidly settled to room temperature, and served mostly to provide the picture of talking over tea. 'They do not understand,' he said, pointing towards Belgrave Road and its Indian continuation, Melton Road. 'All this could not have happened if we had not tried so hard then.' And it could not have happened without that Englishman Alberts, Dhanjibhai said, or without that man he remembered only as 'Punjabi Bhai'. Like all Gujaratis, Dhanjibhai added 'bhai' to names, even when he could not remember the name of this Punjabi chap. I too had learnt over years to add 'bhai' (brother) to every Gujarati male name. It was the Gujarati declaration of every man a brother, a 'ji' with the respect but with less deference and distance. It was tradition also to add 'ben' (sister) to women's names, but that for a male is a trickier addition. Besides, it suggests an age above youth, and you wouldn't want to suggest that to a woman, or to announce safety from yourself. Not adding a 'ben' is not necessarily a signal of dangerous intent, but why rule out those sometimes delicious tensions through this vaguely homely tradition of adding safety titles to a name?

Dhanjibhai and his friends had been working as coolies at a timber yard in Leicester, like all the other Indians they knew, until they ran into Alberts.

'He was the manager of the spinning mill on Frog Island. He gave work to one Punjabi bhai. The Punjabi bhai was the only Indian we knew who had a proper job, he was not a coolie. So we spoke to Punjabi bhai, we asked him to help some of us. So he spoke to Alberts, and Alberts agreed to take two more Indians. He decided he would train them for three months in the mill. You know what we did? We sent two of our men who had already worked in mills in Navasari in Gujarat. The men picked up in two days what they would have learnt in three months' training. Punjabi bhai could not believe it. Alberts could not believe it.

'At the end of the second day the two men told the rest that Alberts had in their presence said things like "very nice" and "very fine". Alberts asked for more Indians to come and work at the mill, so more of our men joined. I also joined. We all taught each other. We used to work on two, even four machines at a time. We would work at night, go on working.

We stayed away from the unions. These British, they work with their mouths, we worked with our hands.'

It worked. Sixty more Indians joined within months, Dhanjibhai said. The factory began to work three shifts, its balance sheets began to balance a little at first and then to unbalance happily. British workers used to complain about working conditions, the Indians were ready to work in any conditions.

'You know, that year when Christmas came, we arranged a party. We called Alberts and his wife, we booked a nice room in Granby Hotel. We decided to present his wife with a gold necklace. We contributed one pound each, some even gave two. Myself, I gave two. When Alberts and his family arrived, we gave them a VIP reception. We gave his wife a gold necklace and we gave his daughter roses. Alberts put the necklace around his wife's neck. Then he gave a speech. He said thank you to us. Then he said something we were not expecting. He said that in the New Year he would take two hundred more workers. He said we could do in one week what a British worker does in one month. He said, the British had ruled India but they did not tell us about your great culture, what you are, and what you can achieve. He said, your work is like magic, I did not know you are all so intelligent. He said the production has doubled, he said the spinning mill had come out of its losses.'

'We were so grateful,' Dhanjibhai said. 'So we said this company is not Bastard. It is Bestard.'

The story spread. 'There was an annual meeting of managers from all factories of the region. We know that Alberts made a speech there praising us Indian workers sky high. After that everything changed. One time we used to be turned away from factory gates, they used to call us mad people. Now they started inviting us in, they would say, come in, we'll sort you out. Then Alberts called a meeting of Indian workers in the canteen of J. W. Bastard. He told us we need workers in the north, in Lancashire and Yorkshire. He told me he will get our people work, but he said we must not let him down. We said, we will never let you down. So groups of our workers began to go north, fifteen people, twenty people at a time.

'People wrote to their families that there is work, come. So people came in one flight after another, and there were no complaints. Why would there be complaints? In the factory that Alberts had, our people would work, you know, eighteen hours at a time even. They would never ask for more. But Alberts would give us two pints of beer free as bonus at the end of the day. I used to talk to Alberts all the time. I took in many, many people. And to our people I said, work hard and help others from your own country. People from mills background came and they succeeded. I used to try and help people so they could work twenty-six weeks in one place. After that they could register on the Labour Exchange and work anywhere.'

Dhanjibhai became supervisor. He did OK working for himself and for the British firm, but he began to work more and more also for the planeloads of Indians flying in. He was worker, fixer and leader. 'I know how to do things for others because I was a *satyagrahi* with Gandhiji. But I know how to do things for myself because I'm from Bombay, I know how to play the game.'

Shires' Share

Leicester lost a little England and gained a little America with the opening of The Shires. Shops flattened out to make way for the mall. Another step in the serial surrender to jeans, burgers and Madonna. Only cricket now holds out against baseball; and football and rugby have not combined into an inter-planetary looking match in the style of American football. It is now tragically normal to go to the mall in Britain, and suggest to the unknown that they should have a nice day. But the opening of The Shires didn't just change the appearance of Leicester, and its style; it transformed the fundamentals of its existence. From a producing city, Leicester has turned into a consuming city. The chimneys have gone cold. The town has stopped manufacturing but it can still buy, and switch to this new way of moving goods around. Because you buy, others buy – mostly import now – to sell to you, and advertise to convince you how much you need the unnecessary. Goods move, money moves, and it's a job for quite a few doing all this. Leicester, like the rest of Britain, does not make to sell, it borrows to buy. The Shires stands at the heart of Leicester, and its new economy.

It has become the official city magnet to draw in people and their money. And because a covered American mall is also a smart place, Leicester can begin to feel good about itself again. Feeling good and moving goods are not always separate things – so America was teaching the world, and now it was Leicester's turn.

The Shires is not quite as big as the typical American mall – what is? – but it's American to detail. The sky was a sharp blue this Saturday; its brightness filtered through the stretching glass roof and bounced off its walls to light up the bustling faces of shoppers below. The English high street is a cold place from where you dip in and out of variously heated stores. American cover made shopping snug and sensible; it brought the street indoors. The mall was to the high street like the American burger to the English sandwich; the Americans had simply heated it into a global business.

As I descended with the light down the 'scenic lift' from the roof-level parking into the arcade below, The Shires seemed to have out-Americaned the Americans. Not in the design; it had the usual square kiosks selling coffee and sunglasses, alternating with benches down the central arcade, with shops on the sides and an entrance or two into a huge chain store that always surprises you with unexpected space. The difference lay in what retailers like to call 'footfall'. It's hard to see such crowds in an American mall, maybe they have too much space, maybe even too many malls. Down here, every minute you stood still you'd be in someone's way.

All of Leicester comes to The Shires at some time. 'All of Leicester' is that multiculturally varied lot; Leicester is advertised now as the city of diversity, and this morning The Shires had drawn all of its diversity to feed into that busy footfall. I found myself making way for white people, black people, Chinese-looking people, Asians of the subcontinental sort, or simply Asians, as most Brits still like to say. Everyone was here under that same piece of sky available through the glass roof, a perfect camera picture of multicultural multitudes. Such a snapshot model it seemed of the way a dream world could be, if an all-are-one is the sort of world you dream of.

I parked myself on a bench across from JD Sports. I planned to be there five hours, until 5 p.m., carrying out what I dared to call to myself a rough quantitative survey, since I wouldn't have to face a methodology lecturer afterwards. I wanted to see how many came to The Shires with their ethnic own, and how many with others. I'd write down the number of people in each mixed group, and who they ethnically were. I would of course never know just how many from which group had wandered into the mall relative to their numbers in the city. I was not pretending that an accurate cross-section of Leicester had set out to parade itself before the approved researcher. If a particular group was less or more inclined to come shopping here than another, and its members mixed less or more with others, what appeared at The Shires would be inaccurate to that extent. But the mall seemed a random enough place to see who might step out in mixed ethnic company.

The first minute was promising. I counted 72 persons passing between me and JD Sports. In the next, 63. Other sample minutes produced mostly between these numbers. If 65 was an average, I would look at 3,900 people in an hour, and close to 20,000 over five hours. No doubt many people would walk by more than once, no doubt later in the afternoon the footfall could lessen, and absolutely no doubt at all that my concentration would fail now and then. But my absent-mindedness would be random too, and blacks and Indians were not more likely to walk in together at 4 p.m. than at two. I figured I wouldn't count a mixed group more than once.

Of course, this measure of multiculturalism, or the lack of it, was purely pigmental, or arose from other visibly ethnic appearances like the 'Chinese' look. Awkward thoughts, these, and an ugly word, 'pigment'. But the debate over multiculturalism rests on them, just as its failure arises from them. Pigment makes peoples out of people, politics out of appearances and, don't we know, prejudices out of differences.

But a sharing of space rather than togetherness was all I was seeing from my bench minute after counting minute. The Shires brought people together, but in an apart way. Almost every group was single-ethnic coded. Group after group from different ethnicities appeared, but almost never different ethnicities within a group. Everything appeared normal, and nothing seemed right, at least not as they said it was in multicultural Leicester.

A white girl in a kilt came to sit on the backrest by my side, boots on bench. She was calling out to her friends, all white, on the first floor walkway in English I struggled to follow. Three Asian girls passed by between me and JD, then another three; there's something about girls going shopping in threes. I reminded myself that I was there to note just the colour coding of passing groups.

But it wasn't remarkable that the white girl who would not use a bench as a bench was talking only to white girls. Or that the threes were all-Asian threes. That's the way it is; it just happens not to be the way the slogans go. In multicultural Leicester, togetherness seemed all closed within a colour.

Over five hours I scanned perhaps 12,000 to 15,000 people. Through this I counted only 44 people in 12 mixed groups. A black guy with a white girl here, an Indian youngster with some Chinese-looking friends there – the rare few sharing more than the roof. Most of these mixed groups were clearly university students, and I was beginning to feel gloomy enough to ask how long this campus-induced hanging out would last. Everyone else came and went with their ethnic own. If this observation was valid, we were talking zero point zero zero something by way of multicultural Leicester.

That people stick to their own is commonplace, you see that every day, everywhere. What struck me this afternoon was the near completeness of that separation. 'Multicultural Leicester' had declared itself different. But Leicester did not appear a multicultural city, only a city of adjacent cultures. Perhaps not even that; just variously monocultural.

With so little to note by way of cross-cultural togetherness, I found myself making the most idle observations instead. White people, I found, walked a good deal faster than Asians. When they walked at the same speed, white people took longer steps. White people mostly looked ahead and moved forward efficiently, like they were going somewhere; Asians looked sideways a good deal more, and walked with more energy lost in sideward sway. Asians walked like they thought they were in a smart place, white people walked like they were in just some place. Asians walked like they would like to be looked at, the whites looked like they didn't care.

Among Asians, no one looked around more than single males; they were there for the shoppers, not the shopping. Indians had an eye for one another, the whites seemed more self-contained. White or non-white, there seemed a higher number of single gender groups, particularly female; girls obviously liked going shopping with girls. Girls in groups usually carried shopping bags; in male groups very few seemed to carry any, nothing like a bag in hand to make a guy boring, or so the guy population seems to think. Whites touched one another only when they were a couple; Asians touched one another a lot more outside coupledom, but almost never when a couple. Many Asian girls linked arms, I saw no white girls who did. Those who came alone were mostly white.

A lot more Indians had teenaged children with them. Many of the Muslim women came with small children. Asian parents kept a close eye on children; white parents let the kids keep an eye on them. Between me and JD Sports that afternoon, all sorts of commonplace patterns that had congealed into clichés appeared and went their way.

About my final observation that afternoon as I got up to leave at 5 p.m., and no earlier, was that no wooden bench is meant to be sat upon that long.

Give Me Ghetto

I wasn't expecting to step onto a metal sheet when Mrs Barot opened the door. She saw my surprise over this metal doormat. 'It's these boys,' she said. 'They had been throwing fire inside and they used to put shit through the letter box. So I put this iron sheet and I sealed the letter box.' She'd obviously been saying this to visitors before, matter-of-fact, like it was just sensible to let shit land on a tin sheet, not a welcoming rug.

My friend Sheetal Singh Gill and I had dropped in at the Barots' house in Northfields, just about a mile or so out from the Indian heart of Leicester around Belgrave Road and Melton Road. But it's a long mile. Northfields is mostly white working class, which is fine if you're white and working class, but the Barots had begun to feel stranded here, as if in hostile land. Gill had lately been very concerned about them. Gill, among the early migrants from Hoshiarpur in Punjab, drove a taxi for a living but his heart was in the job of getting concerned. Which had made him, of course, an early member of the old Indian Workers Association, whose left of centre views had migrated nicely from Punjab. Gill had been trying to help the Barots for a while, without much success.

A few steps into the house, our feet now on carpet, we sat down to wait for the husband Kanubhai Barot. He came downstairs on a banister lift. One way or another, his wife said, he had been unwell ever since they moved into this house.

Mr Barot seemed in his late sixties. Gill had told me he had retired now from many active years in the Indian community. Since he came to Leicester in 1978, he had been joint secretary at the Shree Sanatan Mandir, one of the bigger Hindu temples clustered around Belgrave Road, and then general secretary of the Gujarat Hindu Association, that umbrella organisation of the many Gujarati associations in Leicester. When too many Indian groups get busy close to one another, someone always gets busy putting them all under an umbrella. It is final evidence of irreconcilable differences presented as collective success.

Barot spent years at the Gujarat Hindu Association making things happen right through the annually packed Hindu calendar where many of the groups got together at least sometimes. He edited two Gujarati magazines – *Amay Gujarati* (Proud to be Gujarati) and *Sanatan Sandesh* (Universal Message) – and was vice-chairman of the Belgrave Neighbourhood Centre, the busiest Gujarati meeting place in Belgrave. Until very recently he taught classical Indian music at Belgrave Road.

Kanubhai's wife had helped him into a straight chair in the middle of the room. Seated, he looked stronger than he must have been; tall and almost tough. But his eyes were fatigued with chronic fear. He had lowered himself slowly into the chair, eyes looking fearfully at the window. The white blinds were letting in some insufficient winter sunshine, but Mr

Barot had no eyes for sunshine, he was looking out by anxious reflex for someone there. The window looked out on a world of trouble.

Mrs Barot sat at the table behind, cleaning *moong* dhal for dinner. An Indian home can't get any more Indian than this – a husband retired from singing and organising community events, at home with his wife preparing dhal. But outside was an England that wouldn't let them be.

'Look, they shoot at my windows with air guns,' Mr Barot said. 'Take a closer look at the windows.' I saw little pockmarks covered with adhesive tape, evidence of several airgun attacks.

'Come let me show you the side,' Mrs Barot said. She opened the door to a little storeroom under the stairs. A window here had more bits of tape with cracks spreading out like some lethal flower. To the Barots every window was a weak spot; to those shooting at them, every one was an opportunity.

'You are not thinking of changing the glasses?' Gill asked.

'I can't go on replacing windows, how many windows can I replace?' Mrs Barot said. 'On each window I will have to spend twenty, twenty-five pounds. How many times will I replace? They will break more. How long can this go on? If they smash the whole thing, I'll have to change it. But this hole with the air gun, we can live with it. If I start replacing the windows, they will make it a point to shoot at them again.' Replacing a glass pane wouldn't just be expensive, it would be provocative. The Barots couldn't win, and they weren't trying.

'But haven't you reported this to the police?' I asked Mr Barot back in their sitting room. An obviously naive question.

'We have, so many times. But they say they can't do anything.'

'How long has this been going on?'

'For so many years. Every week there is something.'

'You said something every *week*?'

'Every week once or twice something or the other happens here. We are fed up, god, we are really fed up. What shall we do? We bought this house, spent so much money on it. It will be such a loss, but I think I will have to leave. Everybody who comes here, goes.'

As we'd driven up to the Barots', we'd seen signs of a fire in the shop next door that served also as post office. As was usual, the owners lived above the shop. I asked if that fire too was some racists' doing.

'Of course. I heard the alarm go off in their house,' Mr Barot said. 'They were away, they had told us to keep an eye. I rushed to the phone to call the police but my line was dead. They had cut the main line. Nobody in any house around us could use the telephone. They broke into the shop, they looted it. Next morning I found a video [player] belonging to the shopkeeper in my garden. When our telephone was connected again, I phoned the police. I told them there's a brand new video lying in my garden and it's about to rain. They said, go and give it in at the post office.'

'You mean the police knew this was the video stolen from the post office?'

'Yes, they knew. The police had come by at about two in the night, they knew what had happened.'

'You mean there was a burglary, the stolen video was left in your garden, and the police asked you to return it to the shop?'

'Yes, they just said go and give it to the post office, or tell them to come and pick it up. We told the shop owners. They came and picked it up. What shall I say? So many of these things happen here all the time. You see, if we complain to the police, it comes into the newspaper. When they come to know we have complained, the next day we will be finished. They will destroy us, they will break our home into pieces, they will burn our home.'

'Has this sort of thing happened?'

'This is what happened at the post office right next to us. They burnt the house at night.'

'Had the owners complained to the local paper?'

'Yes, the earlier tenants had complained and it was written about in the local newspaper. They were abused endlessly and driven out. You should never let anybody know that you have a problem.'

The attack seemed to have been part punishment. The Punjabi family who had taken the post office and shop had decided to confront the children who had kept vandalising it. Mr Barot knew better.

The Punjabi couple was younger, and angrier, and that was their fault, Mrs Barot said. 'When the kids came and sat on the wall and shouted at her, she said don't make noise here. A white person will not take that kind of talk from us, will they? She kept scolding them, so they would do it more and more. They used to write dirty things on their door, like black bastard, Paki bastard. She used to clean the wall. Then they would come and write more. One lady told her, don't react, they will do more. But she kept stopping them, and it became worse and worse. So the couple got fed up and left.'

The racists then went for the Barots, again. Someone needed revenge for what their Indian neighbours had dared to do, Mrs Barot said. She was downstairs watching TV that day when she heard the door rattle. 'I thought my son is here. He has a key so I ignored the noise. I heard someone trying to open the door again and again. Then I went to look. I saw a hand coming in through the letter box and there was a fire in the hand. I shouted, "Who is it? Who is it? What do you want?" They ran away. Afterwards a man and a woman came from the police. I told them what had happened. They said they will take a round in the evening, but we should be careful. That was all.'

There is only one family the Barots say they can turn to – their white next door neighbours. 'He said that if we are attacked and the phone goes dead, we can bang loudly on the wall. They are very nice. We take chicken to their place sometimes.' The couple was kind, but they were elderly and struggling to get by. The Barots could turn to bang on their wall if the phone went dead, but the couple could do nothing to stop the Barots getting attacked. Still, while those they dreaded were white, this white couple was their only hope in trouble, even if they had very little to do with them most of the time.

'Now you know why so many people are moving out of here,' Gill said. 'Why our people like to live with our people.' He had been telling me for a while that Leicester is not that comfortably Indian in these parts. And why there had to be an Indian Leicester.

Gill lived in another part of Northfields, down a street many Indians had moved into. From a white point of view, it was an Asian mini ghetto; for Gill and his neighbours, a little street fortress where their families were relatively safe.

Many spot that safety too late. 'People come from London, from Manchester, they see that this area is very quiet, very nice, the prices are good, so they buy,' Gill said. 'Then they realise where they have come. And then it's hard to leave. They have invested money, and they cannot find a buyer because nobody is willing to pay anything close to what they paid.'

The Barots wanted to move, but property agents knew why. 'They have brought the price of this house so low that it is becoming difficult to move,' Barot said. And he had other problems. 'Now that I am disabled, I can't get a mortgage. Where will I find another house to live in? I get so angry with all this. I say the government should give us a licence for a machine gun. I tell you, I will shoot these people.'

'Children' seemed the most terror-laden word the Barots knew. 'It's the children we fear the most,' Mr Barot said. 'You know, they are children, but they have the dirtiest abuses. What are their parents doing? These people just leave their children to themselves. They don't care what they do, whether they study or not, that they are harming others or even themselves. They just leave them. The elderly people here, they are all right. We just want the local council to do one thing. Make this an estate for the elderly. We will be all right. It's the only solution. Just take these children away from here.'

'How old are the children?'

'They are all just ten to fifteen years old.'

'Do you report them to the police?'

'I cannot say which child did this. But we have told them that it's the children who do it.'

'So what do they say?'

'They say they cannot do anything. Under the law they cannot take action against a child.'

'So that means the children can legally do all this to you?'

'Yes, that is what they say. We just want them to take the children away from here.'

It was not a suggestion Mr Barot has pursued seriously. If white British children were to leave an estate in England because an Indian had objected to them, *The Sun* would find a headline the government wouldn't want to read. The Barots had done all they could to fortify the house. Now they just waited, for that weekly assault, for time to pass, for just something to change somehow.

A lid screwed on to the letter box would now keep out a white hand with fire and the envelopes packed with shit. But there were some defences the Barots had abandoned. They'd stopped trying to hold up the fence. Again and again the fence at the back of the little house had been torn down. White gangs would walk into the little lawn, bang on the door at the back near the kitchen. They shouted abuse in the day and at night, at home, outside. The insurance did not cover fencing because they said it's not a part of the house. Also, the Barots could not protect their car. A week before I met the Barots, a window of their car was smashed, the stereo taken away.

White people's cars also got broken into in the neighbourhood, but too many things happened at the Barots' house that don't to white persons. 'They abuse us when we step out. We don't use the front street any more. We take a short cut from the back to try and avoid them. It's not safe to even drive along this road. They hate us. They are jealous. They say we have a house, a car with a radio and stereo. Sometimes they don't have money in their pocket for a meal. They don't like it, they hate us for it, they want to destroy it for us.'

Mr Barot knew hundreds of people in Leicester, but none who could help. Some members of the Gujarat Hindu Association were on the police board in Leicester. 'They have been saying that the police should send people in plain clothes to keep an eye on the situation. But nothing is happening.'

The leader was now a fugitive. The man of music now dreamt of a machine gun. 'The community supports people,' he said, shaking his head, 'but they don't get into these problems. If somebody is harassing me here, what can they do? Nobody gets involved in problems with the police or the white people.'

'Would you be happier in Belgrave?'

'Oh yes, if they try that in Belgrave, our people will get together and beat them up. But out here in the middle of all of them we can do nothing.'

'Is this why so many Indians stay together?'

'Yes, this is why you have the ghetto system, why everyone stays together, so that if anybody attacks us, we can get together and do something. Here there's one of our homes alone on one street, someone alone in another corner. What can we do? We can do nothing. Unless we sell this property and go away, or give it to somebody for free and go away.'

'So are you planning to sell and move?'

'We would lose our life's savings. If we had a house in Belgrave, we could sell it easily and at a good price. I think I will call an estate agent, try to exchange this for something else somewhere.'

From here, Belgrave looked like home.

Kashmir Cab

Councillor Parmi Bhai, now walking into the school hall at Abbey Primary just off Belgrave Road, was the first of the two brave Indians who were going to do something about this whole Kashmir thing. The other was Councillor Paul Sood, expected soon; he had only to drive down from his travel agency on Belgrave Road, unlike Parmi Bhai who'd driven up in his taxi from Southampton. The two Labour men had been listening to party MPs say the kind of things about Kashmir that Pakistanis, rather than Indians, would like to hear for too long now. In this simmering civil war within Labour and within Britain between British Indians and British Pakistanis, Indians, they'd decided, had been too civil too long. The Pakistanis were calling meetings, meeting MPs, writing to them, lecturing at universities, lecturing in mosques, demonstrating outside India House, outside 10 Downing Street, raising Kashmir in council meetings, sourcing funds for Pakistani centres, promoting this, pushing that. Were Indians less Indian than Pakistanis were Pakistani?

Indians had been too un-Pakistani about this, Paul and Parmi had decided. They'd both invited me to this meeting to record what they spoke of as a historical change in the making. Leaders from the Hindu-leaning Bharatiya Janata Party (BJP) in India would arrive every now and then, breathe fire and sentiment on Kashmir and return. But political movements are nothing if not local. All these MPs needed to know that Indians had votes too, more than Pakistanis. In this British civil war, one side seemed to have forgotten its own ammunition. I was on time, which meant I was the first to arrive at the hall. The caretaker had cheerfully let me in: 'Come in, mate, they should be along.' Parmi Bhai walked in soon after, with that look of a man who's called the meeting, you can tell them apart at every meeting.

I'd known Parmi Bhai off and on for years. His parents had named him Paramjit Singh Bahia, but everyone knew him as Parmi Bhai. He'd been elected to the city council in Southampton on a Labour ticket. He spoke often of troubled relations with the party, and not just over Kashmir. The party apparently considered him some local loose cannon. Only because, he said, he was a 'committed sort of chap'.

Parmi Bhai had given up his day's business for the meeting. A four-hour drive from Southampton in his red Citroën taxi showed how committed he was to this meeting. Outside of his taxi, he was very much a politician. He was fair looking for an Indian, you might almost think he was white unless he stood next to a white man. He was in his fifties, and balding between the silver grey hair around his ears in the standard style of a man who matters. In a dark blue suit over an immaculate white shirt with spotted red tie, with an important-looking briefcase in his hand, here was a man who has things to do, and take note.

Paul Sood, then contesting to be a Labour councillor, soon walked in. Sood, who had made it to middle age with a still-surprised look on his face, had found the hall for the meeting, it was in the ward he would contest. We stood chatting a while, waiting for the rest. In a while two more turned up, Ajit Doval from the Indian high commission, and Saleem Gillings, the Jamaican chairman of the National Association of Race Equality Councils.

'He's here as observer,' Parmi Bhai told me. 'Important chap. My buddy.'

But no one else appeared, and it was getting significantly past time for the meeting. Sood figured the reason. Clocks had been put forward an hour to move to summer time. 'Our people, you know, they must have forgotten,' Sood said. 'They'll all be here an hour late.' He looked a bit agitated, fearful that his guests may not be so forgetful after all. He and Parmi had prepared their speeches; the audience was missing, but for me, and I was only there to take notes.

Parmi Bhai and Doval exchanged looks, and Doval tactfully took Gillings out for coffee to give the rest time to turn up.

Parmi had been waiting for just the moment when Gillings would pass hearing distance. 'Where's everybody, *bhenchod*?' he said to Sood.

That word. So much more than its crass translation as a chap who sleeps with his sister. It's the Indian subcontinental male's way of underlining strong sentiment. A bonding word, that in fact bonds also the Indian with the Pakistani male; the partition never did divide such essential vocabulary. The word establishes cultural commonality along the way of speech, and the feeling of the moment in the way it is spoken. Like most swear words, it's usually the first defence against the unknown, and it comes from the gut. It's something said, the way the gut wants it said, before you can start thinking of something to say. All cultures are miserly in their allowance of such words; there are usually just a very few, and this one is ours like no other. It's a word that almost always stops short of vicious abuse; it's exclamation, greeting, it expresses surprise, relief, affection, astonishment, warning, or as Parmi Bhai said it to Paul Sood, impatience and reproach.

'I don't know, I told everyone,' Sood said. He'd written to 130 Indian councillors, he said, then he had phoned them. Almost all had promised they would come. The front rows had been reserved for the councillors. The rows were vacant, and there was nobody at the back who could be moved up.

We heard some steps, and Sood smiled. 'See, they're coming.' A man with a Hindu tilak sitting large on his forehead walked in; that bright red spot on the forehead is in women traditional style, on the male the mark of regular prayer. And if a good Hindu does not come to a cause like this, who would? It was Chandubhai Bhatt from the Hindu Council of Leicester.

'Where's everybody?' he asked.

'There's a little confusion about the time change,' Sood said.

'You mean everybody has forgotten?' Chandubhai looked at his watch brushing against rolls of *rudraksh*, the prayer beads in their Hindu version. He was not convinced, and his forehead creased up around his tilak. We were all beginning to sound a little loud in the empty hall, and Sood was losing faith that British Summer Time would save the meeting.

'Maybe it's because it is Mother's Day,' Sood ventured. No one said anything, and Sood looked like he wished he hadn't said it.

Some whispering between Sood and Parmi led to hurried telephoning, that produced another two men who arrived with their wives and children. They sat for a bit, then wandered in and out, waiting for something to happen. Sood was looking out of the window, and seeing only failure. Two young girls turned in from the road towards the hall.

'See, they're coming,' he said.

'Why you are counting the same people again and again?' Parmi said. This time had he said *bhenchod*, it would be in an angrier incarnation. The girls were from the two recently arrived families.

Parmi was blaming Sood, but Sood would not be blamed. 'What is happening here today in Leicester has been happening for 1,300 years in India,' he said, speech-like. 'What is wrong with us, do we have blood in our veins or water?'

'Too much water my friend,' Chandubhai said. He'd seen it all before. 'If they were doing a meeting on Kashmir they would have collected thousand people in half an hour.' They. The Pakistanis, of course.

'It's these Gujaratis,' Sood said. 'They can go on getting pushed and they'll do nothing. That's why they got thrown out of East Africa.'

Vasant Kalyani, photographer for the *Leicester Mercury* walked in. Sood and Parmi were trying not to look at his camera, but Kalyani was sympathetic. '*Badokidogo*, we used to say in Tanzania.' What will be will be.

But Sood had found some rescue. Sheetal Singh Gill, that saviour from the Indian Workers Association walked in. He headed the local taxi union, of mostly Indian and Pakistani taxi drivers. The Kashmir agitation had brought him here just before a cab drivers' meeting called later in the evening. The taxi drivers had a fight on their hands. They'd been driving their cheap Japanese cars profitably, but now the council wanted them to buy the Austin FX4s, familiar as the London cab. Those cabs cost £24,000 each, twice the price or more of a new Japanese car. Taxi drivers usually bought used Japanese cars for a few thousand, and the new requirement meant that taxi drivers were in for it. Gill was leading the agitation against the London cab being forced upon the streets of Leicester, and no doubt a capitalist imposition on struggling migrant workers.

'Do something,' Sood said to him. The emptiness of the hall added silent weight to his words. He didn't say it with hands folded, but there's a way of saying such things without using your hands. Gill left, and returned 15 minutes later with about twenty taxi drivers. Some numbers at last, but I saw the problem immediately as they walked in, and so of course would Sood and Parmi; a good number of the taxi drivers were clearly Pakistanis. We now had an Indian meeting on Kashmir, against Pakistan, where about half the audience was Pakistani.

Gill had meant well, but this was always going to be a danger if an Indian meeting on Kashmir had to borrow bodies from a meeting of Leicester taxi drivers.

'Let's get it done now,' Doval said to Parmi. He wanted it to end quickly.

If a meeting meant someone speaking and someone listening, we had a meeting now. Sood stepped onto the stage and took the chair in the middle, with Gillings sitting on one side, Parmi on the other.

Sood was chair, and left the speech to Parmi, who walked up to the mike and launched into it straightaway after a quick welcoming. 'Where is human rights when they harass us at Heathrow? And they got audacity to tell us about problems affecting us? They lecture on Kashmir. What right they have to talk without full facts?' He had mentioned Kashmir, but said nothing about it. He spoke very speech-like, and I admired him for speaking as though there were more of us.

'It is Mothering Sunday, we have adopted some of their customs here,' he said, hoping this would explain the missing Indians and their absence of interest in Kashmir. 'This is Mother's Day but nobody thinks of Motherland Day.' He paused, as speakers do before thunderous applause, which we'd have had if we weren't so short of hands.

'Comrades, you know what is first thing I do when I get up in the morning?' Parmi paused again, and it was good more people weren't around for embarrassing guesswork. 'I get up and go to bathroom.' We waited to hear what next.

'There is mirror there, big mirror. I look my face into it. Then I ask that mirror: "WHO AM I?" Mirror tells me, "Parmi you are black and don't you ever forget it." After that I have coffee and I know I am Indian. And I know I'm not going to apologise for it.'

Parmi was not going to apologise for the small numbers either. 'Mahabharat [that most epic of Indian mythological battles] was won by five Pandavas. Guru Gobind Singh [the last of the Sikh gurus] created an army out of five. Christ also had only twelve–thirteen. We can start from small number but if we have faith we will succeed, opposition *will* fail.'

Parmi was getting into the mood and no one seemed to notice that he'd forgotten all about Kashmir. 'The biggest problem is racism. Even prime minister admits it.' Parmi continued. 'You know what we are all farting for?' I knew Parmi, and so I knew he meant 'fighting', these things happen when you carry your accent as accompanied baggage. 'I will always be farting for the have-nots. When they needed soldiers we became soldiers, when they needed workers we became workers, when they needed services we became doctors and nurses. When economy was collapsing, we had the tricks. British leaders go to lay wreath on the memorial of Gandhi, but they never talk about virginity tests here. Remember, Chair, how we ran that campaign?' Chair, recently the *bhenchod*, nodded the way leaders do when momentous matters are on their mind.

But now the taxi gang was getting up to leave. They had made a meeting of this, and it was time for their own. All twenty or so were filing out. 'Wish you luck with the taxi meeting anyway,' Parmi said, mid-speech. He had to let the remaining six or seven of us know that this was not a walkout.

Now Parmi turned to Kashmir. The real speech could begin only after the audience was gone. He raised a sheet of paper and waved it around. It was a statement by Labour MP Clare Short. She had always been critical of India over Kashmir, and she'd just returned from Pakistan with more to say that was less than kind about the Indian government. 'It is downright wicked fiction by a woman in a dream world who only looks what she wants to see.' He paused, then said, 'Clare is not fair.' He waited, aware that he'd again said something that demanded applause pause. 'If she is not living in fool's paradise where the hell she is living? I have paper here that says 7,817 people have died in Kashmir from terrorism. That's hell of lot of people, Clare. What if so many had died in London and Birmingham and Guildford? But they don't mention about it, that's what makes me sick. And they are pouring fuels on burning fires.'

In the audience the two women who had come in with their men had stopped nudging one another and whispering, they were actually listening. They had been patient. But Parmi's speech continued mostly to the walls of an empty school. 'When cold wind starts blowing in subcontinent, Indians and Pakistanis here start sneezing, I tell you. But we are all victims of racism. Clare should start farting about that, I tell you.' This was now becoming a communication between Parmi and the mike. Finally he stopped.

'It was a bad show, how did you manage it?' Parmi asked Sood, down where the audience should have been.

'You see I did not publicise this meeting openly.'

'Why not?'

'If it had been on the local radio there would have been Khalistanis, there would have been everyone.' Meaning, a Pakistani demonstration outside, with still perhaps no meeting within. And so we had a secret public meeting. Parmi and Paul had still done their bit for Kashmir, it was the others who hadn't.

Turban and Trouble

It would have been another of those gray and dull mornings in England without the pink and peacock blue of the Indian women's dresses on the pavement in front of the gurdwara, the Sikh temple, on East Park Lane in Leicester. Or the yellow so prominent among the turbans this Sunday morning, the yellow of protest, or at least the colour to make a point in. It was right to pick a turban in that yellow, because the turban was what the meeting at the gurdwara this morning was about.

Somewhere in boring Brussels a bunch of Eurocrats had made the wearing of helmets compulsory in factories and other locations considered high-risk. To a Sikh that order came as an overhanging threat that a helmet must replace the turban at these locations, and this is what the Sikhs were gathering to talk about.

The ruling from Brussels set off a first dispute between Surinder Singh Dhanjol and the steel factory where he worked in Wolverhampton. He had refused to replace his turban with a 'hard hat' in the factory area. So he was confined to the boiler plant and then offered small administrative jobs that he declined. Finally, he was sacked. He appealed to an industrial tribunal in Birmingham and lost. That led to this meeting. Because it was not about Dhanjol any more, it was about every Sikh's right to wear a turban everywhere. To threaten a Sikh's turban is to threaten his honour and his rights.

I ran into Dhanjol in the gurdwara basement where a quick exhibition on the historic Sikh struggle had been set up. It showcased mostly paintings of Sikh strength and sacrifices over centuries, first in the face of oppression by the Mughal rulers of India, down to Operation Blue Star, when Indira Gandhi ordered the army to storm the Golden Temple in Amritsar in 1984 to end a rebellion by a force of Sikhs demanding creation of a separate Sikh state in Punjab to be called Khalistan. That rebellion was led by Jarnail Singh Bhindranwale, and this exhibition had the usual pictures of Bhindranwale carrying a Sten gun popular among Sikh groups who still think Bhindranwale a hero.

Dhanjol appeared an unlikely leader in that line of Sikh struggle. At any other place Dhanjol would be the eternal uncle, but here he was the uncle who had dared. He was being led through the exhibition by a big man with aggressive looks and an assertively tied turban. He was speaking words to match. 'If our struggles and sacrifices end, Sikhism has no meaning,' he was saying to Dhanjol, just ahead of me.

Dhanjol, the now unemployed hero, had been talking the language of sacrifice. 'I can give up my life but not my turban,' he had said on BBC Television. He now belonged to the subject of the exhibition he was walking through, unexpectedly comfortable amid the paintings of blood and torture.

After a short walkabout through the basement, I followed Dhanjol and his fiery companion to the gurdwara hall upstairs. The large hall was filled with people and that unique gurdwara fragrance that comes only partly from the food in the *langar* hall around the prayer hall. Dhanjol joined the group at the front end of the hall. He'd lost a job but found leadership.

The fiery man, Santokh Singh as he was introduced, began the meeting. 'They want us to take off our turbans and wear iron caps. Raise your voice against iron caps.' He spoke in Punjabi, at a pitch just right for anger. Voices went up after he spoke, saying nothing much. Santokh Singh now got louder by the sentence. 'They are testing us, they have attacked some of us already. If we don't take up the challenge, we'll all be under attack tomorrow.' Santokh Singh was loud but brief.

Lt. Gen. G. S. Clair was introduced to address the packed hall. He had retired, we were told, from the Indian Army in 1987. We all heard that unmentioned year in that statement – 1984. The general had been therefore a serving officer in the Indian army in 1984, and had not resigned despite Operation Blue Star. Everyone let that pass. He still had the authority of a general, and an upright military manner you don't challenge.

'Ours has been a very honourable association with the British empire for centuries,' the general said. 'There was an understanding we had with the British government after they took over from the East India Company.' After the uprising of 1857, that is, when some Sikh forces backed the British to set up crown rule over India. 'We were valued for our valour, our bravery. It was a very honourable profession. And then how many of us gave our lives during the two world wars to keep the Union Jack flying?'

For the general, as for many soldiers in Sikh families, that history tied in with family history. 'My father was in Third Skinner Horse in the cavalry. He served in France till he retired in 1942. My two brothers fought in the Burma War. I lost a close relative in Burma who was reported missing. I have a lot of associations with the British empire.'

The general now turned to the point that Brussels had missed, that now the British were missing. 'When I was in the cavalry, we were never told to wear helmets. Bullets and shells were flying then – we would have needed something thicker than those plastic helmets they now want us to wear. Then we wore what the gurus gave us, we are proud of that. We have sacrificed our elders to uphold the empire through the ages, the British must now recognise our right to wear our turbans.'

It was only a small return the Sikhs were seeking for the forgotten debt. But there are no returns to be claimed for dated valour, and lives lost. It was OK for a Sikh to expose his head to bullets in the cause of the empire. The Sikhs then were good for the rulers, and so the rulers were good to them. Now Sikhs have only a few votes. But they were going to make them count.

Britain has all sorts of doubts about the EU, but it was not about to sacrifice the EU for summoned memories of Sikh heroes who had fought to keep Britain intact through the world wars. There's a Remembrance Day, but it is not spent remembering Sikh soldiers. Or thinking that they might in those days have been better off in helmets. A fair bit of history hangs on that question of helmets and turbans that Brussels had never begun to suspect.

More speeches followed, saying much the same things in routine anger. But everyone was waiting for Kashmir Singh, the one known for knowing everything about the turban in Britain, the intellect of the separatist Sikh voice.

Kashmir Singh, suave and suited, rose to the mike. 'In 1968 Sikh drivers and conductors struck in Wolverhampton because they were ordered to wear caps instead of turbans,' he said, at a considerably lower pitch than the one Santokh Singh had produced. 'They won.' Kashmir Singh was the more forceful for speaking softly, his elegance promised content. The Wolverhampton case was of course well known to the Sikhs there, it's part of collective memory among British Sikhs. Driver Tarsem Singh Sandhu had been sacked then because the rules permitted only clean-shaven staff. Another driver, Sohan Singh Jolly, had threatened to burn himself if rules weren't changed. A supporting protest rally was held in Delhi. The Indian government stepped in to plead with the British government. Under all this weight, the managers at Wolverhampton bus depot gave in. This then cleared the way for Sikhs at other bus depots.

More turban trouble lay ahead, Kashmir Singh narrated. In 1972, Sikhs were told they couldn't ride motorcycles wearing turbans instead of helmets. 'This was ordered by the Conservative government,' Kashmir Singh told us. 'The government changed, but the Labour government didn't listen to us. Then we promised to support Margaret Thatcher and she promised to support us. Finally they changed the law in 1976 and we were allowed to ride motorcycles wearing turbans.' That you never ever see a Sikh riding a motorcycle is another matter. It was a battle won.

The campaign continued; it had to. A new struggle began in 1984, quite a year for Sikh struggles. A new law made helmets compulsory at construction sites. 'For five years after that we were writing to the government, we wrote two or three thousand letters. We had hundreds of meetings. We were supported by the Khalistan Council, the International Sikh Youth Federation, Akhand Kirtani Jatha, Akali Dal, Ramgarhia Board, gurdwaras, Walsall College students, Wolverhampton School students, Cambridge University students and so many others.'

And, again, the Sikhs won. They were granted exemption from helmets on construction sites under the Employment Act of 1989.

This now was the new round. If a battle on motorcycle helmets could be fought and won a little unnecessarily, Kashmir Singh offered a string of reasons for the need to win this one on factories.

He presented several scenarios: a Sikh policeman is not normally required to wear a helmet. So what if he is chasing a thief who runs into a factory? The policeman cannot enter. If he does, he will break the law himself, and the thief will run away because a Sikh policeman would have to end the chase at the entrance. A Sikh lawyer cannot represent Dhanjol. The lawyer might want to see the factory in Wolverhampton himself. If a Sikh judge like Mota Singh has to investigate what happened in the factory, he cannot. And what of a Sikh on a jury? What if the jury had to visit an accident site in a factory? The Sikh on the jury would have to be replaced.

With each scenario the problem looked bigger and bigger. A Sikh architect could design a factory and watch it come up, because under British law he could enter a construction site. Once it was built he could not enter it under European law, because in its completion it had progressed from construction site to factory.

A computer engineer could set up hardware in a power station when it was being constructed. Once it was safely built, he could not enter. If he installed the hardware in time, he could not inspect the software later. A Sikh railway worker could not legally shunt a wagon any more. A Sikh householder could cut the branches of trees in his garden, but not if he was employed to do so.

A Sikh doctor could not treat anyone in a factory site accident. A Sikh ambulance driver could not drive to a factory area. Sikh teachers may sometimes have to show children a factory. They could not go; neither could Sikh children in class. How would Sikh businessmen win construction contracts if they could not visit what they had built? Kashmir Singh's final scenario: if right here in this gurdwara they had to paint the walls higher than six-and-a-half feet, the law said they could not do it wearing turbans. Who in Brussels would have thought of all this?

He concluded with the argument that if this was all for the health and safety of Sikhs, they still did not need to replace turbans with helmets either for health or for safety.

Again, he had masses of data handy. Smoking 200 cigarettes a day means a one in 200 risk of death. Natural causes above age 40 bring a one in 500 chance of death, flu one in 4000, road accidents one in 5000, accidents at home one in 10,000, accidents at work one in 20,000, natural background radiation one in 40,000, head injuries in construction work one in 500,000, head injuries in construction work to British Sikhs one in 50 million, and in non-construction areas where the new European law applies, less than that. So what was the fuss about?

And what if that less than one in 50 million chance were to come to pass? Kashmir Singh had worked that out too.

The Health and Safety Executive in Sheffield had put the turban to a safety test, he said. For impacts to the front of the head the turban gave 141.7 per cent better protection than a helmet. For impacts to the back it gave 95.1 per cent protection, to the side 77.1 per cent, and on top 31 per cent.

And that 31 per cent figure would have been better if the *kanga* had been considered, Kashmir Singh said. The *kanga* was explained to some local white leaders in the gurdwara hall as the 'wooden comb at the base of the knot of hair' within the turban. And the figure of 31 per cent would have been better if a *padka*, a scarf sometimes worn within the turban had been included in the test. So the hair tied up and strengthened with a *kanga* and a *padka* would have fortified the turban that much more. And, he said, the turban tested in Sheffield should have been six to eight metres in length, not four and a half metres. Besides, he argued, the length of the hair makes a difference; the longer the hair, the safer the Sikh.

Kashmir Singh was not done. The turban had other reasons to do better than a helmet, he suggested. The constructional shape of the turban provided better vision. It sat higher than the head, so that the top of the turban would come into contact with structures before the head. And the turban, Kashmir Singh said, was never removed to scratch the head, as a helmet might be.

He signed off citing British authorities on the greater safety of the turban. Lt. Gen. Sir Reginald Savory had written to a science officer to say he had known Sikhs pick bullets out of their turbans during and after battle, and that in fact the turban absorbed the shock of a bullet possibly rather better than a tin helmet. Col. H. A. Hughes said of his regiment in the North-West Frontier Province that consisted entirely of Sikhs that he had no more head wounds here than in any other battalion wearing steel helmets.

Through the meeting, my view on the turban was changed for ever.

The point about the turban was fine, but there was something about the meeting that said it was about more than the turban. That Khalistan question was hanging around the meeting. Maybe it was Kashmir Singh's matter-of-fact reference to Khalistan groups among others. Or the pictures of Bhindranwale downstairs, or the ominous looking chaps at the back of the platform from the International Sikh Youth Federation, later proscribed by the Home Office as an organisation that may support terrorism in its demand for the creation of a Khalistan.

The hidden Khalistani push came to the surface at another meeting, later, at the Guru Nanak Sikh Gurdwara in Wolverhampton, a little further west from Leicester in the Midlands. The meeting was called principally by a new group, the Sikh Secretariat. The brains behind it, again, Kashmir Singh, I was told by friends before I headed out to Wolverhampton.

The Khalistan stalls set up outside the gurdwara were fair advertisement of what to expect at the meeting. I can't remember another market where so many stalls all sold the same things – Bhindranwale videos, tapes, posters, books. The stalls had taken up quite a few spaces in the gurdwara car park.

It was a bright Sunday morning, just right for stalls of a happier kind. The gurdwara is just across from a church, but the traffic down the road carried mostly Sikh-bearing cars headed for the gurdwara. The Wolverhampton sun had very much more of Bhindranwale's stern face to shine on than church bells and good Christians going to church.

Bhindranwale's face meant something to me. I had spent years reporting for the *Indian Express* on terrorist violence in Punjab and Delhi. I'd reported from Amritsar and around Punjab during Operation Blue Star. And I had managed to beat curfew and the June heat to get to Bhindranwale's village in his village Rode in Punjab the day it was announced he had been killed.

It was a tense day; an army helicopter circled above, and a group of about two hundred or so Sikhs had gathered at Bhindranwale's house. My friend Kanwar Sandhu from the *Express* had also made it to Bhindranwale's village. We'd been welcomed warmly, given a hot meal and invited to rest; that particular tradition of Punjab had been kept up for an absolute stranger, and in Bhindranwale's house, on that of all days. I felt a good deal less welcome at the gurdwara this Sunday morning in the West Midlands in England than in Rode village in Faridkot that day.

Among the few outsiders at this Khalistan mela were two white English girls in the foyer, heads covered with scarves, in blue T-shirts that said HALIFAX CAR INSURANCE. They were selling car insurance within a picture gallery featuring martyrs and brutal Indian police. They handed out cards with smiling faces on them, pictures of happiness as known only to those who would have Halifax to call if their car were to run into another.

The girls must have been sent to tap the 'Asian' gathering here – Britain had managed to make Bhindranwale too 'an Asian'. The poor smiling girls were not going to get far; the Sikhs coming in might have one view of Bhindranwale or another, but car insurance was not going to be what they'd take away.

That there were two views on Bhindranwale was becoming obvious. Many Sikhs were coming in for the regular Sunday morning prayers, and then just leaving. They weren't staying on for the political speeches booming through the gurdwara. Someone on the mike was seeing this and not liking it. 'People have given the last eighteen, twenty years of their life for this, and you find it difficult to give ten minutes.' And this from those who should be showing the Sikhs of Punjab what true Sikhism is. 'There is no true Sikhism in Punjab. We should send them models from here. Let them follow our youngsters from here.'

I stepped into the gurdwara office to look for Kashmir Singh, but found only two quiet and unhappy looking men. 'This is the gurdwara office,' one said. 'We don't know anything. We have nothing to do with what they are saying.' 'Ask someone in a yellow turban, don't ask us,' said the other.

Donations were being announced between speeches. I heard all sorts of figures: £25, £11, Coventry £4,000, Southampton £2,000, Singh family £300, the Wolverhampton gurdwara £2,500. If all this was true, it was adding up nicely.

The voice over the mike was now becoming a bit hoarse, a low-key roar that sounded earnest and heartfelt. 'When two of our people shot Indira Gandhi, they hanged them,' he was saying. 'What was the fault of those thousands of Sikhs killed in Delhi? Nobody has been punished for that.'

I found myself in sympathy for once with a view over the mike that morning. After reporting the assassination of Indira Gandhi I had had the misfortune of reporting the killings in Delhi over the next couple of days. More than three thousand Sikhs were killed, but no justice followed. I filed three affidavits before a Supreme Court Commission on killings and interventions by Congress leaders who at the least did nothing to stop the killers. The Commission dismissed my affidavit on the ground that I could not produce an independent witness to testify that I'd been there to see what I saw, that I could not produce a log book from the *Indian Express* to establish where exactly in Delhi I was and at precisely what time. I could, in fact, have added to the arguments on the mike, but the angry voice would hardly have wanted me to. This meeting was not really about right and wrong; it was about a certain way of being Sikh.

Someone else had taken over the mike by the time I went upstairs to sit down in the hall. He was comparing the Delhi killings with the three thousand or so who died in the 11 September attacks. 'You see how they feel...' he was saying. Americans, America. How they had honoured and remembered the dead, and continue to. It sounded like a telling difference. New York had dealt with those deaths by mourning and remembering, New Delhi had dealt with its by forgetting and moving on. Not just the government in Delhi, most Sikhs too. Sikhs should learn from New York, he was saying. 'That is the way we should remember the thousands who had died.'

Much of the anger arising behind the mikes was aimed at Sikhs in Punjab as much as the Indian government. 'We have seen how their corruption ruined Punjab. They have sold us to Delhi to fill their pockets. Now we have seen Punjab handed over to killers.' With the Congress government in Punjab, that is.

Next came anger with Sikhs in Britain; any Sikh who did not want a Khalistan was traitor. 'These people are getting grants from the British government and filling their pockets. The Home Office must be told who are the people they are giving recognition to. We have to come to some decisions and tell the government here. If they don't care about us, then we have to think about who to vote for. If they cannot think of the good of Sikhs, keep them out. So that they don't damage Sikhs any more.'

The meeting was going to make a point to local political leaders, and they had turned up to have the point made to them. Labour MP Rob Marris was called up to the mike, but not before two announcements, the first in Punjabi and the second in English. In Punjabi: 'When the MPs come, give them a good impression. Don't get up and walk off in the middle. Or they'll think you're not interested.' In English, for the MP: 'We are ever so pleased to see you here.' Here was an MP, the announcer said, who has 'lived up to our expectations'.

Marris did, even if he spoke rather carefully. 'I can see Khalistan is an issue dear to your hearts,' he said from under a white handkerchief covering his head, since a turban could not. 'Those in the Indian subcontinent who peacefully and democratically push for self-determination for that part of the Indian subcontinent, their opinion for self-determination, their right to ask for an independent Khalistan shouldn't be suppressed.' It would not be right for parties in Britain to decide whether there should be self-determination in what he called 'that part of the Indian subcontinent'. 'But it would be right for people to democratically and peacefully express their opinions.' This was welcomed with slogans of 'Khalistan *zindabad*' ('Long live Khalistan').

More local leaders were called up, and in between Khalistanis took their turn at the mike, to keep the mood up. The speeches all began at the high end of a pitch, and moved up from there. Everything began with 1984, the year of Operation Blue Star, the assassination of Indira Gandhi, the Delhi massacres. Everyone spoke of the injustice done to the Sikhs. Many ended with a loaded demand; in Britain, they said, Sikhs should be counted as Sikhs, not as Indians.

Shadow Conservative Party minister for international development and women's issues Caroline Spelman rose to say it was 'extraordinary' (British-speak for 'outrageous') that 'the government has not cared to find out how many of you there are'. The Labour government should monitor Sikhs separately and 'if they fail, it will be a task for a Conservative administration to deliver on'.

Papers I'd picked up outside spelt out these demands in an eight-point Sikh agenda. The agenda asked for more Sikh MPs, lords and councillors, more and better jobs in government and what not. But item number six wanted to 'seek action from the UK government on the continuing abuse of Sikh and other minority groups' human rights by the Indian authorities' and to 'highlight the lack of justice for Sikhs in India following the massacre in November 1984'.

Item seven was openly about 'self-determination for the Sikh nation'. It wanted to 'make known and explain the reasons why Sikhs want to establish an independent sovereign state of Khalistan to the British public, political organisations and the UK government.' And it challenged the British ban on Sikh organisations such as the International Sikh Youth Federation.

I left the meeting less surprised by what I'd heard from the Khalistanis than by what the British leaders had said. The promise to find out 'how many of you there are' was of course far from innocent. One change in the census form could dent the figures for the Indian population in Britain. It could fall sharply from around 1.2 million if Sikhs were made one category and Indians an alternative other. It would be the beginning of a political storm between India and Britain. This was explosive stuff, and it wasn't about numbers; the Indian government would see this as recognition for a break-up of the country, and a provocation like this wasn't something the British government was likely to contemplate.

It was a relief to get up to leave, and not just because I'm no Khalistani. Of all the Khalistanis I'd met, this was the least friendly lot. I'd often spoken to Jagjit Singh Chauhan, the Sikh who had spent years in Britain talking Khalistan. An engaging man, great for a chit-chat now and then. He'd made a similarly fiery speech at a Khalistan meeting I'd attended at the Sheehy Way gurdwara in Slough, just west of London. But he saw no reason to be unpleasant to me because I didn't share his views. We always found much to joke about in Punjabi. We shared outrage over the 1984 killings and I agreed that Indira Gandhi had done more to mess up Punjab than anyone else. But with this new lot it had never been possible to talk enough to disagree. If I wanted to talk to any of them, I must be a government agent who'd come to find out something. If I didn't, it must be that I was a government agent who therefore didn't want to hear what they had to say.

I left almost beginning to miss some of the nicer Khalistanis, particularly Sewa Singh Lalli, that Khalistan President-in-Exile among so many such presidents at the time. That's how his letterhead had described him in ornate and therefore presidential looking font. Sewa Singh Lalli had promised me a 'very big post' in Khalistan because I had given evidence against Congress leaders and the police in the Delhi killings. The last time I called him he was away delivering eggs. He did not return my call. Knowing him was the closest I ever got to picking up the phone and calling a president. He just disappeared, and with him my political career.

The Halifax girls, that morning's picture of innocence, were gone by the time I stepped out. Someone should have mentioned to them that between them and the cars they wanted to insure stood some little matter from the past, and a chap called Bhindranwale.

Gujarati Goblin

Christina Rossetti's poem 'Goblin Market' answered some questions for Tina about growing up a Gujarati in Leicester, about being an Indian in Britain and being seen as one. She remembered it vividly from that time years back when it had become an issue at university, I could see that as she talked about it. She was about to begin a job teaching English when I met her for coffee at Bobby's restaurant on Belgrave Road; just the thing for her to do by the sound of it. And she had much to say about anything she talked of. She seemed hardly to pause to breathe, let alone to sip that coffee we saw go cold between us. But she did falter when she spoke of that poem; the time her literature class discussed 'Goblin Market' at Leicester University.

'I remember that particular seminar,' she said. 'We were talking about…we were talking about…a poem by Christina Rossetti. Something about a blonde girl with a red mouth. It's about loss of virginity or something… this that and the other… I'd interpreted it as being totally different. I talked about the loss of innocence, but I talked about the loss of innocence in a non-sexual way, because that's just how I am. And I had like ten faces staring at me.'

She had been talking about growing up in Leicester, as a British Indian in an Indian part of Britain, the sort of situation when clichés start to get a little mixed up. But more than hyphenated labels, it was the poem that told her how very different she was from the ten white faces she remembered staring at her. I was staring at her now, they would have stared at her for all the wrong reasons, not because she was so duskily magnetic. Thoughts had drifted into my mind as we sat down: what if I had been young enough for her? But they drifted out fast. After coffee, she would leave for a life of her own, I'd leave only with some tape-assisted notes.

She was talking about the class. The teacher had called a male student to make his presentation. 'He went into this very explicit explanation of the loss of virginity… and this, and that, and you know. His interpretation. And I said, no, I don't think so, and one of the girls started laughing, and she said something like how many of us take this point of view… who'd be for Tina basically… and they didn't agree with me because they didn't think like that.'

The moment stayed with her. 'It suddenly occurred to me at that point that my thinking and theirs was so different. I felt stupid because of that. Also, my tutor didn't explain that you can have different interpretations based on culture and life experiences. So that opened up my eyes quite a bit. What I found difficult was that all the rest of them had a white perspective rather than an Asian cultural perspective. So my thinking in a lot of areas is different.'

As she saw it, the differences arose because of the way she grew up. She took me through some milestones of her life rapidly. The coffee had long dipped past drinkable temperature, and I left it at that because the same would happen to the next cup. Coming from her, some labels and notions took form and flesh.

'I went to Abbey Primary, and I used to love it. My experience of going to school was my first glimpse of anything English. At home everything was in Gujarati. We didn't have a television, didn't have a video. So I had no exposure to anything English. It was really strange. I didn't speak any English at home. When I went to school I learnt English. I didn't have any friends, I just had my cousins. I talked to my grandfather in Gujarati because he didn't speak much English, and I talked to my cousins in Gujarati.

'Then when I went to school, we had teachers who were white. They were my first interaction with white people. On Saturdays my mum would take us to the city centre for shopping. We would see white people there, but wouldn't interact with them in the same way. Also, in my class we were mainly Gujarati kids, maybe there were one or two white kids. So it didn't feel like there were other kids like white kids or black kids or people from other backgrounds.

'I was about five or six when my father bought a TV. I got glued, it used to fascinate me. You know, the early morning children's programmes? And they were all English kids on TV. If there was a jingle or something, I'd be singing it in school. And people would say, no, I should be singing something else. People from my community, the Prajapati community. We used to go there quite a lot. I used to sing there, I used to sing Gujarati songs. I always thought that I was living in one world, and on TV it was another world. There was my home life, and there was my outside life.'

That could have been such a sound bite, I thought, journalistically. A disrespectful thought, disrespecting of her life as she'd lived it and tried to think it through. What I was reducing to a slogan had been for her a struggle, I saw it in the reach of her eyes from our coffee table to those experiences she had tried to make sense of. Now she had found clarity. She wasn't just some differently coloured Brit; she was what she saw herself to be, a Gujarati Brit.

'I feel very comfortable and easy being with other Gujarati and Indian people,' she was saying. I looked more than I listened sometimes, and only partly because I could do the listening later. She was warm, her eyes were exceptionally alive, her face was comfort-inspiring. 'It's not so much an issue now because I've been working for the last four or five years. I've also lived in London for a little while. I don't know what it is, but there's always a sense of ease with Indian people, I don't feel like I have to explain myself. Because culturally people understand what I am talking about.

'If I talk to a friend who is Asian I can talk about a wedding, I can talk about my mum saying something to me about food or whatever, she or he would understand. If I say this to someone who is not Gujarati or Indian, it takes a little more explaining, I feel I'd have to apologise for myself, and I'm more happy being on the Indian than on the white side of things, you know.'

It was circumstantially the easier side to be on. After Abbey Primary, Tina went to Rushymead Secondary, where, she said, about 96 or 97 per cent of the students were Indians, Gujaratis. It was only when she went to Leicester University for three years for a combined honours degree in English literature and the history of art that she encountered overwhelmingly white people. 'It was a very lonely experience. I was the only Asian on the course among two hundred plus.' English literature is a popular degree at Leicester University, but clearly not popular with Indians.

She took with her to university all the experience of growing up in Belgrave, and that meant she read a different 'Goblin Market' to that read by the white students in her class.

We left Bobby's, and I wanted to believe, for some silly reason, that she did not always order coffee and then ignore it. I couldn't of course wait to go back and read that poem by Christina Rossetti, the Victorian woman who had dared suggest sex in verse.

The poem begins with Laura, who can't get her eyes off a bunch of goblin men selling their 'wares'. She thinks what she might be missing.

'How fair the vine must grow
Whose grapes are so luscious…'

Lizzie offers a sisterly warning.

'No,' said Lizzie, 'no, no, no;
Their offers should not charm us,
Their evil gifts would harm us.'
She thrust a dimpled finger
In each ear, shut eyes and ran:
Curious Laura chose to linger
Wondering at each merchant man.

Laura wants their wares, but has no gold to buy them with. But
the goblin men have an idea.

'You have much gold upon your head,'
They answered altogether:
'Buy from us with a golden curl.'
She clipped a precious golden lock,
She dropped a tear more rare than pearl,
Then sucked their fruit globes fair or red:
Sweeter than honey from the rock,
Stronger than man-rejoicing wine,
Clearer than water flowed that juice;
She never tasted such before,
How should it cloy with length of use?
She sucked and sucked and sucked the more
Fruits which that unknown orchard bore,
She sucked until her lips were sore...

Later, the men

Hugged her and kissed her;
Squeezed and caressed her;
Stretched up their dishes...
Pluck them and suck them,
Pomegranates, figs.

BRIDELESS IN WEMBLEY

Sister Lizzie saw the temptations, but held firm, in a way. She

> Would not open lip from lip
> Lest they should cram a mouthful in;
> But laughed in heart to feel the drip
> Of juice that syruped all her face,
> And lodged in dimples of her chin,
> And streaked her neck which quaked like curd.

Back home,

> She cried 'Laura', up the garden,
> 'Did you miss me?
> Come and kiss me.
> Never mind my bruises,
> Hug me, kiss me, suck my juices
> Squeezed from goblin fruits for you,
> Goblin pulp and goblin dew.
> Eat me, drink me, love me;
> Laura, make much of me:
> For your sake I have braved the glen
> And had to do with goblin merchant men.'

Was this a poem about loss of virginity or about loss of innocence? I'd probably vote with the white classroom against Tina. Why did it feel like a betrayal of her just to have the thought? But perhaps this most basic of possible readings of the poem – most base, really – was not what the poem was really about.

The poem wasn't after all Victorian soft porn, even if it could softly provoke pornish thoughts. Reading this as a poem about loss of innocence, as Tina did, does pretty much cover discovery of sexuality. Loss of innocence could include the loss of virginity, but more. Finally it mattered only that Tina had read it differently from the others.

Hema looked more waif-like than ever under her immense cap this afternoon. The weather was defence enough for it, even indoors at the playhouse across from the Abbey Primary School. Christmas was coming up, and it was snowing wetly.

The playhouse was a pretty enough place; it could belong to a Christmas picture postcard if there'd been a little less rain in the snow. Or if the air had smelt different. Christmas on this Leicester street came mixed with the aroma of Indian spices from Gelani's store across. Which meant the place smelt right, because Hema was telling a Christmas story in Gujarati with enough English thrown in for kids who might not know Gujarati. The most English of stories was a good one to offer in Gujarati because everyone knew it. So they would figure what the Gujarati meant.

Hema worked some days in the local library and some as a storyteller, especially for Gujarati-born English children – or English-born Gujarati children – from the Abbey Primary. She was telling her story to children waiting for their parents at the Belgrave playhouse. She was going to write it on the blackboard, and part act it. They would copy the story down in their books.

'CHRISTMAS NEE VARTA' she wrote on the blackboard, A Christmas Story, and began to tell, and sing, it, repeating the English often in Gujarati to get each to make sense in the other.

Once upon a time there were three children. It was Christmas Eve and they were waiting for Santa Claus.

One child said: *'Kyan chhe Saanta Klaus? Maru* present *layinay kayarey a vasho?'*

Another: 'Oh yes, when will he come with our presents?'

The third: *'Jaldi aavey to saaru.'* [Good if he comes early.]

Hema sang a song that the three children sing together, 'Who is coming on a Christmas night...'

Suddenly, a child says: '*Koi aavyu*! Someone's here! *Kadara Saanta Klaus hosay*! I hope it's him! *Chalo door molisay savay joyay!*'

'Yes! Let's have a look!'

They open the door.

'*Aato koi Saanta Klaus nathi.*' [No, it's not Santa.]

From outside: 'Of course I'm not Saanta Klaus. I'm the Christmas tree!'

Song: 'Oh Christmas tree..'

'But wait! There's someone at the door! *Havay to Saanta Klaus jo hosay!*'

'Let's open the door!'

'Oh! It's not Santa Klaus!'

Voice from outside: '*Hoon to ek pari chhoon* [I'm a fairy]! *Hoon tumhare maate ek ek present lavi chhoon*! Here you are, you can open them tomorrow.'

'Come quickly, let's open the door! Who are you?'

'*Hoon to* Rudolph *chhoon.*'

'*To Saanta Klaus kyaan chhe?*'

'I don't know! I'm looking for Santa too!'

Song: 'Rudolph the red-nosed reindeer...'

Rudolph: '*Aamey thaaki gaya chhe, havey am sui jayiye chheyay.*'

Before he can sleep there is a cry outside.

'Help! *Bachavo*! *Koi mane bachavey*!'

Song: 'Where Santa got stuck up...'

A figure appears at the door. '*Maney bhookh lagi chhey, khaavanu aayo.*' [Please, I'm hungry, can I have something to eat]

'Hooray! It's Santa!'

'*Amara present lavyo*? Where are our presents?'

'Oh, *pahila maney to bhookh lagi chhe*, I'm so, so hungry.'

'Here's something to eat.'

'Good! And here are your presents!'

Mums had been gathering and waiting for the story to end. 'Thank you, Hemaben,' said the first mum who stepped up to collect her kid. They must hope Hemaben's stories continue to have one common ending for the children much later in their lives, that in England they don't lose Gujarati, even if they grow up to care little about Santa.

From the Cradle to...

Leicester has learnt to keep it Indian all the way from nurseries to nursing homes.

Grow old along with the old. The best is over, but it's not so bad in one of those Indian homes in Leicester, the sort we thought were only for white people to grow old and unwanted in.

'We are now one another's family,' Sushilaben said at the Mahatma Gandhi house, just by Belgrave Road. She was one of those abandoned '*masis*', as elderly Gujarati women are rather dismissively called. Like the rest she too had once thought home would always be where their children are. Now she knows differently. 'Let them not come to us. We do not wait for them any more.' 'Them' was of course not just her children, but the children of others with her like her. And 'we' the new family of everyone here who had lost theirs.

She did not look like she was waiting for the children either. Mahatma Gandhi house had brought the beginning of a new life, even if it was near ending. Sushilaben was remarkably not depressed, and she looked quite at home in the reception room by the front door. Almost like it was her drawing room.

'My grandchildren were growing up, they needed the rooms,' she said, as we stood talking by the door. Like all

63

masis, she was dressed in a simple sari under a large shawl. 'My children put me in the drawing room but it did not look nice when guests came. So they sent me here. They said they will see me every weekend. Now nobody comes but it's all right. They never looked after us but now we are here to look after each other.'

Sushilaben invited me into the reception room. A frail and very elderly man walked slowly up and joined us on the sofa. 'They didn't want me then, I don't want them now,' he said. He too had forgotten his family, as they had forgotten him.

Two other women walked up. 'You want to bring your parents here? Wait,' said the woman who had sat nearest to me. She walked down the corridor and returned with a man who looked elderly but not retired. He was the manager. 'There are no rooms just now,' he said in Gujarati-East African English, that Africa-processed Gujarati clipping of English words is unmistakable. 'You will have to wait for one of us to die, and there are plenty waiting for rooms before you.' But he offered reassurance. 'We keep getting vacancies.'

We moved into the common room. A portrait of Gandhi and a map of India had been hung on the wall, they must do their bit to make the inmates feel at home. A lone man was watching TV as I walked in with Sushilaben and the others. His wife had died years ago and his son went back to Kenya, Sushilaben said. Everyone was known this way – when abandoned and by whom. But he said nothing about being abandoned as we sat down together to talk. 'We all get along very well. Singhs, Muslims, Gujaratis of all castes, we are now one family here.' Finally, everyone had come together in this pre-death club. Why did I think they should be more depressed than they were?

The common room began to fill up as we chatted about life in this house. A man introduced as Bipinbhai walked up with some difficulty; he'd been partially paralysed after a stroke. Like almost everyone else, he wanted to talk about his life; most of the time nobody wanted to know. He said he'd come to Britain during the Uganda expulsions of 1972 with a brother and seven sisters. Over the last three years only one sister had bothered to call him. 'We were like one family there. Here I don't know what happened. It must be this country. What else can it be?'

'We like it here because we have to,' said Sushilaben's companion, the one who had gone to call the manager. 'You don't always get what you want.'

'What do you feel about your son who sent you here?'

'No, it was not him, it was his wife. What could he do?'

'How do you spend your time here?'

'We do what we would do anywhere. Get up, make breakfast, clean, cook lunch, sleep, come to the common room for tea, watch TV, have dinner, then sleep again.' Kumudben was waiting only for days to repeat themselves, for as long as they would.

But two days in a year are different. That's when everyone is taken out in a bus on a day trip. And they had the Christmas and Diwali parties every year too, so that was two more days other than the usual. That made four days a year to wait for.

The road must have been named after the new nursing home it led to. Asha Marg, the path of hope, led from Loughborough Road to the home for the elderly managed by ASRA (Asian Sheltered Residential Accommodation). The new home had answered a growing need. Unlike Mahatma Gandhi House which stood on an old street, this one was custom built for the growing population of the Indian elderly, and it provided plenty of parking space for families to visit parents. Wasted space, mostly. A few cars on weekends was all it saw.

Inside the office of the home, with its smart new walls and sloping roof in a new style unconvincingly following the old, the manager produced a report on the need for a home like this, and for more such. The report spoke of the 'myth that Asian people in this country are able to care for their old as well as their young under one roof because of the extended family'.

The truth, it said, is that 'some Asians are treated degradingly by their children and such treatment would include granny-bashing, taking away of supplementary benefits, not giving them enough food to eat, locking them out, making them do the housework and so on'.

Children were making orphans of their parents, and these elderly orphans were being adopted by the state. 'The state is our mother, the state is our father,' said Niteshbhai, a resident assisting the manager. 'The children know this, they know their parents can stay somewhere for free and get enough money to live on. They say why should they look after us when the state can do it better?'

Ashaben, making lunch in the common kitchen, told me she'd never been better off. She was nearing 70, and said she'd moved several homes over the past three years because the next one always seemed better. She had almost too much money. 'We don't know what to do with the money we save.'

'In India the children have no choice but to be tolerant. Where will they send their parents?' someone at the door said. 'Maybe that is good, maybe not, I don't know. Here the government will cremate us. We will die on our own two feet.'

Young Faithful

The stillness on Asfordby Street broke quite suddenly a few minutes to five. Doors opened, little girls all in black with only their faces visible stepped out, carrying copies of the Quran. Boys about the same age – seven, eight years old – in mosque-ready gowns and Muslim-only caps emerged with them from the rows of houses strung together down the street, from little lanes to the side. They scurried down to the flat red-brick building joined to the row of houses down the street – the Jam-e-Mosque, the green letters on its white board announced – and then turned into a little lane by its side to the classrooms at the back. It was 5 p.m., time for the madrasah.

At the end of the street, close to the mosque, four men in long white robes and long black beards watched protectively. Only a few of the children were escorted by elders; it was safe enough for the rest on their own, the kids had the streets to themselves, and the parental were in any case keeping an eye. A white police van drove out from the police station about a hundred yards further down from the mosque, an occasional car drove by. But it was a quiet road that took only neighbourhood traffic.

A little girl in black burkha and hijab over her sports shoes walked down a side street to the corner where I stood by the Islamic bookshop, across from the mosque. 'What are you going to learn at school?' I asked. 'I'll be learning the Quran, and I'll be learning Arabic,' she said. 'But aren't the holidays on?' 'I'm going to *our* school.'

The school after school, that is. Through term time the kids come back from regular school about 3.30 p.m., and head out to school at the madrasah from five often until eight for their daily switch from secular to Islamic education. There's a switch of schoolbags too. Two little boys walked by, carrying bags with 'Madrasah Bag' printed below a sketch of a mosque. I took a quick picture.

Before I could speak to them, two of the four chaps who had been watching over the kids came up. 'You are talking to the children, you're taking photographs, you can't do that here,' one of them said angrily through his glasses. 'The children are getting intimidated.' They possibly were, but these chaps were getting a little intimidating too, and I gave up my roadside post along with my plans of trying to talk to the children inside the madrasah. I was expecting to meet some children at the next madrasah I was headed for on Sutherland Street in Highfields close by.

The entrance was through a side door on Sutherland Street, a fifty-yard lane that dips in from St Peter's Road. The building looked like any of the other houses around. It had served as a mosque for many years before the Muslim population in Highfields and around far outgrew it and turned to the spanking new mosque on Conduit Street near the railway station, or the many other new mosques that came up in Leicester. But the Sutherland Street mosque continues to draw the faithful, and the students to its madrasah. Abdullah Patel, who I'd been told by an Indian Muslim friend was the teacher here, welcomed me into the madrasah.

Patel wore a round Islamic cap, and his grey-black beard angled outward below his ears before tapering tightly down under his chin. Through his glasses I saw the sharp eyes of the knowing kind of teacher. I knew a little about Patel through my friend. He drove a taxi for a living, but he was really an Islamic scholar, and education secretary of The Islamic Centre in Leicester that ran madrasahs at this and other mosques. Patel and another man from the mosque invited me into the main classroom.

'Holiday season,' I said, unnecessarily. There were no kids around.

'Only for this week,' Patel said. 'Some mosques give some time off, some do not. We will be starting our classes next week.'

'And then classes every day and weekends?'

'Only from five to seven, Monday to Friday. But we are planning classes on Saturdays also for the older students.'

'But isn't it too much for the children, after their regular school?'

'Some younger girls get tired by the end of the day, that problem is definitely there, you will see them yawning. But most find the Quran very easy, because it is a miracle of Allah. And so after a long day at school it is not stressful. Children just six or seven years old recite it fluently. At times even I am surprised.'

'But does it affect their learning and their results at the main school?'

'Not at all. Their hard work is not going to waste, it helps them do the national curriculum better. It increases their talent to learn more at day school. We say it is important to earn your bread, be successful and have a decent life. You cannot rely on social security all the time. But it is important to be successful both in this life and the life after. If you neglect Islamic education, you will not be successful in the life after. The deeds of this life will mean reward by the Garden or punishment by fire. So both are important, and we give this concept at the madrasah.'

'But are the kids being forced by parents to come to the madrasah?'

'The children are conditioned to the madrasah system. Parents do not have to force them, they see their brothers and sisters and other children coming, so they also come. Children have this psychology of copying.'

'What do they learn here?'

'By the time children from our madrasahs are thirteen or fourteen, they will have read the Quran many times over, all 6,666 sentences of it. It is obligatory for our children to read the Quran, even if they don't understand it.'

'Is that all they learn?'

'We teach Urdu as a language, but Urdu based on Islamic thinking. We teach Arabic as a language, and we teach Islamic history and jurisprudence – *deeniyat* – and we teach children how to offer *namaaz* and perform their prayers. Every year we run a mock exam and then a regular exam, and children get prizes for doing well, and certificates they can keep in a nice frame.'

'And do the boys and girls study together?'

'Until they are eight or nine years old, then we put them in separate classes.'

'Is it compulsory for the girls to wear long dresses?'

'Girls need to wear a large, loose dress that does not reveal the size of their body parts, otherwise you may look at them with the devil's eye.'

'Could a long loose dress mean also salwar-kameez?' I asked particularly because this dress, something like a long tunic over loose trousers, is considered a quite modest dress.

'Oh no, not above the age of six or seven.' From then on children would begin to become young girls.

'Do you have other events at madrasahs, like sports?'

'We have football competitions. And we have races at the annual sports event. But girls have to keep their traditional dresses.'

'And do most Muslim kids go to the madrasah?'

'Some say ninety per cent. I say about ninety-seven per cent.'

We talked a little more. Patel was kind enough to give me a copy of the Muslim Directory as I got up to leave. I saw later that it listed 18 mosques in Leicester, almost all with madrasahs attached. That was among close to 800 mosque-madrasahs across Britain and more than a hundred listed Muslim schools where the national curriculum is taught alongside Islamic studies. Ninety or 97, there is no doubt that the overwhelming majority of British Muslim kids go to a madrasah after school.

But the Muslim Directory offered other information I wasn't expecting to find. The only pictures it prints are from Kashmir. One shows Dal Lake in Srinagar in Indian Kashmir whose 'serene surroundings are occupied by 600,000 Indian troops!' Another shows a soldier, with the caption: 'Indian soldier, weapon ready and watching high street shops!' A photograph of a funeral comes with the caption: 'Another number added to the genocide!' The directory has been produced with support from the Muslim Council of Britain, the main contact point for government dealings with British Muslims.

Another picture shows a soldier apparently searching somebody, with the caption: 'Palestine? Chechnya? Burma? Algeria? Tunisia? Iraq?… No, Kashmir. Indian soldiers harassing the civilian population. Muslims the world over are being subjected to occupation, oppression and torture.' The directory includes one picture from Pakistani Kashmir – of a fruit seller at his stall, with the caption 'Fruits of the world!' Religious teaching was obviously leading also to some kind of political spillover.

There have been more ominous signs of this kind of extension. None of the 7 July suicide bombers in London achieved much by way of regular education. But they were regulars at the Masjid-e-Umar mosque on Stratford Street in Beeston in Leeds, and its attached madrasah. And Leicester has had its share of terrorist leanings arising from its madrasahs.

In a study of places of religious worship in Leicester, Prof. Richard Bonney from the University of Leicester points to the discovery of a small Al Qaeda cell in Leicester in 2002. 'Brahim Benmerzouga and Baghdad Mezaine were sentenced to eleven years each after conviction for using credit card fraud to raise thousands of dollars for Al Qaeda. They were accused by the Crown Prosecution Service of working together to make military equipment, false travel documents and recruitment material. The two had details of nearly two hundred different bank accounts in their possession, and Benmerzouga had some sixty films covering suicide bombings and martyrdom, including videos of Osama bin Laden, the jury heard during the eight-week trial in Leicester.

'The key organiser was Algerian Djamel Beghal, who, according to *The Independent*, apparently cultivated young Muslims through a local mosque in Leicester. He also quietly built up the network of supporters among foreign émigrés, who used the local Indian and Pakistani communities as cover. Specifically, Beghal is accused of recruiting both British "shoe-bomber" Richard Reid and would-be 11 September 2001 hijacker Zacarias Mousaaoui.' Reid in turn was reported to have been in frequent attendance at a madrasah at the Finsbury Park mosque in London. As Bonney points out, 'that there is, and has always been, a connection between religion and politics is clear.'

'You're late,' the teacher said, like she'd said it before to the little girl who'd just walked into the classroom, and like she'd be saying it to her again.

The girl walked up to her desk, took off her pink coat and sat down. She said nothing, she had heard that from her teacher before, and she must know she'd hear it again. She didn't look like she minded being late, or then sitting down in class as the only girl without hijab. She was going to need some reclamation.

The teacher, naturally in proper black dress and hijab, continued. '*Bismillah ar-Rahman ar-Raheem...*' (In the name of God, the compassionate, the merciful – the opening phrase for all 114 Surahs in the Quran, except Surah 9). She went line by line through the Surah she was teaching the class of eight- to ten-year-olds , and the class repeated each line after her. They were memorising the lines, and they were learning to recite them right.

The two girls nearest to me at the back of the class were moving their lips, and saying very little. The teacher saw this, and perhaps she saw me see this as well from my seat at the back. She walked up to their desks, and now they had to repeat after her. With the teacher away at the back, two boys in the front celebrated their new-found freedom by starting an argument, because boys will be boys even in an Islamic school. That every kid would sit immersed in the Quran equally and absolutely was only a cliché I was carrying.

The teacher heard the arguing. A sharp tap on the desk where she stood, and the boys were back to their recital. The kids all had their textbooks before them, with the selection from the Quran they were memorising. But most were following the teacher without looking at the text. After some time, she stopped and let them continue on their own. They did; most had done a pretty good job of memorising the Surah, and for their age they were speaking the lines pretty much as teacher did. Who would not want to, and get picked on as the black sheep of the class?

'You need to read it, you need to remember it,' the teacher said as class ended.

I took an empty seat next to a boy as class ended.

'What were you reading?' I asked.

'The Quran.'

'But what from the Quran were you reading?'

'This,' he said, pointing to the Arabic text.

'But what is it saying?'

'Are you Muslim?'

'No. But what is the text saying?'

He said nothing. He got up and left.

The head teacher was kind enough to guide me to another classroom. I was at the Sunday school at the King Fahad Academy just across from Acton where London begins to get north-west. The Academy which runs regular school weekdays was obviously set up by the Saudis, with the Sunday school run through the Central Mosque at Regent's Park. Its students are from all over, as I saw in the classroom I'd just left, and the one I'd walked into – black, white, Indians, Pakistani, Arabs, everyone was learning Arabic and the Quran.

A male teacher in this classroom, in mandatory gown, beard and cap, was teaching children off English letters on the blackboard how to speak the lines of the Quran right.

'For those who cannot read Arabic,' he was saying. 'When you see one "a", no stretching, when you see "aa", then stretch.'

The students, a little older here, about ten to twelve or so, followed.

'*Gad aflaha maann zakkaaha*,' he wrote on the board. 'And "*maann*" has a nasal sound you have to practise while reading the Quran. It's called the *ghunna*.'

He asked a boy in front to speak the line. He did just fine. 'Very good, *masha-allah*,' teacher said. Others got the line right too, and the next. '*Wa qad khaaba mann dassaa haa*.'

We were soon into break-time, and he set memorising the lines taught as homework for the week. The kids were out of the class fast. I stayed on with the teacher a little.

'What were they learning?'

'The Al-Shams Surah.'

'But they were reciting it, do you also teach the meaning?'

'No, we do not. It is only after they have memorised it and learnt to speak the lines correctly that we give them a general overview of the meaning. If we also start translating, it will get too much for the children.'

PATEL POWER

Cornered

Why don't Indians ever play football?
Because every time they get a corner they put up a shop.

That old joke tired out some time back. Behind the till of every corner shop, it was thought, was an Indian. Mostly true. It is also true that behind many Indians and certainly most Patels at the corner shops was Babubhai Patel.

If you can allow an exchange of a Mars bar for small change to produce a legend, it would have to be Babubhai. It's too early yet for the Museum of London to find a place for Babubhai Patel, but one day it must if it is to record what isn't visibly grand but still defines London. He alone did much to change the face of London after he turned some of Britain into a nation of Patel shopkeepers, a few thousand of them. In the world behind those shop tills he's known as the 'guru of CTN' (Confectionary, Tobacco, Newspapers). London wouldn't be what it is today without the corner shop, without Babubhai Patel.

Tucked into these stores, the corner stores, was often the post office. Babubhai learnt, then taught, how to make that unsung marriage of shop with post office work better than the English ever could. Like so many business ideas it was simple. Babubhai mastered the business of shop leading into post office past goods and goodies, making a shopper of the post office visitor for those few steps.

Babubhai told me his rags-to-riches story in the office of his company BA Finance, on Garratt Lane near Tooting Broadway Station. Like all of these stories – and there are about as many of those stories as there are immigrants – it did not really begin with rags. But Babubhai's story was not his alone. His was the business of multiplying it for a few thousand others and changing the way London, even Britain, does this sort of business.

Babubhai's office didn't show that success, and what it didn't show advertised his style. He played himself down as he played down his office. You wouldn't suspect he was guru to anyone unless you were in the CTN business yourself. He'd be that short, balding figure in a room you'd probably notice last. The understated helper, and that was his success. 'My father always used to say, help others and others will help you. Because they will come back to get your help.' For a fee, naturally.

Babubhai had worked out ways to cut costs way below anything that English shopkeepers who preceded the Patels thought possible, and improve the productivity of pennies in ways they could never visualise. The two together are known recipe for a shop's success, but some things Patels knew that the English never did. He zeroed in on every penny on every product, on every cost. And then leave it to everyone walking in through the door to do the multiplying. And they did.

But Babubhai offered more than cost-cutting tricks; he could tap the capital to launch into the business in the first place, a reputation he brought over from Kenya. He knew how to channel loans the Patel way and even the Asian way in Nairobi through Standard Bank, now Standard Chartered Bank. When a Patel off the boat from India wanted capital, it was Babubhai he'd turn to. When he wanted investment advice, it was Babubhai again.

It worked well in East Africa of the sixties, but did not last. 'My post got Africanised,' he said. So he sent his wife and children to London, and followed two years later in 1970. He landed with two assets: he knew banking, and Patels knew him. Off-the-boat Patels had needed him in Kenya, now off the second boat in Britain they would need him again.

Within a month of arriving in Britain, Babubhai told me, he set up a small finance company at Trafalgar Square. Easy for arriving Patels to find him there, everyone came to Trafalgar Square to send home that pigeon picture. At the same time he got together with two other Patels to buy a sub post office on the far less spectacular Trafalgar Road in Greenwich, south London. Repeats of the lesser Trafalgar was the product he would sell at the real Trafalgar address. It was a business waiting for Patels.

'The three of us bought it on a goodwill of £5,500,' he said. With the goodwill paid, there was steady income for the three Patels when weekly wages could often be as low as £15 a week. Plus – and it was the discovery of this plus that changed the face of London – Babubhai found that real income came from sale of newspapers, chocolates and drinks at the post office. The post office became only the hook to get customers in, and very soon what the chocolates brought in made post office fees only extra income.

'The margin for the sales was a minimum of twenty per cent. The volume was good.' Babubhai looked pleased even in retrospect. When a Patel says volume was good, he is usually taking in a fair bit of money, though all money is small in relation to what could be.

The partners rapidly bought three other sub post offices. In 1973 they disbanded the partnership, and each Patel set up his own business. Babubhai went on with the business of getting others into this business. He wouldn't buy shops; he would make it possible for others to buy theirs. His was the corner shop consultancy.

'So many people came to see me. I used to give them advice – how to buy, how to get finance, who to approach. I used to do all this for them and after that I used to give them training in my own sub post office.' Budding Patel shopkeepers would be taught how to restrict pennies going out and invite more to come in. A training college unlisted in London's records had come to exist for the expansion of Patels.

'My office became like a doctor's waiting room,' he said. A 'those-were-the-days' look came over him, and I could see the lightest of smiles in the eyes behind those glasses. In that rush of the seventies Babubhai said he got more than 2,000 CTNs going and at least another thousand later, after the immigration wave from East Africa had subsided. All that in turn set off more businesses. 'Once these people set up, they told their friends and relatives. Then they train, then we again finance, see, that is how it goes on.' The Patels advanced rapidly into London's corners, and changed life around them.

Babubhai offered consultation without a consultation fee. 'First I would find out a good business for a client in a good location. Then I would negotiate for them. I would always bring the price down more than they would ever pay me in commission. Then I would arrange for the solicitor, the accountant and the stock-taker. Then I would arrange the finance and then the insurance. I would only take commission from the client on completion.' It didn't end there. 'I would monitor the business for the next six months to make sure it was going well.' And to top all this, 'I used to give them courage.' When had pre-Patel London ever provided service to match this?

The banks came to know Babubhai Patel, and that money given through him was money for the bank. Babhubhai showed pictures of an award Natwest presented him 'as one market leader to another'. Banks, he said, competed to be his best friends. 'Other branches of Natwest, other banks also began to come to me. I never had to go to a bank, the managers would always come here.' He tapped on his modest table to make the point.

'But if business was so good, why were white British people selling?' I asked.

'You see, they used to employ staff and close at five.' Babubhai saw that as reason enough for failure. How much more backward could anyone get than to run a business, employ staff and close at five? A Smith employing a Jones were both unsuspecting then of the profitability in a Patel couple's togetherness at the till.

Other weaknesses in the British character showed up. 'Those were the days of the recession, and they thought everything was going to fall apart. So they sold everything and went to live by the sea.' Babubhai waved a hand in the general direction of the English Channel.

When white Brits see a recession, they look at figures that don't add up, they look at the headlines, and head for the sea. A Gujarati comes into his own when margins shrink. With their backs to the shop wall, and loans to repay, the Patels did away with staff and with downing shutters at five, and with not raising them on weekends. They made pennies add, from customer after customer, day after day. The surrender of London's corners to Patels was soon complete.

K. D. Patel stood before me, an unexpectedly athletic looking shopkeeper at his shop near Clapham Junction station. He was telling me what Babubhai had done for him. This is what he remembered of a fateful conversation with Babubhai Patel years back.

'Babu kaka, I want to borrow £550,000 for this shop I have seen.'

'How much money do you have?'

'£10,000.'

'You have '£10,000 and you want to borrow £550,000?'

'Yes.'

'No problem.'

Memory condenses such exchanges nicely, and makes neat stories of them. Like most Indian stories, they improve in the telling. But whatever got said between the two, K. D. got the money. His shop at Clapham junction today has an annual turnover of a few million pounds.

'I have never seen a banker, I never want to see a banker,' K. D. told me. 'For us there is only Babu kaka.'

K. D.'s shop was fighting off, successfully, a number of Goliaths to corner business. 'I have a Marks & Spencer store third door from me. Walking distance I have twenty-four-hour Asda, I have Somerfield, there is Woolworths, there is Superdrug and now a Sainsbury's is opening up. They are all my neighbours.' He spoke with a show of apparent lightness in the face of grim matters. A man set to conquer adversity through just everyday work.

The Goliaths have the economy of scale on their side to price several products lower than most Patels can, but K. D. was not David for nothing. 'Main thing I have is location.' It could hardly be better, just across from the station. 'You have 3,000 trains a day passing through here. All of them do not stop, but many trains stop.' The ones that don't each carry so many missed pennies. But that's just railways, that's life.

Without scale on his side, K. D. still undercuts the big guys. 'We also make some products cheap, and keep some others not so cheap. These are just tricks of the trade, everybody does it.' If his shop was nearer, people wouldn't cross the road to save a penny or two; by the station customers need to save seconds, not pennies. So he'd tailored his services accordingly. 'We give really fast service at the till. If you come into our shop, you do not have to wait. Because we need your money fast.' Well-matched hurry on both sides.

He knows what sells fast. 'I know they love chocolates.' So he stocks about two hundred and fifty varieties. *Lots of chocolates for me to sell, lots of pennies for me to make.* And K. D. is taking on the Goliaths with all sorts of other extras. Like an offer to accept gas and electricity bills. 'If I process bills of £15,000 a week, I get only one hundred pounds commission. But that is still £5,200 a year.' If you multiply every recurring income and expense into an annual sum, all income is good, and no expense too little. Penny wise, pound very wise.

K. D. said he'd started off with one shop in Streatham bought with his three brothers through Babubhai Patel. 'Then also he arranged the finance for us – no security, nothing. Then we got another shop on the same road and then a supermarket in Dulwich.' Then, as usual, each Patel brother set out on his own. Now the three brothers have a shop each, and their sister three. Each has invested the profits in several properties to rent out, and the value of each has risen.

K. D. works 12 to 14 hours a day, and says he likes it. 'People in this country, they don't want to work, that is why depressed.' But he is working away only because it's working out for him. Not every Patel has a shop nicely across from a railway station. And not every David Patel has triumphed in the face of the expanding Goliath chain stores.

'The Patels can stop London,' Vinod Nakarja had said when we met somewhere. When he left that line hanging in the air and invited me to his shop to find out how, I just couldn't resist.

Some days later we were talking behind locked doors in the little post office at the back of his shop in Gerards Cross, just off the road to Oxford as you leave London. We were in the post office because the wife was handling the corner shop part of the business, and business must go on; Vinodbhai was happy to talk to me but not if he had to lose money at the same time. And we had locked ourselves in because there's money in the post office, this is London these days, and you never know.

London wakes up. And what's in the papers? Can't buy one, the Patel shops round the corner are all closed. Yes, the *Metro* is free, but those would all have been taken by now. What a way to start a day. These Patels.

No morning milk, no tea. How long can milk last even in the fridge? Can't buy the train ticket at the store either. Buy at the station, then. But now what a queue. What if you miss the train? Those few minutes in the morning make all the difference. And the Patels had to do this on a Monday when everyone buys their weekly pass. The scare was in the detail that he added up dramatically. What would London be like…?

Face after face appeared outside the toughened glass as we talked, they wanted stamps and the usual at a post office. They saw two Asian men talking inside, without a clue that one of them was painting scenarios of bringing their city to a halt. They were lucky Nakarja's thoughts hadn't touched their lives.

No, the Patels won't stop London. But in the imagined discomfort Patels can bring to Londoners, Nakarja (another of those Kutch Patels who find it fashionable to drop 'Patel' and take up the village name) saw the power of the Patels.

But why would he want to treat London so? 'I will tell you.' I waited while he sold some more stamps to some dear old ladies. 'Nice day for a walk,' he said to the nearest of them. 'Yes, not bad at all,' she replied. These things need to be said to dear old ladies; they visit post offices more than anyone else.

Nakarja would tell me all, but only by and by. Customer is king, and I was only a reporter.

'*The Sun*,' he said. 'The newspaper *Sun*.' I was from India, and he had to make sure, because what do people from India know. '*The Sun* carried an article that was so abusive of Hindu gods, so abusive. I told them that day that I would not sell the newspaper.' Not only not sell, he would show *The Sun*, and show London, through his Newsagents Action Group, NAG, that others would not sell it any more either.

'A few Patels, they agreed, but the rest, they did not want to know. You see, our people, they have never been united, that is our problem.' *The Sun* got away with it and London was let off because Patels would not unite. Indian history was repeating itself through shops that remained open as usual.

NAG tried to get Patels to unite for the sake of business if not for Hindu gods.

'Look at this.' He held up a packet of Bombay mix. 'Do you see?'

'Yes,' I replied. 'Bombay mix. Why they call it Bombay mix I don't know.' I was missing the point here.

'You see the price, thirty-five pence, printed on the packet. So they are telling me at what price I should sell, they are fixing my margins for me. More and more, these fellows, this is what they are beginning to do.'

The Bombay mix was eating into pricing strategies. Pricing every product to the penny is a carefully considered calculation, depending on competition, location, volume, the preferences of the area, and that balancing act of what you will price low to keep them coming and what you can mark up to swell profits. Those decisions have to be taken, and constantly reviewed, over each of a few thousand products. When manufacturers stamp a price, they limit the shopkeeping genius of a Patel. These decisions were abusing their business choices, not just their gods, and still Patels were doing nothing.

NAG never did become an effective group. It ran into what Nakarja thought were Indian cultural fault-lines that had stayed so long they'd become genetic. So, like India disunited and so colonised earlier, the Patels were not united in standing up to 35p marked on a pack of Bombay mix. Each Patel thought only of his Patel shop. Nakarja's plan failed because customers who run into closed doors may have memories, and no one is in the business of counting how much money you could lose from each displeased customer, certainly not over something silly in *The Sun*. NAG failed because Patels were in the business of keeping shops open, not closed.

Nakarja was holding up the view that Indians were divided and as a consequence played too easily into the hands of the divide-and-rule game the British so loved. These two taken together, and they usually are, must add up to one of the oldest Indian moans. It's migrated quite smoothly to Britain. Every time a Brit does something that does not please all equally, they are dividing and ruling.

Several Patel businesses have failed before the advancing Goliaths.

The race does reach an end point. The first Patel shops started opening late, and then the supermarkets began to open late. The Patels opened weekends, and then laws were changed to let the big guys open weekends. Then the Goliaths began to be open 24 hours, and now a few Patels are beginning to open twenty-four hours. The Patel was likely to be nearer you, but now watch the space: a biggie is coming to a corner near you.

Babubhai figures that CTNs with a turnover of less than £7,000 a week are beginning to close. One small-shop Patel after another has been telling him about the pinch.

Tightening margins need higher volumes to redeem them. When sale volumes fall below a level, the fewer pennies that margins leave don't add up. Cost price needs volumes to sink it sufficiently before sale price. If you can't buy enough, you can't buy cheap enough.

On the other hand, overheads are beginning to take too big a bite from gross income, and Patel after Patel shopkeeper adds up these woes. Local taxes have doubled in some areas. Electricity bills are higher, and everyone needs 24-hour freezers. Banks are beginning to charge now for small-level commercial transactions, and the cost of credit for bulk buying is now higher. More competition means you need to spend more on getting your store to look good. More crime means the cost of security has gone up, along with insurance premiums. The days are long gone when some customer could walk in and ring a bell just to pay.

But, as with most things Indian, the moan is greater than the loss. 'Our people grumble, but they survive,' Babubhai had said. They even flourish.

I ran into Nakarja at a swanky hotel party a week after we spoke. He came in an expensive car, wearing a black *bandhgala* all golden around the collar. Not the picture of a man whose business is falling apart. In any case, by now a CTN Patel has a career of profit behind him, a house to live in, and rent from another two, with mortgage mostly paid off. About the worst that can happen to him now is rich retirement.

As the biggies come in, more and more Patels are selling. And who is buying those shops? 'Sri Lankans,' K. D. said. 'You see, when they compare in Sri Lankan rupees, a pound is a big thing. And they work day and night. They keep their shops open till twelve at night. There is no family life.' Sound familiar? But unlike the Brits who had retreated before the Indian invasion into their corners, sea breeze is not for Patels. Property in London is far more invigorating. The Patels began to buy property in the seventies. Since then, house prices have shot up as much as fifty-fold.

The Goliaths pulling down Patel shutters are getting some help from the younger Patels. One survey among Gujarati retailers showed that only six per cent of the children of first generation shopkeepers want to run their parents' business. 'My children see me working fourteen hours a day,' Nakarja said. 'I have never had a holiday. But they want those holidays. They want proper jobs.'

K. D. Patel's son has studied to be a pharmacist. At shop after shop, the same story is repeated. These Patels went one way, their children are going down about three or four – pharmacists, computer programmers, accountants, solicitors. Younger Patels are stepping out of their parents' corners. No, the Patels cannot stop London. But London is not going to be able to stop the Patels either.

In-house Innings

A cricket match where every player was a Patel… to the *Daily Mail* this had been an ethnic scoop. To a Patel cricketer in England, it was just a way of life, and there would be another all-Patel cricket match this Sunday, a Patel friend had told me. Which had brought me driving up north of Northolt looking for the cricket field.

The little crescent I turned into just after leaving the A40 had been renamed India Gardens, but had not yet been renamed on the *A–Z*. 'They will do it officially and all that,' the Patel on the phone giving directions had told me. They had put up their board already because Patels are known for their enthusiasm, officials are not. Maps would catch up by and by. On the map I'd be turning into Harvey Road, with Peacock Park further up. On the ground I was driving through India Gardens to the cricket fields of the Shri Kutch Leva Patel Samaj.

I'd come to watch a match, inspired by the predictably tickled story in the *Daily Mail* about a match where every player was a Patel. An accompanying picture of the teams was captioned 'Patel vs Patel'. Which Patel beat which mattered only to the playing Patels; I can't remember that the paper much reported on the cricket. The story was not about cricket, but the many-ness of Patels, and no doubt immigrants. So many immigrants now that just Patels can play just Patels. A friend at the Shri Kutch Leva Patel Samaj, the SKLP as it is more manageably known, told me a match like that was not that unusual because Patels more than other Gujaratis have a thing about cricket.

Immigration and cricket were of course brought famously together through Sir Norman Tebbit's version of test cricket, about the only thing he will be remembered for. So an Indian who migrated to Britain and then took British nationality must no more cheer India but England (since Scotland, Wales and Northern Ireland have remained mostly immune to the game). But cricketing loyalties never did migrate. I've never once seen anyone Indian-looking cheer England against India. *The Times* in one such Test front-paged the picture of a banner by Indian fans at Lord's: 'We've failed the Tebbit test, and we're proud of it.'

The Times picture suggested disloyalty and the *Mail* story the numbers that might be disloyal. But the *Mail* didn't know what Patels did, that a Patel vs Patel match is made possible not just by the many-ness of Patels, but by the many Patelnesses. It's Patelhoods within Pateldom that make that kind of match possible, usually between one kind of Patel and another.

I drove around to the parking lot by the sports grounds, large enough for two, maybe three, cricket fields, and parked by a maroon Ford with the number SKL1PP; a number just waiting to be grabbed at those auctions; he would have only his own to bid against, and they could be talked to.

It was a bright day, all green and golden, as only an English summer day can be. Not the kind of day a cricketer likes to pass unpadded. A couple of padded Patels came into view as I walked round to the pavilion, thwacking away at balls in net practice, which does not always need a net. The other players were hanging around outside. Everyone was in the usual cricket variation of off-white; it looked like the start of a very serious day's cricket.

The pavilion was a small, simple block with a lunch table laid out already in the veranda outside the changing rooms for 'Home' and 'Away'. Players were walking in and out of them. The match of the day, a notice announced, was between the SKLP, the home team, and the Muktajivan Cricket Club. The Shri Kutch Leva Patel bit I figured out a little; Shri, a far more respectful Indian version of 'Mr' to both people and associations, of course announced something venerable to follow in the old Hindu tradition. Kutch was a northern region in Gujarat. Leva and Kadwa prefixed kinds of Patels, and I've heard the origins of those two claimed as far back as Luv and Kush, the two supposed sons of the god Ram. The Levas were descendents of Luv, and Kadwas of Kush. That would make the SKLP Ram's progeny through Luv in a certain part of Gujarat. The name Muktajivan meant nothing to me.

Someone should know. The only other man as idle as I was, at least for the moment, was a player who stood by the lunch table surveying the field. Just the man for the first hello of the day.

He introduced himself as Naju Lalji from the SKLP team, which would bat first. He was to come in at number five, he told me, which gave him some time as surveyor. And a quite picturesque surveyor he was too. Two gold earrings on one ear established him at least as intended cool, and dragged what might have been an approach to middle age back towards youth. His cricket cap sat lightly above his shaved head. Silhouetted against that vast stretch of green and gold on the sunny field, he appeared more a profile than a person. He looked dashing enough in a way approaching middle age, and if he played as he looked, he could be the dream of some Patel woman getting on a bit.

'So who's playing today?' I asked him.

'We are playing the Muktajivan Cricket Club.'

'And you are the SKLP?'

'Yes.'

'You are the Patels, and who are they?'

'They are also Patels.'

'So all the players today are Patels.'

'Of course.'

'And you are the home team.'

'Yes, but they are also the home team. We share the ground.'

'If you are both Patels, and you are both home teams, how come you are separate teams, and one is called Muktajivan?'

'Because they go to a separate temple. We go to the Swaminarayan temple at Harrow, they have their own.'

'So they are not Swaminarayans.'

'No, they are also Swaminarayans, but they go to a different Swaminarayan temple.'

'Why is that?'

'Everyone believes in Lord Swaminarayan, but there are different gurus, you know.'

'Are they Patels from a different part of Gujarat?'

'No, we are all Patels from Kutch. We come from a group of twenty-four villages in Kutch. They also come from the same twenty-four villages. You see, we are like different branches of a tree.'

I was being slow figuring this out. Both teams were Patels, both Swaminarayans, which meant they were followers of the nineteenth-century saint from Gujarat, Sahjanand Swamy, whose followers worship him as Bhagwan Swaminarayan,

God himself. Both were from the same 24 villages of Kutch in Gujarat. But they were different kinds of Swaminarayan Patels who went to different temples. That point of separation had made this match possible.

I wanted to ask more but Naju seemed to be tiring of these explanations. In any case, the game had now begun. In a fashion. No one was scoring runs and no one was getting out. For a forty-over-a-side game, it was a slow start.

But before the game took over I had to ask Naju the obvious question: if he was a Patel, why was he called Lalji?

'Of course I am Patel,' he said. 'It's like the Singhs. There are so many Singhs who do not put Singh in their name. But they are Singhs, no?' It is usual for a Sikh name to end with a Singh, but not mandatory, and the lack of a Singh does not make a Sikh any less a Sikh. Every Sikh could be a Singh, but not all surname themselves only Singh. There are of course Singhs who are not Sikhs, but that's just mandatory Indian complication. And so, it seemed, with Patels. Poor Britain still does not suspect that there are very many more Patels in its midst than people with Patel in their name.

I turned to watch a second game of Patel sons now progressing in the net practice area. Naju too was watching. And this appeared a pleasing sight he did want to talk about, rather than explain the obvious about sharing Gujarat, a region of it, a cluster of villages within the region, a surname in principle if not in name, a god – but not the guru, not the temple.

'Cricket is our religion,' he said. 'We have already picked up sixty-five kids for sharp training to become proper players. There are three hundred more on the wait-list.' I thought he was looking at England's future, and a Patel future through it. If England is nurturing 365 colts of just one kind of Patel, one of them will show up on television one day. If Monty Panesar did, can a Patel be far behind?

There was movement on the cricket field. The first SKLP wicket fell. Out lbw, Naju explained; he had been keeping an eye on the big game. The opener was walking back to the pavilion with that hard-done-by look batsmen out lbw always wear. 'It was high,' he said walking into the pavilion, tapping a point almost at hip level. 'Don't worry,' said Naju. 'No one out lbw is ever out.'

The wicket relieved Naju of further discussion. He nodded his cap in my direction and went in to pad up. He stepped away unhurriedly, out of respect no doubt to number four. That left me as one of only two spectators. The other was a Ms Whatever Patel in a blue denim jacket sitting ahead of me outside the pavilion, her legs stretched out on another chair under a shawl. By her side, a chap in white was keeping the score on a register.

She was the only woman on the grounds, and could end up more watched than watching. Her long brown hair flowed straight, more or less, into a butterfly clip before finding freedom again over her jacket. Her profile was shaped very much by Gujarati genes, rounded, pleasant and undefined, and whatever her first name, her last would surprise no one. She would be seen as nice-looking anywhere, but here she was prettier because she and she alone brought femininity to the field. It couldn't be just me who was especially aware of her; the Patels in white must all have noticed her even if they had a lot more to do than I did. Heroism is not heroism if it goes unwitnessed. Her presence brought an odd intensity to the game.

Out on the field the Patels were playing out the usual cricket rituals – repositioning caps, pulling up gloves, waiting with arms folded between panther-like dashes, combining strength with subtlety, speed with elaboration, finding time for swing, time for poise, luxuriating in that balance of ease and energy that only cricket allows.

A couple more batsmen had walked back, and now Naju was out there batting. He did it in style, but not for long. He walked back, not quite the same man. It always takes something out of you when you score less than you'd like to. He resumed spectator position in the pavilion a little droopily just when the game was picking up some life because others were now scoring busily to beat the early stillness.

The last of the overs were played out, and it was lunch. Ms Patel had gone into the pavilion a little earlier to move sandwiches from the kitchen to the lunch table. I went to sit by the scorer.

The scorer was Kirit Patel, a Muktajivan man; square and steady, virtuously unflamboyant. A small scoreboard by his side carried on top the logo of the Muktajivan Cricket Club. It must be about the holiest cricket logo in the world: a very Hindu-looking face, with a cricket ball sitting as a tilak. Below the ball, made so holy by its placement, sat a deep vertical 'U'; on this face of cricket it marked the wicket where the nose should be. Two bats took the place of eyes towards the top on this face of cricket, just towards the top of the 'U', and three wickets below the 'U' offered a sparse, toothy smile. This was temple cricket, and like the local Middlesex league games, this was in a league of its own.

Kirit had not kept score very happily. SKLP had scored 176 runs in their 40 overs and his register showed that 18 had come in the last. He looked doubtful that the blank page on his register kept for his Muktajivan Patels would beat that figure post-lunch. From what he told me about the Muktajivan Patels, he would have good reasons for his doubts. Theirs was not a world of 65 colts training and 300 waiting. 'We have about thirty-six players now, and about twelve to fifteen youngsters.' Not a lot to choose from. The match, and the future, was going the SKLP way.

Naju, who'd got over his low score by now, was preparing for the SKLP future, handing out low catches to his colts in that familiar cricketing arc.

'They just love it, and we love it,' Naju said as I stopped by. 'Keeps them off the streets. Are they taking drugs? No. Are they eating junk food, sitting in front of TV? No, they are right here, playing cricket with us.' In the game of cricket lies the building of character and the perpetuation of Patelhood of the SKLP variety. The little colts were falling into teams of divergent Patel kinds before they knew it.

Over sandwiches and *gathia*, that Gujarati snack that Britain has come to know as the noodle-like ingredient of Bombay mix, Naju told me that the England and Wales Cricket Board was paying to promote Patel cricket at their grounds. The ECB had provided a grant for preparing the ground and the wicket, and every now and then it hands out a little more here and there for bats and pads and the rest. But the SKLP was doing enough for its own cricket. Company billboards, meaning sponsorship and money, lay stacked by the side of the pavilion, waiting to be set up around the field for the bigger matches. Every Kutch Patel with a business worth the name had sponsored a board. The players' shirts were sponsored by another Kutch Patel businessman. One way or another, money from every successful Kutch Patel was doing something for SKLP cricket.

That of course is no guarantee of results, on the principle that New Zealand can beat India. The proportion of numbers to success ceases to matter past some early critical point. But if a Muktajivan club had to choose from 35, and SKLP from a few hundred, it would always be advantage SKLP. By the end of the day it was an easy win for SKLP.

Muktajivan were much the senior team, they'd had a team since 1969, Kirit told me. The SKLP was set up only in 1985. But something had changed in the world of religion, and cricket followed.

Muktajivandas, the Swaminarayan swami who set up a sect of his own in the 1940s, died in Bolton on a visit to Britain in 1979, I learnt from the book *An Introduction to Swaminarayan*

Hinduism by Raymond Brady Williams. Muktajivandas had left the Ahmedabad sect of the Swaminarayans, itself one of the factions that the Swaminarayans had split into. He then set up his own institutions and temples, which came to be called the Swaminarayan Gadi.

'Although the group is relatively small, the devotees seem to be very loyal and lavish in their support,' Williams writes. 'In 1957 they celebrated a golden jubilee of his birth by giving him a gift of his weight in gold, ten years later they celebrated his platinum jubilee with a gift of platinum, and when he was seventy he was weighed against five types of jewels.'

Muktajivandas was among other leaders in the Swaminarayan faith believed by followers to be an incarnation of Sahjanand Swami. In October 1972 he proclaimed he represented the personification of Swaminarayan Gadi, the sect he set up, and came to be treated as God by his followers.

Despite the lavish adulation of his followers, the Muktajivan following has remained small compared to the SKLP Swaminarayan Patels from the Ahmedabad sect of the Swaminarayans, who go to a temple in Kingsbury in north London. The SKLP have grown, and have a smart new Swaminarayan temple to show for it just off Kenton Road. Numbers have brought money, and a better cricket team.

Just two different ways of being Swaminarayan had produced the Patel vs Patel match of the day. Didn't Naju say cricket is their religion?

Milk, Murder, Marriage

One kind of Patel would kill their newly born daughters by drowning them in milk, and so another kind of Patel keeps away from them in London today, and neither of these Patels will marry into the other if they can help it. So the two Patels were saying, though it took me a little time to figure that out because I found that at first hard to believe. The hangover of that nineteenth-century quarrel, they were saying, had been part institutionalised in London, because the Patels from those child-killing origins were set up largely as an association in Tooting in south London, and the other Patels as a federation in Wembley.

Dr M. I. Patel, industrialist and former sheriff of Mumbai, as Bombay was later Indianised to be, had no doubts about this at all, and since my friend K. D. Patel had introduced M. I. to me in one of the more spacious of his many drawing rooms at his house (he would, I guess, have liked the prefix palatial) in Wembley also as historian, I was listening carefully. K. D. himself, the former Tory councillor from Brent with a petrol station or two, and certainly two concurrent wives, was not a man to be taken lightly either.

'These Patels from the six villages, they used to kill their daughters,' M. I. told me firmly. We hadn't met to talk about this, but the conversation had naturally come round to the ways of Patels by and by. 'They always thought themselves very superior to the others. What superior, when they would kill their daughters?'

And this, he said, is affecting Patel lives in Britain here and now. 'The hangover of these things continues a long time.'

M. I. Patel was in London on his way to a lecture tour in the US, and looked very much the businessman on his way to a lecture tour of the US. As the industrialist, he said that his Patel Extrusion Group manufactures among other things the tubes that companies pack toothpaste into. Just as necessary as the toothpaste, when you think of it. He'd squeezed enough profit from those tubes, and found himself time for politics and history.

'It was called the practice of *doodh-peeti*,' Dr Patel said, literally, 'a girl given milk to drink. When a girl child was born, they would

95

just kill her. They would place the child's head in a pan of milk and drown her. I have seen it with my own eyes.' A consequence of such murders as widespread practice, he said, was that 'the population of girls in those villages came down so much.'

I wanted to know more, but K. D.'s hospitality and the compulsions of two busy Patels came in the way. But of course if something like this were true it would be known to many more than two Patels.

That those six villages in the Charotar area of central Gujarat that M. I. spoke of were quite different from others is clear from just a few brushes with London Patels. Back in Gujarat the six had grouped themselves into the Chha-gam, the Six Villages. Other village clusters had formed in Charotar too – the Baavis-gam (Twenty-Two Villages), the Sattavis-gam (Twenty-Seven Villages) and so on. But the Chha-gam lot had the money and power, they were the ruling elite. It was inevitable that the rest would resent the assumed aristocracy of the Chha-gam Patels.

Migration to Britain did nothing to erase those differences, it might even have drawn out memories fading away within Gujarat itself. So Patels whose forefathers lived in the Twenty-Two Villages have set up their own group, the Patels from the Twenty-Seven Villages one of their own.

The Patel Association centre in Tooting has long been associated mostly with the Chha-gam Patels, the Patel Federation centre in Wembley with the rest of the Charotar Patels. But do memories of murdered infant girls stand between a Wembley Patel and a Tooting Patel?

'I was born and brought up in one of the "Six Villages" of Patidars (another name for Patels) of central Gujarat mentioned frequently in this book as practising female infanticide,' Prof. A. M. Shah from the Department of Sociology at Delhi university wrote in the foreword of *Female Infanticide and Social Structure: A Socio-Historical Study in Western and Northern India* by L. S. Vishwanath published in 2000. 'Throughout my childhood I had heard about the practice of *doodh-peeti*, the drowning of female infants in a pail of milk, in earlier generations in my village.'

The British of today know of Patels as a plentiful kind of Gujarati Indian. But Vishwanath writes that the colonial Brits of the nineteenth century knew a good deal about the Patels under their noses – and of this practice of *doodh-peeti*. They took occasional steps to discourage the practice but did little to stop it, at least to begin with. Vishwanath writes that no one knows how far back that practice went, but the British discovered it both among the Rajputs of Gujarat and the Lewa Patidars, that one lineage of Patels drawn from Ram's son. And among the Patidars, he writes, particularly among the Chha-gam lot.

'The middle and higher-level status groups in each of these castes tried to maintain their status and avoid substantial dowry payment which hypergamous marriage (a marriage of a girl into a family of higher or at least equal status) involved by resorting to killing of their female children,' Vishwanath writes. 'The problems of the top stratum in these castes were compounded by the fact that in addition to high dowries, the high-status lineage had to find eligible grooms in a restricted circle of elite families within their caste. Generally, therefore, the higher status groups practised female infanticide more extensively than the lower status groups.' This happened to such an extent that the female population crashed.

Milk became by tradition the murder weapon for some time, Vishwanath writes. But there were other ways of killing newborn girls. Why give the little things poisoned milk, when you could give them nothing at all? 'In fact, the newly born infants were so vulnerable, that neglect which took the form of refusal of the mother to feed the female infant, or exposure to heat or cold were enough to finish them off. After the passing of the Female

Infanticide Act, census officials were reporting that castes which practised female infanticide were "resorting increasingly" to neglect of their female children to escape detection.'

What Vishwanath wrote every Patel knows, it was just I who didn't. But Vishwanath's pages of history were continuing into London today, it seemed from conversations with Patel after Patel. Quite obviously no Patel is killing infant girls in London today through poisoned milk or otherwise. But just about every Patel I spoke to about *doodh-peeti*, after my chat with the two Patels and the dip into Vishwanath's pages, knew about the practice. For the Patels not from Chha-gam, this was the way of 'those' Chha-gam Patels. Just about every Charotar Patel has a clear sense of being either inside the Chha-gam circle or outside of it.

The practice of *doodh-peeti* still only gets whispered about if it comes up at all; but the differences between the Patels whose families originate from Chha-gam and those whose do not, stand out in separate buildings, in separate parts of London, and as a Patel showed me, in bold print.

The 624-page directory of the Sattavis-gam Patels in Britain, one of the bigger of the non-Chha-gam cluster of villages in Gujarat, recalls the story of the separation of the rest of the Charotar Patels from Chha-gam, lest their kind of Patel forget. The directory, which sits in the home of every Sattavis-gam Patel, reports a historic resolution:

> A conference of Patidars from Charotar was organised under the auspices of Mr Shepard the then Collector of Kaira and Commissioner of Northern Region on 8 February 1888 at Dakor with the pious objects of abolishing Dowry and Girls' Infanticide.

Approximately 10,000 Leva Patidars of Charotar were present at the conference. Mr Shepard proposed a resolution for reforming the oppressive and expensive marriage customs and traditions. Villages which were considered of higher social status opposed it while those at the lower strata and ruined by bad customs and dowry welcomed the proposal. Not only this, those Patidars with hurt ego decided that girls should not get married in so-called high-status villages.

So that no Patel from any of the other cluster of villages would want a daughter to marry a Chha-Gam Patel.

That resolution came to have the sanctity of a declared constitution among the villages. The first clause of the constitution reproduced in the directory says, 'Those villages who have entered into this agreement and signed beneath should not get their girls married in those villages of so-called higher status, or others who did not enter into this agreement. Villages who are a party to the agreement should not keep any social relations on good or bad occasions or directly or indirectly.' Penalties of 1,000 to 4,000 rupees – a fortune in nineteenth-century India – were laid down for anyone breaking the code.

That was then. But the recall of that resolution in a London directory now was no doubt a message. It anchored a far more serious game of Patel vs Patel. And just the existence of the two broad groupings of Charotar Patels in London announced the reliving of that old division. The Patel Association run first from Archway in north London and later Tooting in south London claimed to represent all Patels, but was seen as dominated by the Chha-gam Patels. So the rest set up a federation of almost entirely non-Chha-gam Patels. Now, in Chha-gam in London, you could hear substantially the National Association of Patidar Samaj in

Tooting; for the rest of the Charotar Patels, the Federation of Patidar Associations in Wembley.

The old rebellion by the 'lesser' Patels came in British-ruled India in the late nineteenth century; a polite revolution by Patels of that 'lesser' origin was repeated in London principally through creation of this Federation on London Road in Wembley. Ruling Patels at both the Association and the Federation speak of a pan-Patel unity but when a first-generation Patel hears of the 'Association' and the 'Federation', he hears Chha-gam in the first, and Charotar in the second.

The Federation lived in a tacky old building off a decaying Wembley High Road. This has been rebuilt in tall and impressive announcement of the new success of the 'lesser' Patels, as no doubt it was intended to be. No success statement can ever beat 'mine is bigger'. London Road says that in this new round in Britain, the supposedly lesser Patels have more than equalised.

'We rebelled against them,' Mr Patel, who would be known only as 'Mr Patel', told me at the Federation office. He looked collectively pleased that his lot of Patels had done the right thing by their forefathers in nineteenth-century Gujarat through a polite repeat of that old rebellion in Britain. As invited by the directory of the 27-village Patels, they had carried out a constitutional obligation. I was a little surprised that the proud rebel leader had wished to remain unnamed. He had called me after we had met. 'You must not name me,' he'd said. I guessed that call was made on the advice of the young Patel shuffling papers to a side as we had sat talking.

'They think they are the super-Patels,' he said of the Association, meaning the uppity Patels of the Six Villages. 'The majority there are from Chha-gam.' When he said Chha-gam, it sounded like a rude word that surfaces straight from the heart. Anything Mr Patel said, he said with certainty. His face must have hardened into a look of immovable wisdom about twenty years ago, and it looked even sterner when he spoke of the Chha-gam Patels. He did not have to say the majority at the Federation are not from Chha-gam, because the Federation letterhead said so. It read like a condensed account of a migrating rebellion.

Patelbhai had given me the letterhead as a short introduction to the Federation. It was a picture also of how the non-Chha-gam village groups had set up societies in London to shadow their old villages. The odd one out on the list was the Sojitra Samaj, the sole Chha-gam representation in this camp of the other Patels. 'It is not very active in the Federation,' Mr Patel said. There and not there, not really an interference. That name on the paper was an idea that a bridge can be built across the two worlds, but it did not appear to be a bridge much in use.

It was an idea which would have to battle against history and memory. He recalled the ways of the other Patels like it was yesterday. 'One thing was clear when we rose against Chha-gam,' Patel said. 'They would kill their infant daughters. They used to exploit us a lot, demand all sorts of things from us. People finally got fed up. So we set up the Sattavis-gam Federation then, and the first item in the constitution was that we would never give a daughter from our village to a Chha-gam family. Whoever did would be expelled.'

Marriage would be the big test. That nineteenth-century divide would become real in London only if the Chha-gam families and the rest still discouraged marriages between one and the other. Could a Romeo and Juliet both be Patels?

The test becomes easy particularly on those five or six occasions in a year when the Lagna Sahayak Samiti, the Marriage Promotion Committee, holds its marriage melas at the Federation hall in Wembley, when Patel singles can book in to look for another Patel to marry.

'We do not distinguish,' Mr Patel said. 'All Patels are welcome.'

'Chha-gam too?'

'Yes. They have started coming. There are so many Chha-gam girls who cannot find partners, so they have to come here.'

'Lot of marriages between Chha-gam and the other Patels?'

'No, no, not many.' He said that like he was underlining it.

'Do the Chha-gam have their own marriage service?'

'They must have it. But we have our own database.'

'Do you share that with them?'

'No.'

'But still, you do keep your meetings open to them?'

'You see, because it can get much worse. You see our girls, they go off with fellows here, fellows there, makes your heart cry. Because if someone wants to marry someone these days, who can stop anyone? The only real problem is if a girl goes to a Muslim or a Punjabi. But times are changing and now we are beginning to accept Punjabis also.' He would have known I am Punjabi, but clearly felt no need to restrict speech. And if you can accept a Punjabi, why not that other kind of Patel? In these difficult days a Patel must consider also marrying another kind of Patel, because it can get so much worse.

But there was an arithmetical angle to this. If this Patel was right, and he was after all only one Patel, then there was a disproportionately high number of single women among the Chha-gam Patels. Because the other Patels, and the other others, would not marry them? And were Chha-gam men not enough, or not good enough?

I took these questions to Babubhai Patel, the coloniser of London's corners for Patels to set up shop, and a father figure to the Chha-gam Patels. Babubhai's office is not far from the Patel Association hall in south London traditionally dominated by the Chha-gam Patels. I crossed Battersea Bridge with the sense for a moment of a man moving from one Patel world to another between which hostilities had not entirely ceased. I even found myself a smug sense of neutrality in this civil war.

Babubhai welcomed me with a smile that had won him friends and business all his life. This time I'd come to talk to him about Chha-gam Patels and not Patel corner shops. If Babubhai could set up shop for thousands, he could set up homes for them.

'Look, this is the application form,' he said. I'd settled down over tea in his office brought by his daughter-in-law who had her desk next to his; Indian businessmen do not look for managers, they look for relatives. We'd talked some shop, and now we were talking marriage, though the two are not always distinct.

On the top left of the form sat the Chha-gam logo, a hexagon formed by six triangles, with the name of a Chha-gam village in each triangle. Babubhai read them out: Bhadran, Dharmaj, Karamsad, Nadiad, Sojitra, Vaso. 'That's my village, Vaso,' he said, very Vaso-proud. He showed what a marriage applicant would do. The form asked for 'Candidate's name, sex, marital status, legal status (UK/USA/India/Africa), birthdate, birth place, country, height, education, occupation, native gam, special interest and desired education/occupation of opposite sex.'

Babubhai next pulled out a folder with a stack of A4 sheets with the title 'Chha Gam Lagna Sahayak Samiti Wedding Candidates List'. The Vaso lot, the list of candidates from Vaso, eligible to candidates from the other five. A marriage within a village was something 'we never do', Babubhai said. Incest. 'You know about DNA, no?' Babubhai said, educationally. 'About same blood? Our forefathers were right, never marry within the family, I mean even the extended family. We have taught our children this. They listen.'

The first page listed nine names, eight of them women, all in their thirties. I flipped through the other pages. Page after page listed a very large number of single women in their thirties and forties. It seemed that the Federation Patels might be right to suggest that many people still do not want to marry Chha-gam Patels. But that still left the question why they weren't marrying Chha-gam men.

I turned back to the Chha-gam women claiming qualifications on the first page. 'BA Modern Studies in civil service', 'O levels and clerical', 'A levels and civil servant', 'BTech, computer, now a travel consultant', 'A levels with a finance planning certificate, now a senior mortgage advisor', 'law degree and idle', 'BSc Honours in applied psychology, now an overseas programme manager', and 'BSc applied economics a housing officer, now in Harrow'. I liked the sound of 'law degree and idle', but I was no Patel, let alone a Chha-gam Patel. There's no way she could say no to me, I'd never even get to see her.

'What is the proportion of single girls to boys among the Chha-gam here?' I asked Babubhai. Apparently innocent, but put to a Chha-Gam boss it was like the lid blown off a pressure cooker. I realised I'd asked an explosive question. 'It varies,' Babubhai said. He was not going to talk any more about this.

Babubhai told me instead how much more of a life the Chha-gam Patels were building around themselves with every passing year. Since marriage to anyone whose family is from the same village would be incest, arranging marriages meant arranging mass meetings with the eligible from the other *gams* (villages), and not your own. And so registers were being filled, and 'meet and greet' events were being held, like the Lagna Sahayak Samiti meetings over on the Federation side.

'We are now about 5,000 families from Chha-gam,' Babubhai said. 'Maximum migration came from these six villages. Everybody cannot know everybody.'

The meet-and-greet marriage meetings are becoming increasingly well-attended, Babubhai said. 'Last time we had four hundred and fifty single people, this time we will have more.' This was my opportunity to ask again about the proportion of males and females. 'It varies,' Babubhai said. 'Never counted. But whatever marriages are taking place are taking place mostly within the group.'

I asked, with the sham innocence of an outsider from Punjab wandering into the world of Gujarati Patels, whether they would network with the Patel Federation up at Wembley for marriages. 'No, we have not joined them.' He sounded like they never would if he had his way. 'They set up separately because they thought the Chha-gam Patels were holding all the high positions in the Association.' On this side of the divide, there wasn't even lip service to a Patel togetherness.

I left his office still with that question: where were all the Chha-gam men?

I thought Subhashbhai Patel might tell me what Babubhai had not. Subhashbhai was a Chha-gam Patel from the Karamsad sixth of the hexagon. A very special village even among those top six, because this was the village, as any Patel would tell you, that gave India Sardar Vallabbhai Patel, the first home minister of India after independence. The time when some princely states in India had thought they would remain independent within India until they encountered some military-like persuasion ordered by Sardar Patel. Karamsad Patels like to say their village gave India Sardar Patel, gave India India.

Subhashbhai Patel was at one time president of the Karamsad Samaj in Britain, and everyone I met said he knew more than a thing or two about Chha-gam Patels. He was recovering from medical treatment when I went over to see him at his house in

Kingsbury but he still looked handsome in a tough sort of way. A little like a villain in a Bollywood film, except that he was imposing rather than villainous.

'So you're from Sardar Patel's village,' I said, complimenting him for possessing an illustrious relative. Subhashbhai immediately told me some stories about Sardar Patel, from a fellow villager perspective. That the village had produced India's pride had done little, however, to stop a substantial migration from that village after independence. To Britain mostly, via East Africa of course. The short Karamsad history done, Subhashbhai reached out to a shelf by his side and passed me a copy of a directory listing 1,300 families of Karamsad Patels.

'I see Karamsad is not a part of the London Road Federation,' I said. 'No, we are not a part of London Road.' Like Babubhai, his tone too added, 'and never will be'. I thought the upturned Chha-gam noses at the mention of the larger Federation had a strong nineteenth-century profile.

The Association had come before the Federation because it was the Chha-gam Patels who began to get together first after migrating to Britain, Subhashbhai said. 'The Federation came up only subsequently. Because they thought the Chha-gam are coming together, so they formed the Federation.'

'But there are a large number of single Chha-gam women, aren't there?' Subhashbhai, in the trained manner of an official spokesman before journalists, offered neither denial nor confirmation. But he did offer an explanation. 'The percentage of girls from Chha-gam marrying within Chha-gam is beginning to go down because they are not getting the right boys. When the parents came here they bought businesses, they bought shops, they bought sub post offices. So many of the Chha-gam boys just went into their father's business, and many more of the girls went into education. So they are not finding enough of educated boys within Chha-gam.' And if there were so many single women among the Chha-gam lot, it meant also that they hadn't married other Patel males from outside of Chha-gam.

I left Subhashbhai's house in Kingsbury trying to figure out which Patel had told me once that Sardar Patel could unite India but he'd failed to unite the Patels.

Some Three

A Khan or an Ahmed with two wives or more would invite only polite silence on the subject, but once K. D. Patel decided on two concurrent wives, Gujarati gossip would buzz a long time. So everyone knows of the Patel with two wives (one of them with him in public, the other never) who always wears white, and Lata, the wife you see in public, in white too.

As a Patel of the 22-village Baavis-Gam, K. D. is not elite Patel. It's the family particulars his entry in the Baavis-Gam Patel directory that distinguish him. Wife: one, and then; Wife: the other. It quite sets him apart from the usual village wars of which kind of Patel you are. There just isn't another Patel who could produce this kind of directory entry. The bedroom curiosity his double marriage excites makes him so much more than just another married Patel.

I'd been to a couple of parties at his house in Wembley; every busybody of the area has. K. D. is the Great Gatsby of Wembley's Gujaratis. His is the unmissable house with three Mercs in the drive and all those white plaster lions on the wall. Some of the lions stand on their hind legs with the likes of a royal shield hiding their testicle vicinity from drivers on Harrowdene Road.

I'd looked in to see K. D. again. 'Kusum Villa' the legend above the front door said. A little like Kusum petrol station (named after the first and more private of his wives). You see the other wife's name everywhere, you never see her.

K. D. let me in and through three large drawing rooms before we settled. I sat on a boring sofa beside a heavily carved *jhoola*, that suspended swing of a sofa so favoured by the rich and holy. K. D., in his mandatory white suit, sat on a chair across. His fondness for white extended unfortunately to white leather shoes, once so favoured by Bollywood heroes. K. D. is not particularly heroic-looking. His dash comes from the lifetime of double devotion he is thought to enjoy, a king among Patels for satisfying two wives when most can barely do the minimum with one. That there is a law on bigamy in Britain is a question no one ever raised because everyone agreed K. D. was special. And no doubt he had found a way to speak of two wives and also do the right thing by law. That would be the proper Patel thing to do.

'So, how two wives?' I asked.

'It just happened. I just don't know how it happened.'

'But surely you do.'

'I fell in love with Lata when she came to work in my office in Kenya.'

'What office was that?'

'Africana Towel Company.'

Everyone needs towels, maybe more in Kenya which is never short of heat or water. To others this was nature; to a Patel businessman it became opportunity.

'Were you married then?'

'Yes, I was married to Kusum. I told Kusum about Lata and then also married Lata with the permission of my first wife. The three of us have been happily married for more than thirty years.' I skipped the bedroom questions because I suspected the guessing would be more engaging than the facts.

K. D. had other things to show off. 'My house,' he said, as he saw me looking around. 'Built over 48,000 square feet. Eight bedrooms, eight receptions. I will ask someone to show you around.'

A young female manager visiting London from K. D.'s IT company in India became my guide. She was one of those tinsel girls in tight jeans that every man fancies, and no woman knows why. We went up what was designed to be described as a winding path through a garden. A single bend in the path meant it did wind once. We crossed about a yard or two of bridge on our way over a pool fed by a fountain. The garden was landscaped with statues of peacocks and of a dog.

'There were real peacocks once, about twelve of them,' my companion in jeans told me as we crossed the bridge. 'But the dog ate some of them. And the climate here did not suit them.' So K. D. gave away the surviving peacocks to the zoo and eventually built memorials in the garden to both the peacocks and the dog. These were the gardens of the K. D. parties, it's where you could get to meet the millionaires who do not get on those rich lists because they know the taxman also reads newspapers.

Up the garden towards the rear stood a white statue, three women in the nude in close embrace. 'From Greece,' my guide announced. It couldn't be just me thinking what I was, even if this was an all-female threesome.

We had reached a little back house, with a garden bar by the entrance watched over by a bronze figure of Cleopatra. We entered a disco hall by the side of a pool that didn't look like anyone ever swam in it. It was there so that a party around it could be called a poolside party. Behind the pool was a little stage, because guests are served speeches too. Both K. D. and Lata have been elected councillors in Brent, and Lata was also mayor.

We returned to the main house and now K. D. showed me around the inside. He took me through bedroom after bedroom, some of them multiplied by mirrors on all sides, inspiring unprintable thoughts. I saw no sign of the first wife.

Back by the *jhoola*, K. D. handed me an 80-page brochure on the couple (K. D. and Lata). It had an albumish picture of K. D. and Lata on the cover, side by side. Under K. D.'s name were printed the words 'Flair', 'Fortune', 'Flavour' in large type; under Lata Patel's, 'Dignified', 'Devoted', 'Dedicated'. Within, just about every page carried photographs of Lata Patel and of K. D. But at last there was one of all three, a posed photograph, with K. D. sitting in the middle in a white suit (also white shirt and white tie) flanked by the two wives in white saris (daring only a little non-white print) standing to the sides, each with a hand on K. D.'s shoulders. Now here was a real man.

The brochure was packed with photos of K. D. and Lata alongside eminent others: Lata Patel variously with the Queen, with Tony Blair, Prince Charles, Amitabh Bachchan. The only pictures where Lata Patel did not wear white were from the year she was mayor of Brent, when she wore the heavy red mayoral gown with that black furry collar. Lata Patel was mayor no longer when I visited them. K. D. was now out of local political life too, so they were both back to white.

With that brochure planted in my hand, K. D. had made sure I'd know them much better. I thought I was forgetting something as I got up to leave. It came to me at the door.

'Why do you always wear white?'

'I like white because it is the colour of purity and simplicity,' K. D. replied.

Who was I to argue?

Holes

The Gujarati inclination to say 'hole' when they mean 'hall' has long been familiar, but I still wished it different when I heard Suresh Kansagra tell the bride's mother that she will like his hole, and so will her daughter. The bride's father replied in the same Gujarati English. 'You have a lovely hole,' he said as the couple settled down in Mr Kansagra's drawing room. 'Thank you,' Kansagra replied.

He'd heard that before, they all say that when they come to him to book the Kadwa Patidar Hall across from the Harrow Leisure Centre. Another man was waiting outside, most likely a soon-to-be father-in-law.

Suresh Kansagra is a large and efficient man and carries the look of one long familiar with his importance. He would; as magistrate, as president of the Kadwa Patidar Samaj, as Conservative Party councillor in Brent. But his weightiness comes at least as much from the hall he takes bookings for.

It's a large and well-placed hall in north-west London, the part of London that becomes more Indian by the day. Built in 1993 by the Kadwa Patidar Samaj, a relatively small group of about seven hundred Patel families from Saurashtra (that elbow of Gujarat that sticks out into the Arabian Sea) the hall has now become the place to celebrate marriage and Indian living itself. How often you get invited to a hall, any hall, is a measure of how connected you are to other Indians like yourself, even how Indian an Indian is. Because halls connect people, and because that has consequences. Two or three Indians can be a pain, two or three hundred are such fun. If there's one thing Indians love, it is to just gather. Indians have never been great adventurers or wanderers, but they've always been great gatherers. In Britain it takes halls to make that happen because that's where the weather pushes you into. So when people want to meet or marry, Kansagra's name is never far from the mind. And for a fee that hall can be anyone's, not just a Patel's.

'People tell me they first want to book the hall and then look for someone to marry,' Kansagra said to the father. 'I am taking bookings eighteen months in advance.' The father nodded reverentially.

I'd dropped in to see Kansagra to talk some Patel matters, but I sat in that room as mostly a witness to his significance, through his hall. Kansagra could talk to me only between fathers and bookings.

Finding a gap, I asked him why he was called Kansagra if he was a Patel. 'I used to be called Patel but I changed that to go back to my real surname. You see, in Saurashtra and in Kutch (in northern Gujarat) many also have their own surnames besides Patel, and either they do not use Patel or they use both. Outside we use Patel but inside we go back to our real surnames.'

'But do all Patels have other surnames?'

'No, in the Charotar area they have the *gam* system. They are known by their *gams*, so they can only call themselves Patels.' But in Kutch and Saurashtra, it announced membership of a world; you could surname yourself more precisely than Patel, while being Patel all the time.

The bride's father paid a deposit of £550. On the wedding day he would pay £280 an hour, for a minimum hire of six hours. Not a bad day's income for the Kadwa Patidar Samaj. Income from the hall has made Kadwa Patidar Patels the envy of other Patels. But it isn't just the income they would be envying. It's what the hall can do for keeping your own together. Anyone not a Kadwa Patidar Patel would have to hire it, but they have it to themselves for free on every one of those many excuses a Hindu calendar throws up through the year for a community to gather. Add the differently coloured dates from the Christian calendar as well, you are in Britain after all. So the more you gather, the more likely it is you will find connections within the community. Just about everyone knows that when people marry, they marry in a hall, but when a group has a hall of its own, they're more likely to have the kind of marriages they want. Patels, like others, have discovered the relationship between space and choice.

A hall has so much to do with the thing called love because what feels like magic can only be made possible by time and space. A hall is love's best friend; it gives you space enough to move in, but not enough to move too far. It's a saturation move. Take a hall and fill it with your own. On those nine nights of Navratri dancing, on those other Hindu festivals; Holi, Janamashtami, Diwali, Dussehra, visiting saints, weekend parties, weddings, birthdays, anniversaries, Valentine's, someone's twenty-fifth this, fortieth that, Christmas, New Year. Could that many years pass before you like one of your own that you see again and again, under official encouragement to flirtation?

Given a hall, you don't need to arrange marriages; you need only to arrange introductions, or even just to turn up. Matchmaking blends with flirtation. An arrangement by parents can feel like love to the introduced; in the end arranged love must feel like any other love.

And that is also why I was in Kansagra's room only as a wandering bum and not some promising groom. The hall had no room for a non-Patel or a non-community specific other like me on all the interesting days. I'd always envied the Patels their hall as I envied all those I'd seen so often headed that way. They had a little world of their own to go to, I didn't. They were in a space with their own, I was out on streets that were strangers. Too often profiles of lovely women in what promised to be lovely saris had passed me by in cars headed that way. Maybe it was the near uniform highlighting in the hair, since that's most of what I saw, or the consistency of the denial, but in time these images coalesced in my mind as a lost chance because I am not Patel. I was an outsider to Patels of every kind, and to every other kind of kind that ever hired that hall. If India had been smaller I might have got in as just Indian. It was in some despair that I watched how much that hall was doing for others.

One father gone, and before the next, I found a quick moment to ask Kansagra how many youngsters marry within their own.

'We are getting about ten to fifteen per cent of our youths marrying outside the community because they meet people in universities and offices,' he replied. Universities and offices are a natural hazard of living. 'That is where people do meet others, what can you do?' He spoke, still focused on the register, his eyes scanning dates and bookings.

If Kansagra was right on the numbers, halls are doing their bit to deliver one Patel to another, to recycle love within a community. They're the weekend counter-magnets set up against the double danger of universities and offices. Every hall is a fortress resisting that modern march towards a mix of people where only individuals matter, not where they come from. A hall is the most practical defence against annihilation of a people who share a past and want to share a future.

The last father had gone, and Kansagra was now going to fit me in before dinner. We'd been talking about Patel-to-Patel marriages, I reminded him.

'Times are changing and you are getting a lot more intermarriages,' he said. 'You have Kutch Patel marrying Charotar Patel, Saurashtra Patel marrying Kutchi Patel, Leva Patel marrying Kadwa Patel.' And I used to think of Hindu-Muslim marriages as intermarriages. In London, a marriage of a Hindu Indian Gujarati Patel to another Hindu Indian Gujarati Patel can be intermarriage, and the 'inter' part of it can be a quite serious thing.

It was different back in Kenya, Kansagra said. He was not a man to talk at length; he was more a deliverer of sound bites. Maybe he was just hungry. 'We used to meet everyone there because we saw everyone as Indian and Hindu. But here everyone got segregated. There are so many of us that there are enough within every community. So everyone says I will go to my own.' That I knew, that we were so many that I would have to be alone.

It seemed now that Kansagra was resigned to the occasional Patel marrying a quite different Patel. The ten to 15 percent might not be statistically precise, but allowing for a little more than 15 was still not bad. In these changing times everyone knows how much worse it can get; there are sadly no Patel-only universities and offices. So better a compromise than catastrophe, better embarrassment than shame, better to stretch your world to other Patels than admit an outsider from the universe beyond.

Kansagra looked past me, he was getting signalled to. But before his meal he had something more to say about communities and halls. 'It means you have a whole community to face. If I am alone and go bankrupt, who cares? But if I am a part of a community that meets once a week at a hall, where will I show my face if I do something wrong? These gatherings are a very great deterrent to wrongdoing.' This was the magistrate in Kansagra speaking.

'Look at the very small number of Indians in British prisons,' he said. 'And the very small number of Indians who go to jail are for some kind of petty fraud, not for violent crimes.'

'Is that because Indians have formed communities, or found halls of their own?'

'I think these community gatherings are keeping Indians out of prisons. They give people something worthwhile and honourable to do with their time.'

It sounded like a good theory to test: how many people who go to community functions, or how few of them, also go to prison? It would be great for a Kadwa Patel from Saurashtra to marry a Kadwa Patel from Saurashtra because only then will an offspring ensure that Kadwa Patelhood from Saurashtra is not history. But if Kansagra's theory stands, it would also mean a good Patel marrying a good Patel. A hall could save you from the wrong Patel, even a non-Patel, and it might also have stopped you going to jail. Marriage and morals and halls are all one.

The groom and bride had driven up in a small red Peugeot – not the usual Rolls, or these days those extended American abominations. The lack of size of this car mattered. One of

115

those American things the size of a bus would never have made it down that little lane from Tooting High Street to the community centre of the National Association of the Patidar Samaj, that Patel group everyone else thought was dominated by the Chha-gam Patels. That little lane had been too little even for the motor garage where the association hall now stands. The Patels bought the garage and turned it into a hall big enough to fit 500 people, but with parking for only three or four cars in front. The lane hardly suffices for visiting Patels, let alone marriage parties. Red lines along Tooting High Street rule out the immediate outside.

Thankfully, I'd taken the tube. Pravin Amin from the association was waiting for me at the entrance, along with the wedding guests. We made way for the drummer, beating away at its Indian incarnation, the *dholak* strapped around his neck. The *dholak* does the essential beat for bhangra, but it provides by tradition a heralding beat, and it was now heralding the bride and groom from the car into the hall. The bridegroom was white. 'You don't have this sort of thing happening very often,' Pravinbhai assured me.

The bridegroom wore a white closed-neck *bandhgala* suit, a style popular with Chinese communists and Indian grooms, the very Gujarati bride a mauve *lehenga-choli* (long skirt and blouse improved by colour and shine) with a good deal of mango-shaped shine on it. Take away the colour and the shine, and the dress was merely a long skirt and blouse, OK for a London office, not an Indian bride. Not a very bridal looking bride. And not a young couple who had just met, or been made to meet. This was obviously not an arranged marriage, and just as obviously not a fresh love marriage. They had only finally married.

Unnoticed by the *dholak* player, a noticeboard just within the entrance was warning about noise levels. It was from the local council addressed to the management of the hall 'requiring you to stop causing a nuisance'. Because next time the fine could be £5,000. The hall stood next to houses at the back, and any wedding here would for their sake have to be a quiet wedding. Parking problems and complaints about loud music top social problems in Britain today. This hall had enough of both.

For the chap with the *dholak* this was a matter between him and his skill, not the hall and its neighbours. He was getting more and more carried away with his wedding kind of beat, and danced on into the hall, leaving the couple well behind.

'Slowly,' the man who seemed the bride's father said to him. 'Slowly.'

'Can't beat this thing slow, you know.'

'No, I mean walk slowly.'

A little procession of six or seven led now closely by the *dholak* player made its way through the dinner tables to the top table. A manager quickly shut the glass doors behind, with the look of a man who does not like writing out £5,000 cheques. The DJ playing *'Hum tumhare hain, tumhare sanam...'* followed by *'Mubarak ho tum ko ye shaadi tumhari...'* was adding to the *dholak* decibels. A love song and a wedding song.

The only white people in the hall other than the groom was a couple with a little baby. If the groom had family and friends happy about the marriage, they hadn't shown up. Or maybe it is Indians far more than white Brits who always know people who'll turn up for events like this. There never was a Smith Samaj to match a Patel association.

The loss of this particular bride to an out-and-out non-Patel was not a loss to the Patel association that owned the hall, Pravinbhai told me as we queued for dinner. This was not even some lesser Charotar Patel group in relation to whom the Chha-gam had become aristocracy that had rented the hall, only a Kutch Patel family from far north in Gujarat, far outside the pale of Charotar Patels where one Patel could be higher than the other. A blessed marriage, no doubt, but it was the Kutch Patels' loss.

The wedding brought in some rent, as other events here must do. But I doubt this particular hall was working as well for members of the association as some would like. If they wanted to come, where would they park? For a marriage to happen, two must meet, their eyes must meet, then their hearts and minds, their families, and not least then the meeting of what are called practical interests arising from a bank and property register. But first they must park.

Who knows, a woman from an Association family, perhaps an eligible Chha-gam woman, never married because she never got to this hall often enough to meet others, because she and that possible someone couldn't find anywhere to park.

The spaceship appeared unexpectedly as I rounded the corner on Forty Avenue, driving west past the Brent town hall. That's what the Sattavis-gam Patel Samaj had built by way of their hall, not the roadside rectangle I'd expected to see. Its facade of glass panels leaned outwards above the roadside in the modern designed way, under a roof that waved up and down with the support of curving white beams. The British Patel from the 27 villages were saying hello to the twenty-first century.

I found The Avenue leading up to the hall, and then space in its ample parking lot. A phone introduction through my friend Harshadbhai Patel, a local Conservative councillor, led me to a meeting with Raj Patel in a foyer brightened by hidden pink lights, and then a walkabout. 'It can take one hundred and fifty cars,' Raj said, pointing to the parking before turning to what was within. He was bursting with fabulous facts about this building and they quickly came tumbling out. I took in such Patel-proud statistics as 3,400 square metres of covered area – 'maybe even more' – at a cost of £8.1 million.

The building was designed to provoke exclamations like 'futuristic' and 'state of the art'. All sorts of angles and curves appeared, relieved by occasional straight lines and squares. Pink lighting marked the border of a large square of wall inset into wall. Raj and I strolled through two large halls around the foyer, all sorts of rooms upstairs and up to the third floor auditorium whose 'cascading chairs' had yet to be installed. The centre was opened in April 2005 and was still being given its last additions.

'We have arrangements to lift a car into the auditorium in case anyone wants to display it,' Raj said. Why anyone would want to take a car to the third floor of a building of the 27-village Patels I couldn't tell. But Raj explained that the space was intended also for commercial use. Round the corner from Wembley Stadium and its business complex, and close to new hotels in the area, the Sattavis-gam centre was being promoted as a conference centre. Much of the £8.1 million it had cost was a loan that would have to be repaid. Renting out conference facilities would pay for the hall, or so they figured; it would also be a centre for other communities to hire. And it was always there for the Sattavis-Gam Patels to gather to perpetuate themselves, like the Kadwa Patels in their hall.

The big dream of just about every Indian community is to get a hall of its own. Dreams sometimes turn to plans, plans raise funds, funds put up buildings. This hall was still a plan when I'd first dropped in to see Harshadbhai Patel at his place by Preston Road, not that far from where the structure was to come up.

Harshadbhai must be about the busiest of the Sattavis-gam Patels. His home office was a mess, which meant both of us were at home in there. Harshadbhai took position behind piles of papers and reference books; he looked like he knew where to unscramble the mess for what, so that was all right. Harshadbhai looked very much the moustached hero on an

Indian university campus in the seventies, and those chaps always knew what they were doing. Harshadbhai was going to show me his plan, and he knew just where that one was in the papers. It was a pamphlet called the '27-gam Patidar Building Project'. The project would get the Patels from the original 27, and now 66 villages in Gujarat's Charotar, a hall of their own.

A list of 'Priorities' sat on the pamphlet by the side of a picture of the model.

A HUNDRED YEARS FROM NOW IT WILL NOT MATTER WHAT MY BANK ACCOUNT WAS, THE SORT OF HOUSE I LIVE IN, OR THE KIND OF CAR I DRIVE...BUT THE WORLD MAY BE DIFFERENT BECAUSE I WAS IMPORTANT IN THE LIFE OF A CHILD.

Below that came the collective plea of the Sattavis-gam Patel leaders to cough up for Patelhood of the Sattavis-gam kind:

How easy it is to forget. Time moves on. Circumstances change. Families multiply. Houses get bigger. What car do you drive? Is it still about survival or is it about wanting more? Perhaps wanting more and sometimes wanting just for the sake of it?

The biggest oak tree perhaps over 100 feet tall and standing up to the tests of nature for more than a hundred or two hundred years. We've all seen them. The oak tree cannot forget its roots as only by its roots does it survive. The nutrients in the soil are washed in by the rain entering through the roots and thereafter the tree is fed and grows and once grown survives all nature throws at it. Unless a rare disease hits the oak tree it outlives man, unless man itself destroys the tree.

Do you remember your roots? From whence you came? Are you better today than you were then? Better fed. Better off. That's as may be but what keeps us all together is the protection of our roots. Call it our culture. In a world where culture is dying and modern fashion dictates a modern style of culture and not always for the better.

We are all about to plant an oak tree in Wembley.

Planning permission has been granted. In East Africa we had our roots, our cultural places to visit, to meet, to discuss. Now we are about to embark on an oak tree that could last 100 years or more. This is bigger than any one of us. It is a chance to come together, to work together for the benefit of us all.

As somebody once said, let us come together now to work today, for all our tomorrows, and the tomorrows of generations to come. Without your support it will not be as good as it will be with your support. Please!

As an elected leader, Harshadbhai knew just what to say to journalist types, and he delivered a short speech answering the 'why' question before I could ask it.

'We need it to keep the young with us in our ways. I have three daughters. Culturally they are not under the influence of the West at all. They speak fluent Gujarati. If they didn't tell you they were born here, you would think they are born in Gujarat.' That, he meant, shows how good they are.

'Once you have lost your language then ultimately you have lost your culture,' he said.

'But can you force Gujarati down the throats of the young these days?'

'It is not question of down the throat, it is question of education. We do not find a lot of youngsters rebelling against our ways. When it happens it is the fault of parents, they do not educate them properly. If shown right direction they will follow. We do not have to tell our young to celebrate Navratri.

They are ready before we are. We want our culture preserved. Our culture gives better life, it gives more secure life. In every way. Socially, financially, in achieving their goals.'

'But how will the building of a hall help the young achieve their goals in life?'

'Because that happens when you are a close community. Then what happens, you see this person, let us call him or her X, who is a doctor. Then I also want to be a doctor. When you are close like this, it brings more and more competition. So then greater and greater good results come.'

He could defend every statement he made. Gujarati students do have some of the best results in schools and universities. Is that because they go to community events where they are under watch, and will get talked about for performing, or not? So that the more of your own that watch you, the better you will do? And the more regularly you go to a community hall, the higher your marks? This theory too needs testing.

Harshadbhai's list of the virtues of a hall was a long one. If you need an anchor in your life, you need a community. And when you have a community, you need a hall for it – you can't talk long in the rain. Community means communication. The hall would do its bit to keep the young in their cultural ways, but it didn't have to feel that heavily driven. It would also be just a place to meet one another. These days community works when you turn it into a club, somewhere nice to go to with your own, away from the unfriendly world outside. A hall can be a hole after all.

ILLEGALLY YOURS

Freshy

He was Kashmir Singh, or said he was, which meant that was probably the one name his mother had not given him. But I had to call him something, and Kashmir seemed best since that's what he was calling himself now.

Over the years that he said he'd spent unnoticed by authorities in Britain after arriving unobserved through East Europe and Italy, he was never going to carry with him the name on his school certificate in Punjab. Or the one he got from university, because he said he had done his Masters in Punjabi before disregarding the British High Commission in Delhi and moving into Britain without the knowledge of Her Majesty's customs, coast guard, immigration and whatnot.

It's an old convention that when you travel illegally, you not only carry another name, but another face so far as possible. Like his fellow Sikh passengers, Kashmir too had cut his hair and shaved off his beard at the start of his journey from Punjab. I 're-turbaned' him in my mind as we walked down Broadway in Southall in search of tea and pakoras, and decided he would look much better as the turbaned Sikh. I saw him in Punjab in a maroon turban, and a substantial but controlled beard, and I saw in him the confidence that goes with that kind of look. Not as he now was under a self-effacing crew cut and the furtive look of a fugitive in his light brown and otherwise interesting eyes. But even without that Sikh look, he must be interesting to women. Or, who knows, because of that non-Sikh look, because even Sikh women have definite views on turbaned men, one way or another.

Never mind the Sikh women, Kashmir would never have made those many thousand miles from Patiala to London under a turban. Nor all the other Sikhs that British ministers and newspapers call 'illegal immigrants', who see themselves more as informal guests making themselves at home. On a trip like that you don't want to stand out in a crowd.

I'd accidentally spotted a number of such guests before while taking pictures in Southall. A fair population of males ducked every time I aimed my camera at them. Maybe a lot of them just happened to have become camera shy at the same time and place, but I thought it more likely that every head that vanished was one that didn't have its mug on a proper passport.

We stepped into the Chandni Chowk restaurant on Broadway. It was a cold and damp day, and you must never let one of those pass without pakoras. They arrived quickly frying hot on our table in the usual pool of yellow oil, and accompanied by cups of tea creased over with the brown film, the curtain that one learns in time to blow gently aside to access the tea below. Firm evidence of tea cooked the Indian way.

'How did you come to England?' I asked, in Punjabi naturally. He'd tell me, he said, because we'd met through common friends and because he could trust me not to be a 'plain-clothes-man'.

'I just could not find a job in Punjab,' he said. 'I used to look in newspapers. And there I used to read about agents who can get you to England. I found an agent, I paid him 400,000 rupees [£5,000].'

'That easy?'

'Yes. The agent took us by air to Moscow. We were a big group, about fourteen or fifteen of us. The agent was there in Moscow to meet us. He had arranged all the passports and visas and everything. But in Moscow he asked us to throw away our passports. We gave them to him.'

From Moscow he said they had travelled by bus and train for a month, halting for the night at tiny places where everyone slept on the floor. At one stage they had to walk long distances in the snow under the eyes of two white agents.

One day, he said, one of the group fell ill and couldn't walk any more. 'One of the agents shot him. He died. I saw that. One more fell ill on the way. He disappeared. None of us knew what happened to him.'

I had no means of knowing, of course, whether all this was true. The route through Moscow and overland through Eastern Europe has been popular for illegal migration for a long time. No one who fell ill on the way could be taken to a hospital, and agents wouldn't want to leave people behind with tales to tell. I told myself he could just be inventing these stories. His earnest manner meant nothing, he must have produced plenty of fiction in that manner whenever required. But there he was then, and here he was now, among so many more, some hundreds of thousands likely. They didn't take the straight path, so it could well have been a ride like this. And, I also told myself, if he felt the need to lie to me, he wouldn't have wanted to talk to me in the first place.

Eventually, he said, they reached the Austrian border. 'I managed to get through. Ten of us got through. It is a matter of luck, how they check and where you can hide. The agents told us this is going to be a big gamble. Two of our fellows got caught, but there was no big checking on that train. We were happy.' The train brought them to Milan. He wandered about a bit lost at the station in Milan, but not for long; a man sought him out and took him away.

'The man who met me took me to a room. I saw many of our own people there. They all lived together. It was so good to meet Punjabis there, I could speak to them in Punjabi and I felt good. For two days I had lot of food and whisky with them. Then they told me where to go to work.' He joined them packing tomatoes and fruit into little boxes, for €5.50 an hour. 'But we worked more hours than we were paid for. We were all like that. If there was work, we would do it, nobody used to count the hours. My friend told them one day we are not like Italians.' At the end of the day there was 'good whisky, very good whisky'.

He worked like this for a year and a half, Kashmir said. Our second round of pakoras had arrived, his story was moving on, and sex had to come into it. 'There was one place, a packing factory. There were girls there from many countries. I did it with one girl. She was a white girl but she could not speak English at all. We used to do it every day under the stairs in the factory. She did everything. In Punjab, girls never do everything. It was very good. My friends used to tease me. They also tried with others but they were not successful. One friend said to me, get me your girl. I said, up to you. He was not successful. But afterwards he was successful with another girl.'

All those days in Italy, Kashmir said he never stopped thinking of England. That's where he really wanted to get to. England had both money and Punjabis, and he could speak a little English too. He once paid an agent €2,500 to take him to Britain, but the agent took the money and disappeared. Then the man who had arranged their stay in Milan offered to send them to Britain. 'We gave him the money, cash in hand. He told us one day, early in the morning, to get up and be ready and a man will come to take us.'

'So that is how you reached here.'

'No, no.' It wasn't that easy.

The man took them to Paris where they stayed at a gurdwara. 'They looked after us very nicely. We also did *seva* there; cooking, cleaning. We did not have to do anything. Agents came to the gurdwara, they said they will take us to England.' They were driven, he said, to a port somewhere and packed into goods trolleys that would be loaded onto trains. But then they were rapidly offloaded because someone tipped them off that trolleys were being checked. They were taken back to wait for another day, another trolley.

'Next chance came after one week. Again we went in a bus and got into the line for the ferry. Then the agent said it is all right this time, you can go. Then we went into a different trolley inside a lorry. There were two others in the trolley with me. We made a little place inside the crates, and we lay down. Then I said it is now up to God. I started to say prayers.

'After a long time somebody opened the lorry door. We came out. The lorry was inside a warehouse. We were in England. We took a train to London. There we took another train to Charing Cross. Over there our people came to meet us. From there we went to Paddington, and from there we came to Southall.'

Southall, the suburb near Heathrow that metamorphosed under migration into a Punjabi transplant, was a new home, and it brought new hope. Platefuls of pakoras later, we were walking down Broadway towards the Southall railway station. Kashmir was taking the train to visit friends in Gravesend. It was a Saturday, and there was no work for him. Until he could find busier employers, he had no choice but to rest.

I don't know a more heartening street than Broadway for a strolling Punjabi in England. To a Kensington Indian this is downtown Indian ghetto, and maybe some ethnic indulgence on a Saturday some time. To Kashmir and me this was natural habitat. Ghettos are reassuring places; they are your world that migrated over, which makes them a comfortable place to occupy. It helped that Punjabis had in effect renamed Southall. It is now 'south' plus 'hall', no more spoken of as 'Sathal', with the 'th' as in 'the'. Punjabis first split that one name in two, then put them together sequentially and logically. It was among the early preferences Punjabis showed of taking England on their own terms. Now everyone says 'south' and then 'hall'.

Broadway consequently is more bazaar than street. A stall on the pavement selling jalebis frying hot and dripping oil blended with syrup, vegetable shops where vegetables do smell like themselves, a watch stall where a toy Sikh pop artist Daler Mehndi can be wound up to sing '*Sadde naal rahoge te aish karoge*', jewellers, music shops competing in range, prices and decibels, and suitcases guaranteed for ten years that would last no more than two, stealing space on what was built to be pedestrian land. Occasionally the bazaar attracts ever-welcome whites amid the bustling Indians. A pity that more white Brits don't head for the flavours, and colours, of Southall. The life of a bazaar is so much more the people it gathers than the goods it's set up to move. Broadway is a 'mall road' of the old world, and everyone knows that mall roads are shopping streets only incidentally, they really are meant for people to parade themselves before potentially noticing others. A bazaar is a place for strangers of the familiar kind, and Southall's the place to feel at home with people you don't know but who're off the same boat. It's a reassuring multiplication of the likes of yourself.

It's the place to be seen, to stare and be stared at. Indians love to look at Indians, to size them up, to slot them, to find in them material for opinion-making. Just to be aware of others and to think they might be aware of you can be treat enough in a country where by unstated cultural agreement no one looks at anyone else. Nothing hurts more than a denial of existence in the eyes of some other. Those are the ways of the 'mainstream'. Southall's the place to forget you were once displaced.

Kashmir and I had turned right from Broadway onto South Street in the direction of the railway station. Not as much of a mall road as Broadway, but with life enough by way of travel agents, restaurants, an Indian supermarket and the new Himalaya cinema. And it has the Suman Marriage Bureau, that oldest Indian hope in Britain of turning stranger into spouse.

'Ever thought of marriage?' I asked Kashmir as we walked past.

'Yes, I have someone in Patiala. I plan to call her here.'

'And if you can't?'

'Then I will go back. But I will not leave her.' Kashmir did not connect his love for the Patiala woman with matters under a staircase in what he had called 'Milan area'. He was talking man's love here; those Milan encounters were just a natural outpouring of Punjabi hormones.

'But some people marry here just to get legal.'

'I don't want to marry here.'

'You want to marry her.'

'Yes, and you know there are also big problems here. The girls over here, their style is much higher than ours. They think they are much above us. They don't like us. They call us "freshy".'

'But there are girls who will marry if you pay them.'

'Yes, agents told us. The girls want £10,000. Where to get the money? And it is big risk.'

'What's the risk?'

'There are two boys from Barking. Came here like us. Both of them agreed through agent. They said they will pay half now and half after marriage. Each fellow paid £5,000 to the girl. The girls said you go back, we will come and marry you and then we will come back. But the girls never went to Punjab.

And they never called the two boys here. They never sent any papers. They lost £5,000. And they lost England also. And after so much difficulty they had come.'

'Were they Indian girls?'

'No, white girls they had met. But Indian girls also do this. They take money, then they don't marry. So now we also don't marry. These girls, they do this just like doing a job. There are so many cases. Now we have become very careful.'

'What about meeting girls. Do you go and have a good time? You know, like in Milan.'

'You know our girls here, they want sixty pounds every time. On Peter Street. Then we are scared of infection also. But still our boys go. But they like more to go to white girls.'

'On Peter Street?'

'Yes, but they come to house also. That way it is good for everyone and cheaper also. In Gravesend also they come to houses. Ninety per cent of our boys like it.'

'But what about just meeting girls?'

'I go into town with my friends in Gravesend. We go to pubs, you know they have mixed pubs here. Our girls also come there. They just call us bastard and freshy. So we say bitch. And all the time there is too much fear of the immigration people.'

'You mean they might send girls to catch you.'

'Yes. Sometimes there are fights. Then you get exposed. Police comes, you get exposed to immigration. Then you also have to spend so much money on these girls. Then also nothing happens.'

'Do people feel really scared of immigration?'

'Yes, it is very dangerous for us. Every time you hear of raids. That means sometimes we cannot find work. And there is so much work out there, and we cannot do it.'

'But how do you find work?'

'There are people who take us. They say to us go here and don't go there.'

'How much money do you make?'

'In construction it is good. The company pays eighty pounds a day. But we get in hand only forty. Agents and company managers take the rest.'

'Did you get some good construction jobs?'

'Yes, in Wembley Stadium. For two months. Then regular fellows came back and I had to go. But still many people had work there. Sad thing is sometimes you do not do any work in the day. And weekend is difficult time, no work. We make about two hundred pounds in a week.'

'Doing what?'

'Anything. I work in packaging all the time.'

'What are your expenses?'

'Rent we pay £125 a week. Four of us share the rent. Then there is food and whisky. Then there is train tickets. Then we have to phone to Punjab also.'

'So what do you save?'

'We save about one hundred and fifty a week.'

'Do you send money home?'

'Yes, to family, they had to pay back loan to agent who I paid in Patiala. I have paid the agent. I have helped family also.'

'Where do you keep the money?'

'Big problem. We have to keep in cash. We are always scared of some thief. So we take turns to be in the house, and nobody looks at the other fellow's money. There is always good adjustment between all of us.'

'Do other Indians here help you?'

'These pukkas hate us. They tell us you have come and spoilt our work, we have spoilt the market. They just don't want to know us. White people are good to us, our Indians are more against us. But some are good also.'

'You got help from the gurdwara in Paris. Do you get help from the gurdwara here?'

'No, no; they threaten us. They say if you come to us, we will report you to immigration.'

We had walked up the flyover and stepped into Southall station past the welcome sign in Punjabi '*Jee aayaan nu*', put up there by a Sikh manager. I asked Kashmir as we sat down on a platform bench if he had a passport. Like I was some immigration officer.

'I have no passport since I gave it to agent in Moscow. Agents in Italy got me a passport there. But it was a risk. I came to England in trolley. Never used the passport I got in Italy. So no identity. Other boys also do not have.'

'Did you think of asking for political asylum?'

'No, they reject. They send us back. After spending so much money no one wants to go back.'

'How many are here in Southall like you?'

'Oh, thousands, there are thousands.'

'And women also?'

'Yes there are Punjabi women, three work with us. But they did not come like us.'

'How did they come?'

'They married pukka fellows here, then those fellows left the girls. They always do that. So girls are just living here and working in the factories. These fellows, they marry girls from Punjab, then they just leave them. Then they cannot get stamp.'

'And the people with you, some have been here a long time?'

'Some are here for eight, nine, ten, twelve years. Now they have become too old to marry anybody, and they are too old to go back. They send money, and they don't even know where it is going.'

'So it is work, work, work.'

'Work and whisky. We really love to drink. Who is there to say anything?'

The smell of alcohol and stale curries had by now wandered into the country meadow the wallpaper had tried to bring into this Southall sitting room. That aroma, garnished by presumable breaking of wind and perhaps of sex, can be quite a force, particularly when closed windows feed it back on itself. I was reeling under its power as I waited for my Punjabi brothers from the next room who, like Kashmir, had taken the trolley rather than the flight to Britain.

Stains of all kinds had added themselves to the heavy black and brown print of the carpet. The carpet was of a colour meant to disguise stains, and suggested long periods of occupation of a place that would never be home. An empty bottle of whisky on the floor was the only thing in the room that looked new; there was probably something new in this respect every day.

An open window could have done something to clear the room's recent history. But cold, fresh air came at a price; it would bring with it a bill for heating the room again. Or, this may not have been a calculated decision at all; home environment must be about the last thing on the minds of Jas and at least six others he was sharing the house with.

I was waiting for Jas on a sofa made of something synthetic; it was the only movable object in that room other than the bottle. Jas was at the moment talking to some others in the room at the back.

After some waiting I wandered into the back room; among Punjabi males, no niceties stand in the way of doing some such thing. It was the bedroom in the sense that the room was a bed. The floor was covered by wall-to-wall bedding for seven or eight. Jas was talking to two of his mates, the rest must have found weekend work or wandered out. I asked for tea and suggested we have it right there. The two chaps did not look very welcoming, and I returned to the other room.

Jas brought some tea in a bit. Like the Chandni Chowk tea, it was heavy on milk, long on boiling. That kind of tea was a bond, so obviously was our language. But we were uncomfortably aware of the great divide between us. They were illegal, I was pukka. I felt almost guilty that I was legitimately in England. It meant I was occupying a dream they'd risked their lives for. I felt like a passenger in an air-conditioned railway coach looking at someone hanging on outside the locked door.

I'd met Jas through a family I've known for years in Southall. As with Kashmir, I needed a strong introduction to open illegal doors. So, to him too I wasn't some immigration officer in disguise. But Jas had not just been willing to meet me, he sounded keen. He said he wanted me to take a message to the outside world. He'd told me on the phone in a nutshell what it was: he and his friends, and others like them, had so much money to give to the British government, if only it would please accept it.

'Main thing here is work permit,' Jas said. His life would turn one way or another on those two words. 'Just think what it would mean. You see how much tax the government would get through us. And with that, cheap labour. And whoever is here, even if he came illegally, he would have a status, he would have papers, he can apply for good jobs.'

Jas said he was a computer engineer, and looked it in his wise-looking glasses over a square and sober face. He was not my idea of an illegal immigrant who sailed through Dover in an unobserved trolley, any more than Kashmir had been.

'And what job would you do?'

'In computers.'

'But are you doing any computer work now?'

'Only a little. Basically, I go where they take me. Mostly farms and factories.'

'Who is "they"?'

'The agents.'

'Are they Indian?'

'Sometimes. But mostly they are white British people.'

'And there are enough people who will give you work?'

'It is human nature. If a company gets cheap labour, then it is human nature they will go for cheap work and save money and make more profit.'

'And you think the government will benefit more than you if you get work permits?'

'Of course. We have benefit here anyway. There is so much freedom. You can eat, drink, do what you like. Nobody asks you, nobody says what you are doing. And this place is much more safe than Punjab. You have full rights, you have full human rights. No problem with police, no racism, people are very kind, people are very fair.'

'But you are illegal, you have no rights here.'

'Even then, there are rights. But, of course, we are illegal, so there are big problems also.'

'Like what?'

'Like, you know, we do not get proper pay. We can work for ten hours and get only thirty pounds. And the agents, they take fifty per cent. Sometimes when it is very hard work they take more than fifty per cent. And this money, all is in black. The government getting nothing. If we have papers, government will know what is going on, they will have benefit of proper economy.'

'But the pukkas will say you are taking away other people's jobs for less money, you are ruining the market.'

'You think anybody will do the jobs we do? Show me one pukka who will do the job I do. Work so hard, never complain. We cannot say anything because we will get exposed. We just want to cooperate with government. Just give us work permits, then we will take care of everything.'

'Forget the government here, you think work permits will be good for you, isn't it?'

'Of course, of course. So many of us people who come here are educated. But they are not getting proper work. One man is an electrical engineer. He cannot find work as electrician also. He works on field with me. And look at the others. They should at least allow us to get education. But everybody is afraid they will be exposed, means they cannot go and learn anything. We have technical graduates here, professionals, computer programmers. But they are working in packing, working in building. This kind of exploitation we face. Main thing is work permit. Otherwise you come here like number two, you live here like number two.'

'And where do you work?' I asked one of the other chaps I'd seen in the back room; they had both walked in to join us. He had the mean good looks of truck drivers on a Punjab highway.

'Same thing, everyone works same thing. We go where agents send us. Mostly building.'

'What kind of buildings?'

'New buildings also, repairs of houses also. There are so many contractors.'

'You know anyone here?'

'I have some relatives.'

'In Southall?'

'Basically it is all of us. We have suffered coming here, only we know how we have suffered coming here. Pukkas don't care about us. So we look after one another.'

'And white people?'

'They are very good to us. Only white people are good to us.'

'Are there many Indians here?'

'Oh yes, so many, from India, from Pakistan. But we are not so many also. Most people are white, they come from Albania. We are nothing before them. You should see them. They do what they like. They get more money also.'

'So it's you and Albanians?'

'No, Chinese. There are too many Chinese.'

'Do you compete for jobs?'

'Yes but many pukka Chinese to help them. They get many jobs. You have Thai girls also, they do those jobs, you know.'

He smiled the smile of one who knows. 'You have girls from Albania also. The girls do light work, they work in restaurants, they work in kitchens. Only Indian girls, Pakistani girls don't work like us.'

'Do you get along with the Chinese and Albanians?'

'We say hello at work. Then everybody goes back with their own group, we don't know where they go. But there is competition. But less competition in the summer. Then there is so much work.'

'How long have you been here?'

'Three years.'

'How long do you plan to stay?'

He looked surprised, like going back was not an option.

'Now I am here, I will stay. It is not easy to go back.'

'Why not?'

'What work I will do if I go back? And what people will say? They make so much fun of people who fail here, people who go back. Then you can never go out again. No chance after that. You should see those people. They can never do anything. And if you go back quickly, no money to pay agent also. My brother tried three times. Never succeeded, and family has paid so much.'

'But is it worth it here?'

'We are happy. We only know about today. We don't know about tomorrow.'

'Do you know anyone who has gone back?'

'Yes, some fellows. They have been here for five years, six years, they have family in Punjab, they have gone back. They could not become pukka. So they went back.'

'So it is only single chaps who come here?'

'No, now the older men also come. Because it is easy for them. They get visitor visas. We can never get visitor visas. They come here, they work for two, three, four years, then they make some money and go back.'

'No one has asked you in three years who you are and what you are doing here?'

'No. People are very nice. And our people also, they don't tell.'

'And do you feel settled?'

'You can never have family life here. Agents, they give very false picture. They say good money, good houses, you will find many girls, you will marry, you will stay. But it is not like that. You go to girl here. What can you say to her? She will not look at you.'

Our chatting went on for some time till we decided to take it up another day. I hadn't asked the truck driver type his name, or the name he had given himself. He came to see me to the door, and saw I had a car to get into. 'I want to drive a car here,' he said. 'Let us see, one day…' He was unhappy, and I uncomfortable. Now he would see me drive off in his dream.

To a Degree

So it was time to go back, I said to Ujjwal, now that his degree was nearly done. It was the mean sort of thing an immigration officer might say. It didn't upset him; he was too chronically cool to be upset by anything. 'We need permission to come here, not to go back,' he replied.

It wasn't something he had just thought up; he said it like he must have known well before he came to Britain that he'd never want to go back after it had offered him what it could by way of education. He didn't come here to return to Gujarat with a British degree of sorts. Something in software engineering from the London Metropolitan University couldn't count for much in India, and he had no intention of testing its worth back home.

We were at the Sakoni restaurant on Ealing Road, that temple of Gujarati shopping and vegetarian eating out. Sakoni and its clones make this almost certainly Britain's longest vegetarian street, which means no Gujarati can keep away from it long. And at £2.50 a meal and £4.50 for an exaggerated buffet, the street makes Gujarati economic sense as well. The restaurants, usually rows of whitely-lit white tables, more eating places than restaurants, price low to go for the turnover. Here, even the less than low-waged illegal migrant can at least sometimes eat out.

Ujjwal was quite at home. He ordered his spiced Indian tea like he'd been promoting it proudly to others for years. Britain is so much easier to deal with when you feel at home, and to a Gujarati no place is home quite like Ealing Road in Wembley. It provides fulfillment by bhajia, and reassurance in numbers. If all those Gujaratis could be here to stay, surely someone as smart as Ujjwal could too. I looked behind his glasses and saw a winner's resolve in his eyes. He was determined to take from England more than he would give it. So far it was all give, and this bothered him.

'You see the fees we pay, the students from here pay so much less. So we are paying the universities. It is an income to government also. The governments must be paying universities, and because of us they will ask for less from government.'

'But the government allows you to work and earn money while you study. Twenty hours a week, isn't it?'

'Yes, officially twenty hours, but people work more for cash in hand.'

'How much do you earn?'

'The minimum wage is four pound fifty an hour, but most people pay less. You see everyone is getting a lot of workers now, students, illegal people. So many people are ready to work for less, for cash-in-hand. There is lot of competition, work is not easy.'

'How do you look for work?'

'I have been going to different areas. First to Wembley, then others. I give my CV, then I call them. I gave twenty CVs, then I got a call from a restaurant. So I work there as waiter on weekends when they need more people.'

'Is that OK money?'

'I get sixty pounds a week. That pays for my living charges here. But I am looking for work in city. I have been there and given my CV to many people. I told them I am ready to work cash-in-hand for less than four pounds fifty, I can work at night also. I have not got a job in city, but I will get. The British people talk to you very nicely.'

'Any chance you will get work in software? That's your area, isn't it?'

'UK has no market in software. Here there is no development happening. No new companies, no new work. Not like India. Here, now, I can get labour work in offices and places like that. Because native British people, they don't like to do basic labour jobs.'

'So for work you will do just anything.'

'Anything. Tomorrow I am going to Heathrow. Going to hotels. I will ask there. At least someone can give me a rejection letter in writing.'

'Why do you want that?'

'Because with that letter I can get a national insurance number. I can show it to other places. It makes me proper you know, legal to ask for work. It can also help me open a bank account.'

'How will it help you open a bank account?'

'Because it is at least something. The banks here, they all want proof of residence before they open account. But we have no gas bills in our name. If there are twelve of us in this house, how can there be a bill in anybody's name? And banks want two utility bills in your name.'

'So what do you do?'

'We cannot just keep money inside pillows all the time. So we take rejection slips, because the letter comes to our address. That is what some people have done.'

'Did it work for you?'

'No, I haven't got a rejection letter in the post yet.' This was the first time I'd seen anyone look sorry over not getting one. But he had managed a bank account, he said.

'How did you manage that?'

'I got a provisional driving licence.'

'And that became proof of residence?'

'Yes. Because you know I don't have a car. Students don't get cars. And look at how I got it. Had to surrender my passport for one week. Then they give provisional licence and charge thirty pounds for it. It is one type of income for government here. Otherwise I have international driving licence even if I don't have a car. So I don't need provisional driving licence.'

'What were you doing before you got it?'

'Twice I had to go to broker to cash cheques. And I had to pay him commission.'

'It all sounds very difficult here.'

'But I will stay here. Everyone here I tell you, we have come to stay. Level of studies in India, too much. And money is not good in India.'

'But you are on a student visa.'

'Student visa? You know, I went to ask for delivery job at a pizza place. And the manager, he came on a student visa fifteen years ago. He is still on a student visa. You know how much money he is making?'

'But don't you want a career in software?'

'Yes, if there is good money in it, why not? I could get a job, then get work permit. If I can get work permit for four years, that's all I want. Then I am here. Pukka.'

'You think you will get work and your work permit one day?'

'Yes, there are agents for that also. They get you work permit even if they don't get you work.'

'What do they charge?'

'One hundred, two hundred a month.'

'But whatever you do, you want to stay here.'

'Yes.'

He looked like he meant it. He had developed a certain ease with things British, and how to work them, and around them, that should have been deeply worrying to an immigration officer if only he could see now just who he had let past his little desk at Heathrow's Terminal 3.

Ujjwal said he discovered the London Metropolitan University – one of those polytechnics now renamed universities – through a universities mela the British Council held in Ahmedabad. Ujjwal, with a degree in computer engineering from Baroda, went to Ahmedabad for the mela because his father, a distributor with an electrical goods agency, had the money and because 'at the end of the day, pound is pound and rupee is rupee'. 'At the end of the day' – Ujjwal was already using London's language. Good British Gujaratis say that about three times a day, and 'having said that' about twice, to announce their comfort with current English.

Ujjwal discovered in Ahmedabad that London Metropolitan University had an agent in Baroda. There on, it all worked out smoothly; the admission, the visa. His father paid up £2,400 as a third of the annual fee upfront, and arranged draft payments for the rest of the year. Foreign exchange was no problem, since India now has those fabulous billions of it. Through the agent network, Ujjwal found also an address for Nilesh who was running those thriving home-hostels for Gujarati students arriving in Wembley. And who could do better than £250 a month for a place to stay, with Gujarati breakfast, dinner and friends thrown in, even if everyone slept a little closer to one another than they might have preferred?

I never did find out whether he was Nilesh, Navin or Naved. When I met him he was Nilesh, but others spoke of Navin and Naved, talking of the same chap. And there was more. 'Actually, he has got another name, Federico Fernando,' said my friend Vineeta who introduced me to him. 'He has that name on a Portugese passport he got from an agent. Portugese is EU, you know.' So is London, and Wembley too. Have one, you have the other.

Vineeta said she knew because she had seen the passport, and that was because she had rented some of her property to him in which he housed Indian students. She didn't know how Nilesh came to have that passport, she knew only that he arrived somehow, and like the rest, somehow overstayed. Now that he was in Wembley, he'd found more local names than Federico bhai.

Nilesh had rented ten or twelve houses and sublet rooms to students from Gujarat. Their dreams had brought him business; in their future lay his.

I met Nilesh briefly a few times, and always only briefly. On a couple of occasions I met him with the woman who said she was his wife, though that was not something he ever said. She told me her name was Chanda, but she was probably Chanda only in the way that Nilesh was Nilesh, because another friend called her Chitra. With the illegal arrivals from India these days, you never know who is who.

Vineeta had been telling me about Nilesh and Chanda as we walked down Ealing Road in Wembley to see them. Vineeta was only one of his landladies because he needed to rent many more houses than just she could offer, and Nilesh just one of her tenants. But Nilesh was her tenant and wasn't. 'Because he never takes the tenancy in his name,' she said. 'It is always in the name of one of his students. That way he does not have to pay council tax. And if there is a problem with the landlord, he can run away.' Vineeta had been thinking about his business because he was behind on rent. If he were to disappear, she might never even be able to name the man who owed her the money.

'He has 160, 170 students, you know,' she said. 'Can you imagine?' I understood that to mean, did I know how much money he was making? She counted swiftly for me. Sixty pounds a week per student in some of the houses, £55 pounds in others. In the house we were heading to, he had 13 students, maybe 15, three to a small, very small bedroom. So £800 a week income, about £3,500 pounds a month and, of course, no receipts, which meant no taxes. He paid £900 a month rent and the usual bills for heating and electricity. He also spent on loaves of bread and milk for breakfast, and a Gujarati dinner of rice, dal, *roti* and vegetables; *shaak* when Gujaratis cook them. But the net added up nicely. And that was just this one house.

'You should see him shop,' Vineeta said. 'He buys damaged oil tins that no one else will buy, he buys the bread from Kwik Save at just 15p for a loaf. And he gets Chanda to cook.' Vineeta figured he makes £2,000 a month from this one house. Multiplied into many houses with students in them, Nilesh was in money. His home-hostel business was flourishing in Wembley. Like all good business, this was a good deal for everyone. And the lucky student appointed house manager by Nilesh paid £200 a month, not even £250.

Vineeta and I turned off Ealing Road and walked down Clayton Avenue to the nearest Nilesh student home. Chanda, plump and unhappy, welcomed us at the door, and to leftovers from dinner for the students. 'I cook for fifteen people every day,' she said. 'There is always enough for one or two more.' We walked through a dark little passage from the front door to the table at the back by the side of the kitchen. Three students – two chaps and a girl – were talking at the table before our arrival bust up their meeting. The leftover dal and potato *shaak* waited for us in large pans. Boiled rice sat heaped up on a kitchen plate.

Chanda heated the food and served generously, and I felt very at home. I'd breathed in my appetizer already on that walk round the corner from the VB Indian Foods Store, across from Fudco, that other supplier of raw material for Indian cooking. A cooked version of those fragrances was all I now needed.

I'd asked Vineeta just short of the door why she wasn't in this student business herself. She whispered to me a lot louder than she knew as those students left the table, 'He has the contacts in Gujarat. He has the agents, he is also an agent. The students come straight to him. They have his house number and telephone number. From the airport they come straight. It is good for students, cheap. And they have so many friends from first day they come here.'

Nilesh appeared briefly. He was slim, not very tall, and of course he had a moustache, the subcontinental guide to the serious male. He had an abrupt way of talking and moving; at least he was always abrupt when I met him, and this time was no different. He quickly fished out his mobile phone, and with him you knew it would be one of the latest, with features that would have amazed me had he cared to show them. Someone wanted him on the phone, he said, and he was gone.

Chanda was not sorry to see him leave. She'd done all the cooking and looked tired and hard done by. This was no way to spend evening after evening.

He was hardly gone before she began to complain. Not about work; it was Nilesh. She was convinced he was having an affair with a girl student in one of the other houses. 'Actually he is having an affair with two girls. But I'm not sure. One, I know, one hundred per cent. Other one, I am ninety-nine per cent sure.' There was hope in that one per cent.

'I am going to leave him,' she said. 'He cannot do anything to me. Because he knows I can fix him.' There had been a quarrel over some money transfers, and there were things Chanda said she knew. The quarrels had led someone to invite Nilesh to the car park at the Sainsbury's store in Wembley and assault him. Nilesh was left heavily, very visibly, bruised.

Chanda was in the confessional mode appropriate between friends on a late evening after rice and dal. She could fix him because she was on pukka ground, she said. 'I have full rights to stay here now. I have got political asylum.' That clearly was not true, because I had gathered from Home Office figures that no one from India was getting political asylum. Who knows whether she could ever fix Nilesh, because he must know a thing or two about her as well.

Chanda said she had arrived from India at the time of those attacks on Christians in Gujarat. She said she declared at Heathrow that she was a Christian facing political persecution, and so needed political asylum. I never heard a word about the persecution she had faced in Gujarat. If she did apply for asylum, then presumably her application went into processing stage. Whether her application had been turned down, or whether she did not apply at all, or was overstaying after a decision, here she was, long past a visitor's stay. It's called disappearing into the system, or out of it.

I had no idea how Nilesh and Chanda turned up in Wembley, only that they were now here. Together, or in such togetherness as they had found suitable, they were running the business of maintaining imported students. I couldn't guess just how many of the students appearing at their doors would later disappear. In Wembley, disappearing is popular business.

Katherine and Cab

Across from the bus garage on Ealing Road in Wembley, Katherine and King's College of London stood to make dreams of England come true, if not of education. For the chap I was talking to by the reception, who told me his name was Inder, it would make true his dream, for now, of driving a taxi in London.

Inder from Ludhiana could, of course, as easily have been Sarabjit from Jalandhar. Whoever he was, he was a student now with an advantage. He had come to Britain to the Thames Valley University for a £6,800 course, he didn't say which, it didn't matter. Since he moved to Katherine and King's, he was paying a fraction of that. With that difference he was 'getting a car to start a mini-cab,' he said. Driving around London, even if that meant driving someone around London, sounded a lot better than sitting in a classroom here and then returning to Ludhiana.

In the hearing of the girl at the reception, Inder gave me a lesson on his roundabout route to acquiring the taxi. 'You have to join a reputed university first for visa. You have to be there six months, because you have to pay half the fees first. Then you can go to a cheaper course.' That second move reduced costs, provided capital and gave him time through a day to start making money. 'But I do studies also,' he said, after a quick look at the young receptionist. She was listening with open attention, and she represented establishment. It was fine for Inder to think and do, but not to talk. We talked a little further, in Punjabi, and he was quickly gone.

That left me with the receptionist, just within the shop-like shutters of the college. The place had more of an academic look indoors because on the outside it appeared too much a shop. Just above the entrance by the side of the name 'Katherine and King's' sat a coat of arms in the shape of a shield. This was a coat of arms for academic knights. The upper half was divided in two sections, with three keys painted in the right half and three flower-like motifs in the left. The middle section tapering below featured a flat black graduation hat, a blank open book, and 'K&K' imprinted in knight font. On a Gujarati street across from a bus garage, with a computer repair shop on one side and a fried-chicken outlet on the other, here was Britain being presented at its most English.

'Who owns the college?' I asked the receptionist.

'A Chinese lady,' she said. Predictably, the receptionist was East European.

'Is she Katherine?'

'Yes.'

'And King's?'

'It is Katherine King.'

I picked up a copy of the brochure from the reception desk. 'It's very simple,' she said in her East European English, before I had a chance to look at it. 'You get the application form on our website, and you fax it to us and send a payment of one hundred and fifty pounds. We will send you a letter of acceptance on that basis. You take that to the British embassy in your country and you get the visa.'

'And if you don't?'

'We will return fifty pounds to you.' Not bad income at 100-a-head if enough people do no more than try.

I sat down to study the brochure. The first page asked the question: 'Why to choose Katherine and King's College of London?' Answer: 'An edge is given to you at Katherine and King's College of London, which makes you stand out among the crowd.' Admission itself would be no struggle. 'An acceptance letter will be issued upon receipt of the application package,' the brochure said. Some minimal education would be required, and this would be checked on arrival.

The brochure promised free collection from the airport to the college, or to student accommodation. And help with accommodation. Cards on an accommodation board in the reception area offered a choice of places at the usual £50–60 a week. And once it has all proved suitably tempting: 'It is your wise choice to choose Katherine and King's College of London

148

as a significant stop in your life journey. Wish you enjoy your stay here at Katherine and King's College of London!'

The website had more. Students can work 20 hours a week, and 40 hours during holidays, it announced. 'In line with the government initiatives to make studying in the UK more attractive, there is a new policy on working visas after the completion of the student's study. All students will be eligible to gain a further 12 months working visa based on the employment being in some way related to the preceding area of study. For further information, please contact student service advisor.' Some courses were as cheap as £1,400 a year, which would in a way make the fee for staying in Britain only a little more than £100 a month. Once there, you could earn as you wanted. Who would clock Inder's hours in his cab at 20 a week and 40 during holidays?

The college website quotes Katherine King, principal, with the qualification 'ACIS', whatever this was, as saying: 'Where there is a will there is a way.' Others, presumably college academics of a sort, also speak up. Julie Samwise: 'I ask God, "How much time do I have left?" and God replies, "Enough to make a difference".' Harry Lee: 'The only real failure in life is to stop trying.'

Education had kept Ushani two years in London now, and still she had no husband. She hadn't enrolled to be single, and looked betrayed by the absence of a suitable man. 'Why don't you suggest somebody?' she said to me as we sat down to lunch at Jashan, one of those Gujarati vegetarian places on Ealing Road, together with our friend Chanda.

Ushani had brought down costs steadily to stretch discovery time. She got herself a transfer from the £7,000 a year South Bank College to an £800 a year place in Ilford outside east

London – with, she said, visa. 'And you know what? I never even have to go there.'

It surprised me that Ushani had not received a productive proposal for all of her two years here. She had the tough elegance of a Delhi girl – what more should a man want? Two blank years had not diminished her confidence, but she was obviously impatient for a marriage proposal from a pukka male for final admission to Britain, and not just from some teaching place for a few months now and then. There could be no right man for her who did not also bring the stamp of permanence on her passport, or 'indefinite leave to remain', as the Home Office so fuzzily calls its equivalent of the American green card. She was determined to be attractive to her right man; if she'd come here to stay and not study, then stay she would and study she would not. If she needed more time in Britain, she'd find it – she had at just £800 a year – and invite opportunity to do the rest. Living in Britain seemed only a state of non-return, but so much better than returning on a one-way ticket.

A Pakistani in the business of settling imported students had explained the game simply. Get a student to take course after course. And after the courses, what, I asked. 'You think my students are such fools that in four years, five years, no one will like them?'

She had glanced more than once at a couple of Indian looking females who'd had taken the next table. They were obviously 'from here'; their suburban-Jamaican style was unmistakable. So too was the look of envy in Ushani's eyes. They were her settled dream. They in turn would have placed Ushani as an off-the-boat Indian. Not through her long brown slit skirt, almost a split skirt, nor her beige sleeveless shirt… It was the Delhi that spoke in her voice that would bring the boat to mind. It's much easier to leave Delhi than have Delhi leave you, and not just by way of accent.

Our Guju-veggie lunch later, Ushani and Chanda took the bus to a home for the elderly where some caring at £6.90 an hour would buy more time. I walked the other way towards the London College of Business and Accountancy that Ushani had said she was considering for the next year if she still hadn't found anyone by then.

I took a short-cut through the parking lot behind the Wembley High Road and then the stairs up to the road, and regretted it, as I always do. As usual there was renewed evidence by the stairs of kidney-processed beer from the previous evening. I tried to make the stairs in one breath, and failed again.

I found the college by Wembley Central Station, round the corner from Somali-owned Internet cafes, next to a vegetable shop. Up two flights of stairs, a door in the corridor was marked LCBA, the London College of Business and Accountancy. The corridor was packed with Somalis. This was more Mogadishu than London. I couldn't see Ushani ever attending college here, but then she only went to colleges she didn't have to go to.

A large man with a substantial beard rose from the computer and bore down on me at the reception. 'I'm Mohammed,' he said. I said I'd come to ask about admission. He gave me a brochure and pointed to a chair. Like the Katherine and King's brochure, this one was for the dream of some distant student, wasted on me because I'd now seen the college. The college was one thing, its brochure another.

The cover showed a happy white boy carrying a happy white girl on his back. The Tower Bridge behind showed just where such happiness could be found. Like K&K, this too had a coat of arms printed on the brochure, split into three sections. This one featured a graduation hat, a blank book with feather and inkpot, and what looked like a folder with the profile of a man and woman on it. Below these ran a wavy ribbon, the sort that things in Latin get written on. The words in English here were far simpler: 'Excels in Education and Training'.

The cheapest course on an accompanying 'price list' was a year's diploma in business administration at £2,000. 'Is that negotiable?' I asked Mohammed before leaving. 'The fee is not negotiable,' he replied, looking up. Then added, 'But it can be negotiated.' That offer stayed with me long after I left.

Several weeks later I mentioned to Ushani that I'd visited her dream college. I mentioned the fee. 'You never go by their price list,' she said. 'If I had to go there, I'd bring it down.' But she would not need to go to this college, she said. Or to any college. 'I'm getting married. I've met this really, really nice guy.'

Chanda later took some of the romance out of it. 'You know he is BSc honours in information technology. Born and brought up here. Parents are from Delhi but they came here forty years back. Whole family is pukka here.' Wouldn't Ushani like to go back to Jashan and have the same two girls at the next table again? Now she would have a passport like theirs. And perhaps unlike them, a husband as well.

The new students head for the 'new universities', now the polite name for former polytechnics. Like the London Metropolitan University, the Thames Valley University, and the Hertfordshire University just north of London that I'd driven up to. A very university-like campus, and after Katherine and King's and LCBA, it looked a proper place for study.

A woman at the reception in the students' office asked me to wait for 'a lady in glasses with quite curly hair, if you see what I mean'. I saw when Alison Proctor finally turned up, after a long wait. I'd asked at the reception to speak to someone about the fees students from India paid. It was a touchy subject; millions of pounds in income for the university depended on it. Some discussions had clearly taken place within on what to say to me, and mostly, I thought, what not to say.

The waiting had given me more than a moment to survey the new money all around. Three glassy new buildings had come up to face the old one. I waited within a tinted glass shell of a building held up by bright yellow frames, very new Britain. A little further up the de Havilland centre, proclaimed proudly as a state-of-the-art learning centre, had just been built at a cost of £120 million.

Our meeting turned out to be a controlled quarrel. The British are particularly good at dressing quarrels politely.

Alison had finally walked in accompanied by a young suited chap, a Mr Fletcher. They walked in like they were ready to leave. They asked me what I wanted to ask. I had a few simple questions. How many students did the university have? And how many foreigners? And what fees did the local British students pay, and what did foreigners pay? My questions, Proctor said, would be answered by the marketing manager, a Mr Donald McCloud, and he was not around that day. But they would get back to me.

Did I need a marketing manager to tell me how many students there are at the university, I asked. I suggested that as someone who's been to a British university, I didn't think this kind of information was difficult to access.

'We have 22,500 students,' Proctor said, allowing the minimal to pass through. 'Of that about 3,000 are international students. They come from eighty countries, but the number of students from China and India is significant. But we also have a lot of students from Pakistan, Sri Lanka and Bangladesh. And many British Asian students. We are very proud of our diversity.'

And the fee for overseas students? 'About £7,900 pounds for a standard undergraduate international student.'

'What about a British student?'

'You say you have been a student here,' Proctor said, sharply. 'You should know.' She looked more than a little accusing, and looked more and more like she couldn't wait to see me leave. I replied that fees vary, and that it had been a while since I was a student.

'It's about £1,100 a year,' she said. 'But, don't forget, parents here also pay a lot of taxes.'

In the same classroom, a British student would be paying £1,100 and an Indian student £7,900. That was the simple explanation why the British had suddenly started to issue so many student visas. It was the reason Ujjwal and Ushani were here, and why Nilesh was in business. International students were being called in to pay to educate the British, and they were paying to build up the new universities. They were paying for these brand new campuses that would remain in Britain long after they supposedly left. With so much foreign money, Brit students could be tempted to universities paying just minimal fees.

Taking the difference in fee at face value, Ujjwal's parents were paying also for the education of six British students they had never met and never would. On a rough calculation, the 3,000 international students were bringing in £23 million a year, about as much as the remaining 19,500 British students. Besides, the university was getting grants from the government, the taxpayer eventually. As Proctor put it, Brits were paying their fees that way too, and so their fee was not as low as it looked.

It was hardly surprising that Proctor and Fletcher did not want me airing these matters, particularly in India. If even a few potentially arriving Indians were to think they were being suckered, and choose some other place, those absences could add up to significant losses.

'Do students find work here,' I asked. To my surprise, Ms Proctor began to offer a little more information.

'There is enough work in the area. But it is at the lower end, labour work in shops and warehouses and industrial areas. There is a lot of disappointment among students, because they come from well-respected families there, and they expect to pick up similar levels of jobs here. But we don't encourage students to come with that in mind, we want them to have their finances sorted out before they come. There are enough unscrupulous agents out there who say don't worry, you will get a job there. But the cost of living here is very high, and working here can only give you those extras.'

Proctor was delivering a warning through me. 'It is very important that people who come this distance know what to expect. They should not come with inflated expectations, and we are very concerned that they come for the right reasons.'

Fletcher must have feared this would develop into a proper conversation. 'Thank you,' he said, and got up. There our meeting ended.

Hertfordshire University, I saw later, had appointed four agents in India, in Amritsar, Ahmedabad, Bangalore and Chennai. But this was not the only new university out there to pull Indian pounds to Britain.

Middlesex University had set up a South Asia regional office in Delhi that offered admission and accommodation. London Metropolitan University boasted 4,000 international students, a great many of them from India. This university too was now suddenly a richer place. It had set up overseas offices in Beijing, Shenzhen, Delhi, Chennai, Dhaka and Lahore. And its old unlovely blocks had been given a dramatic new look by way of a centre designed by Daniel Libeskind, the one who designed the memorial to the World Trade Centre in New York, the Jewish Museum in Berlin and the Imperial War Museum in Manchester.

The coloured steel of this 'little jewel' of a campus, as Libeskind called it, has made London Metropolitan University quite a landmark in its drab neighbourhood. It would be right to put up a plaque here, at Hertfordshire university, and others to thank Indian and Chinese students for paying so dearly to transform teaching shops into universities. If, after all this, some Brits still cannot get themselves a decent education, no one can say many thousands of Indian parents did not do their bit to help.

Legally Married

When Manjula said she'd found true love at last, no one took any notice; she found true love about three times a week. 'His name is Shakti,' she said. 'You must meet him, my other friends have all met him.' I said sure I would, as I had to the many other true loves of her life I never got to meet. She'd never had a boyfriend, and some of her friends had got so far as to talk of ex-boyfriends. We would indulge the declared new loves of her life a little patronisingly. Now Shakti had come along.

But Shakti was for real. She met him at the Hare Krishna mandir in Leicester, and everyone saw that they met again and again; in Leicester when two Indians meet, various other Indians see, and take note. In time Manjula came to worship Shakti more than Krishna. She knew he was an illegal immigrant, but love can blossom independent of landing papers, or the lack of them. It did for her anyway.

Manjula's mum Preeti was getting more worried by the day over this true-love-at-last. She asked me home in Leicester one evening to talk to Manjula and to Shakti. She wanted me to quiz Shakti and talk some sense into Manjula implicitly. They no doubt were anticipating some interrogation, and had worked out how to deal with it, I guessed right up to the last minute. They turned up eventually.

Shakti was a big and shifty guy with very short hair, and if he too had found true love, it didn't show. He did not look pleased with the summons, he was there because an intended mother-in-law could not be wished away, and avoidance was not an option.

'How did you come to UK?' I asked.

'I came on a fake passport. I threw it away after I came here.'

'Who gave you the fake passport?'

'There was an agent in Jaipur. I paid him 800,000 rupees [£5,000]. Plus the air fare.'

'You from Rajasthan?'

'Yes.' That much at least seemed true, because he spoke that kind of Hindi. He did not speak English at all.

'The passport must have been a good fake. Why not just use it, why did you throw it?'

'No, it is too risky. And anyway its date was running out.'

'So how do you plan to stay here now?'

'I will just stay. Maybe if I marry Manjula then I can stay.'

'You want to marry Manjula just to stay here?'

'No, but that way I can stay.'

I thought I'd been spared the burden of playing some Poirot-like detective, that we had here something like plain confession. Manjula heard, of course, but didn't look like she minded at all. She was in giving mode, and her love would shower on him the legality he needed. After what I heard, I now wanted that meeting to end fast, I couldn't wait for him to leave before turning to Manjula. He had, after all, said what we'd been saying to her again and again, that he wanted to marry her just to settle here.

'I don't care,' she replied. 'I love him, and I'm going to marry him.' There is never anything left to say after 'but I love…' Shakti must have been very sure of her to have said what he did, the way he did.

Preeti's friend Raksha dropped in later that day; around Belgrave Road people always drop in without calling. Phoning first is too English.

Raksha too was determined to save Manjula from herself. We all were, but there was nothing we could do. The only way to stop the marriage was to have him deported. She had called Crimestoppers, a substitute for calling the police in non-urgent matters. She gave them Shakti's name, his address, and told them he was an illegal immigrant, that he had arrived on a fake passport, and had said he did. The man on the phone took the information, thanked Raksha, and that was it. She thought he hadn't sounded interested. She was right. Weeks, and then months passed by. Shakti lived freely in Leicester, and continued to work in a woollens factory along with many other illegal arrivals like him, and continued to see Manjula.

For his own reasons he was now in a hurry to marry, and so of course was Manjula. You don't see that much blind love these days, but here she was. She said Shakti had asked to be introduced to her friends. She had, and then told us he proposed to two of them. Then he proposed to her sister. None of the others wanted to know him. And after all this, Manjula said she loved him.

Finally Preeti gave in, Raksha gave up, and before I knew it I was shopping for an engagement gift for the couple. I picked up some vouchers from Marks & Spencer, as dull and functional as a gift can get. I chose a card that said 'Tying the Knot' but I stopped even as I started to write something in the card. Dear Manjula and… who? He had said his name was Shakti. Maybe he was Shakti, and had used another name for the passport. But Shakti was all I knew, and that's what I wrote.

I was back in Leicester the day of the engagement. Manjula glowed in the red sari she had managed to wrap around herself, a mother's caring quite obviously missing from the way she wore it. When a near-bride wears a sari like she is wrapping cloth around her, something is not right. Manjula, naturally, did not see that. 'This is the happiest day of my life,' she said as I sat down on a floor cushion in the sitting room. Nobody else in the room said anything. There were just about a dozen of us. I looked around and thought of everyone not there; most of the close family and friends weren't. Preeti had not thought it the sort of engagement you make much of.

Preeti's boyfriend, very much a white Midlander, sat next to me, very all-seeing but saying nothing. I exchanged a despairing glance with Raksha, who had tried so determinedly to stop the marriage. The next-door lady sat next to her on the sofa. A few others I didn't know had dropped in. Raksha's husband, a white Hare Krishna devotee, came a little later in his usual white dhoti and kurta. '*Hari bol*,' he said. Some '*Hari bols*' floated back to him.

Shakti was last in. He walked in alone, camera in hand. He wore dark trousers and a light grey cotton jacket that sat so badly on him it could not have been his own. Getting into that jacket seemed the only special effort he made that day. He sat down on the sofa in a corner by the little bay window. He was with us and he wasn't. We all looked at him, he looked at no one.

It was now about twenty minutes past the auspicious 3 p.m. that Manjula had fixed for this first formal connection to Shakti. She went upstairs and fetched two tiny red boxes with the engagement rings. She called Shakti up to her by the door and handed him one. He took the ring he was to put on her, and for the first time looked around. Manjula had her hand out, she was waiting for him to put it on her finger. But he didn't know which finger it should go on.

Preeti stood up from the floor, held up her daughter's hand and presented the ring finger. He slid the ring onto her finger like he was placing it on some little stand so it doesn't fall off. Then it was Manjula's turn. He held out the forefinger of his right hand. Manjula struggled, but the ring did not get far. Preeti again corrected the finger, but the ring wouldn't get on to his ring finger either, it was way too small.

'Didn't you check before buying your ring?' The question from the lady who had dropped in from next door cracked the strained silence over what we were seeing. 'Take it back to them, they will enlarge it for you.'

Manjula didn't care about the misfit ring – she was a heap of ecstatic giggles. She reached out and gave Shakti a hug. She could have been hugging a tree for all the response she got. 'His turn now,' the neighbour called out. Shakti made a move like he wanted to hug without touching, and since that was not possible he did something approaching a hug, and rapidly recoiled into his space. All of us came up to give each of the pair some sweets. We took turns to take photographs for Shakti, with his camera. The photography was the only thing he was taking seriously.

Lunch followed in the back room. Vegetarian, without onion and garlic, in the proper Hare Krishna way, because Raksha had been handling the kitchen. Shakti sat by himself on a chair nearest the door. He finished fast and left first. Raksha had some quiet words to say later: 'Best wishes for indefinite leave to remain.' It was Shakti's big day: he had just got engaged to a British passport.

The engagement lasted, though Manjula had time to 'see through' Shakti as everyone wanted her to. But she was making arrangements for marriage. It was agreed that they should marry in Rajasthan. Months later, they did.

Manjula returned a bride, and Shakti returned later, this time on his own passport, to live in Britain legally. They would have to stay married at least a year for Shakti to stay on. The marriage did not last – if it ever began as anything that could be called marriage. Mother and daughter engaged a lawyer to advise whether they should seek annulment or divorce. And this time Manjula supported a push from family and friends that her much desired husband be deported.

But Manjula put that experience behind her easily enough on the face of it. The last I met her she said she had found real true love, someone she was now seeing in London. A chap, she told me, who had just arrived from India, and wanted to settle in Britain.

Dinesh was going to 'expose' Shah Rukh Khan, the biggest Bollywood star, and when they get that big, Bollywood starts to call them superstars. Quite a challenge to take on. Not only was Dinesh much better looking than the superstar, but once his new film was out the public would also see how much better an actor he was.

Dinesh looked film-set ready in the kitchen of my friend Sharda, whose daughter Anita he had proposed to. He wore an off-white silk pyjama and shirt, with a blue sash around his waist, really a *dupatta* meant originally to be draped over shoulders to negate breast profile, and now inevitably in its variations a style statement. In any case, not something a male ties around his waist, and not to wear in a London kitchen. I've only ever seen it worn by men for a village dance in a Bollywood film. Dinesh could, because he was Bollywood ready.

He did not think himself good-looking without reason. He was on the short side, had those clean, boyish looks that never fail to charm and a winning sort of smile when he looked at mother and daughter. He did not smile at me, or even look.

I'd asked him what he did for a living soon after joining them at the table. That's when he said, looking pointedly at mother and daughter, that he would expose Shah Rukh Khan. He would do so for a start as the 'counter-hero' of a film being produced in London. It would be released soon, and it would show up Shah Rukh Khan for what he is not, and Dinesh for what he is.

'I am going to create a new concept in Hindi cinema,' he said. 'You wait and see.' He would not only act, he would produce films and he would write the script, because the script in Bollywood cinema is rubbish.

'You mean you'll be hero, producer and scriptwriter?' I asked.

'Oh yes, why not?'

'But are you planning to do this in Bombay or here?'

'No, I plan to make the films here.'

'In Hindi?'

'Yes, in Hindi.'

'But won't that be expensive? I mean, it would take a million pounds, or maybe some big fraction of it.'

'That is not a problem, there are people here ready to finance my films.'

'Like who, Indian businessmen here?'

'Yes.'

'I know most of them but I don't see any of them putting a few hundred thousand pounds into a film here.'

'That's because they haven't seen my ideas yet.'

It was an act, and not a very good one. The mother had been finding his outpourings of optimism worrying for some time now, and she'd developed strong misgivings about the marriage to be.

Dinesh and Anita had met at the temple on Lady Margaret Road in Southall. Anita called one day to tell me about this meeting with the man of her dreams. She had a role in a Krishna play at a temple in Southall, and she ran into Dinesh just as she was heading for the changing room after the show. He told her he loved her role, they exchanged numbers, and it was not many days later that he told her he loved her. And she loved him, and didn't they look good together. And weren't they blessed to have met at a temple.

Within a month of that meeting at the temple they were talking marriage dates, and Sharda had invited me to talk wedding matters through with them. Really, to check him out; I must be more detective-like than I'd thought. Something told her, as it told me quickly, that this chap in the kitchen was not the hero Shah Rukh Khan was waiting to concede stardom to. Only Anita looked pleased. She was in love and, to her, Dinesh was already a hero. The wedding was to take place in a couple of months.

Dinesh was already very much at home. It was that sort of home too; Sharda was strong on entertaining, and her lounge was intimately lit to dissolve distance among people. Her kitchen offered guests a parade of mostly successful experiments. All was as should be in this happy home except that the lovely Anita was pushing thirty and had not found anyone. Now that too seemed sorted, except that she had found a dubious hero.

'You see, he has no family here, we do not know where he is from, we do not know anything about him,' she told me, after the lovers left for an evening out in Anita's convertible black Golf. She had been asking Dinesh to say more about himself, and what she heard made her uneasy. His story was that he was from Nepal, but had lived in India because his father was an officer with the Indian army. He had begun studies in India, but family responsibilities came in the way. He then went to Singapore, studied hotel management but stopped just short of completing his degree. Now he had come to Britain to study. Where or what, he would not say. Sharda was becoming uneasy every time he took her daughter out, which really meant when she took him out.

'Three weeks back I asked him to show me his passport,' Sharda said. 'He said, no problem, he will bring it the next day. He said the university has kept his passport. I asked him which university, he did not say anything to me. Then I asked, can I talk to your family in Nepal? I said we cannot think of marrying unless we have met your family. He gave me the number. I called and I spoke to his mother. I told them that we are thinking of, you know, that he and Anita could get married. And you know what the mother said? She said don't believe anything he says. And you won't believe, she said she will feel sorry for any girl who marries her son. This is his own mother who said this.'

'Did you tell him what she said to you?'

'Yes, I told him. He said, don't worry aunty, my family is like that, they have always gone against me, they have gone against my studies, they want to go against my marriage.'

'And what does Anita say?'

'She is crazy about him, she believes everything he says.'

'What does he do here?'

'He works as a waiter. He says he is earning some money until his film comes out. After that he will be big. But it is not easy to become Shah Rukh Khan. Main thing is he has no job or qualification.'

'And Anita doesn't mind that?'

'No, she says she can work extra to earn for both, she says she will earn money to educate him if he does not make it in films, she says we can use our savings to put him in business. He says so many nice things to her, and she has gone crazy about him.'

'Does she believe everything he says?'

'No, she cannot. Because about his degree he was saying one thing, then he was saying something else. In front of her. I told him. And he said, sorry, he was telling lie about it. I asked him why did he tell lie? He said he was sorry about it.'

Sharda was determined to cure her daughter of this craze. They made a deal. He had lied about his university degree, and they would let that pass. But if he lied also about his passport, that would make him a pukka liar, and an illegal immigrant. It would mean he wanted to marry Anita because he wanted to settle in Britain. Maybe he really liked Anita too (it was hard not to), but it would mean he had a migration motive. So if he could produce the passport, the marriage was on, otherwise not.

He never did produce a passport. He would call Anita night and day, he would text his love. But there was no university, no job, no passport, no qualifications, no money. And no sign of the film. Mother and daughter were devastated in their own ways. They left for Bombay on a six-week holiday, Sharda wanted to get the daughter's mind off her hero. The time away worked. They returned, Anita changed her mobile number, and changed her mind.

The search for someone eligible, and legal, for Anita began again, but this time it was not at the temple.

CIRCLES

Nine Nights

'You are not, please, you are not going to match-make for me,' Kalpana was saying from the edge of the back seat after we finally made it to the car. The edge was all she had because we were giving her friends a ride to the first evening of Navratri, those nine nights towards the end of the year when Gujaratis meet for their group dancing in circles of all sorts. The crushable silk of her mauve *lehenga-choli* deserved more space, but *lehenga* management in a crowded car is an art all Gujarati girls learn in time. It's a consequence of family going out as family. Happy little problems, these, that Indians run into so much more than white Brits.

It was the time of the year when everyone deserves to be a Gujarati. After tonight there would be eight more Navratri nights to come. And nine more if you add the *poornima* night (of the full moon), making ten in all, and even 11 if you were a spectacular enough dancer to go through to the competition at the end. I figured there'd be a quarter of a million Gujus, and quite a few non-Gujus like me doing the Gujarati thing these nights, crowding into cars headed for Navratri dancing around Britain. It's when you wish cars were bigger than they are.

My friend Harshad wasn't coming, which meant he was not being a good Guju. He had been driving buses all week, he said tiredly. His 17-year-old son Ashwin wasn't Navratri-ready either. Blame the parents, since 'blame' it is in the Gujarati world, that he'd grown up more Londoner than Gujarati. His hair was long, he played football, and he played in a rock band. We would look at him and ask if England was going to claim him forever, or Gujarat recover him at least a little.

That put Harshad's wife Vijaya, his brother Ashok, their daughter Kalpana, who had just turned 21, her two friends and me into one car. But that little problem was not on Vijaya's mind; it was that Kalpana was 21. Vijaya had shown all the signs of readying Kalpana for a husband. She'd been dressed with almost bridal fuss. That this had delayed us was only another minor problem; brides, not even near-brides are expected to dress in time. Count in the mandatory rounds of 'why don't you' and 'I told you' when an Indian family steps out. These too had been flying mostly around poor Kalpana.

Mum was determined to prevail over the unwise confidence of her daughter that she could do her own thing; and daughter was determined to grow out of the controlling ways of parents. A global kind of conversation which gets amplified for Gujaratis with marriageable daughters at this time of the year. Nothing would push away that constant doubt from the back of mum's mind: did the daughter have a hidden boyfriend? If she did, maybe the right guy at Navaratri could out-magnet him. Over these nine nights they'd all see she was single, and they'd see how very nice she looked. She should have proposals enough, properly routed through 'community leaders' and parents, well before the ninth night was done. To the 'settled', Navaratri brings more of a reassuring sameness. For an unattached Gujarati girl just over 21, these nine nights bring promise of the new. Husbands are in the air, and on the floor. The future dances circles around her.

Parking at the Harrow Leisure Centre was full, always a sure sign of an Indian event, confirmed by the population of Mercs

167

and BMWs. We found a slot eventually, and stepped towards the hall. The women raised their *lehengas* just that bit above their sequined sandals past puddles from the afternoon rain. I found myself stealing more than a look or two at those light silver *payals* circling Gujaratan ankles, such a world above the soaked grit of the parking lot.

We could hear we were late because already the band was playing '*Pankhida, tu urhi ja*', that theme song of Navratri. We excused our way through the crowded colours to the stepped seating to a side, originally intended for spectators of some game of basketball, now adapted to Indian requirements. We joined the outer ring of spectators, five or six circles deep. The *garba* circles were going round in another five or six rings on the floor, the first of the two big dances of an evening, the *dandia raas* follows later.

The fascination of the *garba* lies in the eddying movement along rings of circling dancers. One circle of single dancers forms within another on the floor, moving clockwise or anticlockwise. Whichever way you go, the circle keeps turning back on itself as it moves along. Arms swing back as you move forward, then they go forward just as the circle changes its mind and decides to go the other way, before moving forward again, all to a set of five sometimes halting steps. The circle keeps going one way when it looks like it's going the other way. It's an optical illusion to a beat of five.

Vijaya and Kalpana didn't belong to the spectators' circle, and they weren't there long. Together they walked up to join the swing of a circle, husband to-be or not-to-be apparently forgotten. Everyone was doing their own thing, and everyone was doing just one thing. That can happen with most couple dances, pairs can move so very differently to the same beat. But the *garba* is peculiarly inclusive. A lazy aunt, or *masi* as Gujaratis might call her, not entirely reverentially, would take the minimal steps to some limp claps to mark the beat, and her neighbour could be swirling along with speed and grace that defies you to look away.

The tempo increased, and the speeding circles began to shed the slower dancers, leaving only the young to build their eddying circles up to the finale. A breather of a dance followed where groups linked arms for forward-and-backward steps, and we then gathered around the little temple in the middle of the floor for *arti*, the collective prayer. A small figure of the goddess Durga rotated slowly on a round pillar, a makeshift suggestion of a temple about five feet high and two feet across. The *pankhida* singers on stage at the far end began the *arti*, and everyone joined in.

Finally it was time for the *dandia raas* everyone was waiting for, the men particularly, and particularly among them, the boys. The flowing circles of the *garba* are best left to women, but this stick dance is a little more suited to male energy – at least the men and boys all thought so. All of us who had been spectators at the *garba* with pairs of *dandias* waiting impatiently in our hands, were now on the floor. Perhaps just the holding of those foot-long sticks was satisfying in a male sort of way.

The large *garba* circles had broken down into pairs of rows of anything from four to many more which stood facing each other. We must have been about twenty pairs in our lot. We would each play *dandia* with our facing partner to a count of five, and then step left to the next facing partner. Your opposite number did the same. At the end of the row we would simply cross over to the opposite one.

A man in glasses with 'community leader' written all over him took a stand behind the mike to start us off with the count. An athletic-looking chap by his side with a *dholak* drum strung from his shoulder, clearly a Punjabi even if he hadn't worn his *karha*, that obligatory Sikh bangle of militancy, underlined each 'one, two, three…' with a sharp smack on the *dholak*. We closed in on the opposite number to the first beat, and away we went.

To Gujaratis, *dandia* steps come with mother's milk. On 'one' you step forward to make contact with the opposite number's *dandia* with the *dandia* in your right hand swinging right to left, on 'two' it's the same with the other *dandia* swinging the other way. On 'three' you step back to tap your *dandias* against one another. On 'four' it's forward again, right *dandia* moving back to tap the opposite, right to left. 'Five' is the step sideways, with a swivel thrown in if you can. Dancers launch all sorts of variations around this basic pattern.

We were a pair of facing rows, not a geometric circle. But we moved within the circle principle because we were only going around one another. Two or three rounds on, I spotted Kalpana in the next circle. I stole a look at her circle every time I turned around to switch rows. I counted up to four chaps in there worthy of further investigation by Vijaya.

The circling through the *dandia raas* meant Kalpana was where she should be. It made the roving eye unnecessary because the circle itself was moving. Every alternate person simply kept appearing face to face for the *dandia* rituals. We were in a real-life slide show, one before the other.

It's the nature of a circle that nobody in it disappears from sight of the other. The circle is for its duration a closed world by the agreement of those in it. The group, and only the group, has been thrown together for everyone in it to share rhythm and ritual and to open themselves to awareness of one another.

Sighting is the first step to eye contact, should two people want it. In a circle you either look or you meaningfully don't, it does not leave the third option of not engaging at all. But in a Gujarati circle when you look, you can't too obviously be seen looking. Eye contact here means corner-of-the-eye contact, and if that happens it can be followed by networking later to take it further. Add to this eye movement the change of direction that the circling rows make possible, and you can begin to eye other circles, as I had Kalpana's. As you go round and round, early research can be fine-tuned into re-search, and that can suggest migration to other circles. Through an hour or a little more of *dandia*, anyone looking for a change can simply leave a circle, and not always do it the courtesy of leaving in a pair.

Vijaya and Ashok quit after some time and headed for the spectator stands. I joined them. From here, every moving circle appeared a rotating catwalk. Everyone in all the circles nearest you could be counted on to be quite close to you at some time. You could take a good long look as they approached and receded, and I had no doubt Vijaya was doing just that. She'd probably forgotten that she'd even heard her daughter's pre-car protests; that was standard youngster noise you learn to step past. Kalpana didn't have a boyfriend, not at least that anyone knew, and if someone suitable was presented to her, he wouldn't be less suitable because the manoeuvring came from a parent off a *dandia* floor.

The evening concentrated that search. Long before anyone joined circles on that floor or abandoned them, we were all already a part of the loose circle that was headed for that particular hall. Like all circles, this one drew to it those it was meant to and kept the rest out, because circles are also remorseless separators; they are society's oldest device to establish inclusion and exclusion. Other circles are drawn far tighter than ours was at this hall this evening. Through Navratri, thousands and thousands of Gujaratis head for halls hired only for members of their own caste. Few can match Gujaratis in drawing circles on an evening so closely in line with the structuring of little worlds.

And no one knows better than a Gujarati at Navratri that you can go round in circles, and still get somewhere; get someone, that is. But not everyone was here looking. For the rest of us, the appeal of the evening lay in the annual sameness it brought. So many faces appeared from Navratri of the year before. We moved to the same steps, to the same music, and with many of the same people. The dance was yesterday once more; it would be more of the same the next day, and next year. It was the time when the year came round full-circle, and slowed down for a week or so.

If Vijaya had made some mental notings, she kept them to herself. The evenings work also when they are not match productive. She had *garba*-ed, *dandia*-ed, prayed and gossiped, and wouldn't find it a failed evening if she left without a son-in-law in the bag. We were a lot of sweaty, happy people by the end of it. A few quick steps round that old path was always going to be a fulfilling enough end in itself.

Harshad was waiting when we got home. He'd seen it all; what might have been the pull of sameness had staled in his mind into boredom. He was the dancer who wouldn't dance because he knew the steps. He didn't want to see the colours because he knew the hall would be colourful. He didn't want to see and be seen because he had seen some, and they him, and the rest didn't matter. When a Gujarati gets tired of Navratri, that Gujarati is tired of life.

Behind the window with the saffron-coloured 'Om' was the engine room that made so many circles go round. Before they moved out, it was the office of the Brent Hindu Council, that handled more people in a day during Navratri than the grand new Wembley Stadium across from its window.

The usual amazing numbers had been circulated for the new stadium: big enough to fit 90,000 spectators, or 25,000 double-deckers and what not. You wouldn't have thought Venilal Vaghela could look at the stadium past that 'Om' and hope to rival it in any way – until into Brent you read Wembley, and Wembley Gujaratis, and what Navratri means to them.

Venilal's office didn't need a board, not with that 'Om' there. And within, it had everything Hindu you could think of. Shiv and Ganesh kept godly watch over the desks, phones and filing cabinets. Copies of a magazine, *Hinduism Today*, sat on the shelves. In a mini-auditorium to the side, an 'Om' painted on a golden sheet took up a whole side wall; a map of India hid most of the wall on the other side.

Britain found a place too in this Hindu scheme of things. A portrait showed the goddess Durga sitting on a globe floating on the sea, with Indian flags in evolutionary stages rising above her; a 'Vande Mataram' slogan in 1906 (the Hindu voice of freedom from the British then), the charkha in 1931 (the spinning wheel that came to symbolise homespun cotton in defiance of imports from colonial Manchester) and the Ashoke chakra in 1947 at the time of independence (the wheel with spokes that now sits in the middle of the Indian flag). The Union Jack lay at Durga's feet.

Had *bhajans* played in the background, they would have been just the right audio accompaniment of Hindu prayer to this picture, but Venilal Vaghela was listening to Schubert on BBC Radio. I've always found Venilal, who has found a way of growing and greying and still looking young, to be a Hindu more of the cerebral than the praying kind; the *karam* yogi, as he said, who would rather think and act than pray and meditate. 'Four "P"s rule my life,' is another of his lines. 'Propagate, Preserve, Practise and Protect.' Which meant that he was always up to one "P" or another before he completed his term at the head of the council, and who knows, still does. His passion, mission maybe, is to push Hindus into British politics, and Hinduism as far towards centre stage in Britain as possible. He helped manage the first ever Diwali celebrations at the House of Commons, and worked with Ken Livingstone, the willing mayor of London, to help set up annual Diwali celebrations at Trafalgar Square.

More routinely, he was the man behind the Navratri celebrations, still the biggest event the Brent Hindu Council organises. The local council pays the Brent Hindu Council, which then pays different groups to hold their Navratri celebrations. Brent is less than half white; the majority of the rest are Gujarati and they've made sure the council uses some of their local taxes to pay for Navratri.

Venilal Vaghela had Africa somewhere in his Gujarati-Hindu hyphen, like most Gujaratis you run into in Wembley. He grew up in what he knew as Northern Rhodesia before it evolved into Zambia. He left for the US in 1964 because 'the apartheid was really bad', he'd told me in the course of one of our many chats. The US offered him a green card, but the offer was accompanied by a letter telling him he was to be drafted. 'I became a draft dodger like Bill Clinton.' He was moving in Gujarati circles in Wembley because he just managed to save himself becoming a Vietnam War veteran – or a name on a casualty list. The British passport he had in Rhodesia brought him to Britain. After this job and that, he came to spend most of his time working with the Brent Hindu Council.

Venilal's office was usefully located right next to an Indian pub, and it supplied the beer and bhajia for our chat about this Navratri. It was right to speak of Navratri in celebratory style. It's the time when religion becomes fun, when praying merges with dressing up and dancing.

Vaghela brought out the Brent borough guide to Navratri celebrations that listed details of who was celebrating where. 'Everything is here,' Vaghela said, showing me the list. Thirty-eight halls had been booked in Brent for Navratri. I found myself looking more at the 'who' than the 'where'. The list read like a guide to the Gujarati caste system in London. Most of the dancing, the dressing and the praying would happen within a caste, and halls had been allocated accordingly.

CIRCLES

Making some calls from the list Venilal Vaghela gave me, I discovered more about the caste system in Britain than I had in years before.

Ashaben Desai from the Anavil Samaj, of which she was president told me they are a group of very special Brahmins from Surat in the south of Gujarat. All Brahmins were special for sitting on top of the caste ladder, but there must be the special among the special.

'You have heard of Morarji Desai?' she asked.

She waited, and I said, yes, I had.

'He was prime minister of India. He was from our samaj.'

'But, as a Desai, wasn't he a deluxe sort of Patel?'

'No, no, nothing like that. He was Brahmin, from our community.'

The community was booked for their Navratri in the gym of Wembley High School. 'Not every day,' Mrs Desai said. 'Our community is not that big here, so we take the hall only on weekends.'

So, on two consecutive weekends a year, the likes of Morarji Desai go round in their own circles in London to be among their own.

The Brahmkshatriya Mandal UK that I called next sounded like an intriguing mix of Brahmins and Kshatriyas, combining the learning of the Brahmins with the martial traditions of Kshatriyas.

'That is exactly what we are,' Ramanbhai Chhatbar from the mandal said.

'How did you come to be Brahmins and Kshatriyas?'

'Because there was an evil man, I forget his name, he decided to destroy all Kshatriyas. So some of them put on the *janau*, the thread that Brahmins wear around the torso, and so they were saved. So we became the Brahmkshatriyas.' Overcrowded Indian history had found in it room also for men of war whose best defence turned out to be a thread around the torso.

'So do you think of yourself more as Brahmins or as Kshatriyas?'

'Originally we were like Kshatriyas, now we are more like Brahmins.'

'When did this thing happen?'

'Oh, long time back, because we are the descendants of the Kauravas and Pandavas.' The warring cousins of the Mahabharata epic.

'What was the profession of the Brahmkshatriyas?'

'Colouring and printing of cloth, especially saris and ladies' clothes.' Some distance from both scholarship and soldiering.

'And here?'

'Lot of people are still in cloth business. But not everybody.'

'But the Mahabharata is very old, and printing is quite recent, no?'

'No, our people have been doing this for long, long time. You see, in our Jedhpur village in Gujarat, many are from our caste. They have been expert in *bandhini* prints and they are expert in printing on *ghagras*, those long skirts. They used to do printing using wooden blocks long back, and some still do it. But now some have come into modern printing methods also.'

'So this goes back to old Mahabharata days?'

'Yes.'

'Your samaj has come together here in Britain for Navratri?'

'Oh yes, for many years now.'

'Do most people still marry within the Brahmakshatriyas?'

'It used to be one hundred per cent. Now ten to twenty per cent are going out.'

Somchand M. Parmar, listed as president of the Gujarat Arya Association, introduced his lot simply.

'We are *mochis*,' he said.

'Does that mean shoemakers, or generally leather workers?'

'Originally shoemakers. But that is not the case now. That was the case thousand years ago. That business has died down now, these days shoes get ready-made in factories and all.'

'But why do you need to get together as *mochis* now?'

'Because we are one community. We are a very big organisation. We have bought property and we are setting up our own hall, cost of £1.2 million.'

'Will that help to keep the community together?'

'That is the purpose of it, isn't it? We have to keep the community closer together.'

'Is it working? Are most people marrying within the community?'

'About ninety per cent.'

It was not a question I would stop asking, and the 90 per cent figure or thereabouts was the answer I would always get. It may not be accurate, but it did at least say something about the dreams of caste leaders and the efforts they were making to see them come true.

The Kshatriya Association was a bit of a surprise on the list. I didn't think there was much of a surviving warrior caste among Gujaratis.

'We are a very large community actually, you see,' said Bharat Vakharia from the association. 'From Navsari, Balsar in Gujarat, now we are in Britain, Fiji, United States, Canada, Australia, New Zealand.'

'But you are all Kshatriyas?'

'Actually Kshatriya is a modern way of saying it. We are all Khatris actually.'

'So what does that mean?'

'We are in the tailoring business. Sewing and stitching was our profession originally.'

'Isn't that more the profession of the Wanzas?'

'Tailoring has so many communities.'

'Are people doing that business here in London too?'

'In London there were quite a few factories, and after coming here many of our people worked in these factories. There was big demand here, and lot of people made a lot of money also. But now nothing is left in stitching – so many cheap imports from India. So people are taking up associated business like dry-cleaning, they have even opened sweets shops, started travel agencies, property business. But still quite a few work as sample machinists, cutters, do repairs at dry-cleaning shops.'

'And you?'

'I have a dry-cleaning business.'

'You have help from the family?'

'My wife is in tailoring, my father-in-law is an expert tailor. He could see a show on stage, even a photograph, and do a cut to match.'

'How do you compare with the Wanzas?'

'They are also very good at tailoring. They are good with made-to-measure and up-to-date styles. We are also expert in many things.'

The Vanza Society London were holding their Navratri separately from the Wanza Samaj UK. The spellings announced a difference that must have resulted from 'organisational issues'. I meant to ask about an elderly Wanza father figure I'd met. I could not find Vinod Tailor, listed as secretary of the Vanza Society London, so I asked Mahesh Sonigra from the Vanza Society UK, another tailors' group.

'He is a founding father,' I said.

'You see, we have quite a few founding fathers.'

'But are they different to those from the Kshatriya Association?'

'We and Kshatriyas, we are same profession, but different clans. Originally we are also Kshatriyas. But now there are different classes. But we also have some surnames in common, like Visawadia and Parmar.'

'What's the point of difference?'

'We have different beliefs.'

'Like what?'

'Our deity is Hingaraj Mata. Her shrine is now in Pakistan.'

'Who is she?'

'Like any *mata*, she was our protector. And also Gopal Lal Maharaj.'

'Are you a tailor?'

'Yes.'

I hadn't expected that many tailors down the list. Certainly not separate tailoring circuits, each arranging their Navratris, and through that marriages within circles of their own kind of tailoring families. Venilal Vaghela was listed in the Wanza Samaj UK. I called him again about the list.

'You see, they took these caste issues with them to Africa in the thirties and forties, and they kept them there. And then they brought the same thing to Britain.'

But couldn't it have changed, couldn't everyone have come together, at least as Gujaratis?

'If we could find a hall that can take 10,000 people, we would bring many into one hall,' Vaghela said.

The caste system continues because London has only caste-sized halls.

Stitches

I drove down East Lane amidst cars full of tailors. I knew they were tailors, or at least born into tailoring families, because those nine Navratri nights begin to announce a car's caste content usually within a mile or so of its destination. The cars down our road were carrying Gujaratis dressed for *garba*, and the school they were headed for had been booked by a Wanza group for their Navratri. Tailors, then.

I pictured the suited men with measuring tapes around their necks as I walked past them to the foods corner, always a safe destination at a Gujarati do even if they serve up just the same dhokra and poori positioned in separate compartments of white plastic trays, the only way Gujaratis ever serve anything. In this respect tailors were no different.

A teenaged lad at the eats corner just outside the *garba* hall had taken a break from talking to a girl, so I asked him who the Wanzas were.

'We were *darjis*, you know, tailors,' he said. He spoke with no hesitation that this ancestry should have brought him dancing here. He must have been 18; he'd begun to find that post-adolescence confidence.

I asked him why he would rather be here than at some hall where the dancing would not be tailor-specific.

'You come here, you play *garba*, you are a part of something, something more than individuals. Tony Blair himself has been talking about tradition.'

'What does the word Wanza mean?'

'I don't know the real meaning. Something with *darjis*, something to do with stitching and things, our grandfathers and others, they used to do tailoring.'

'So Wanza must mean tailoring or something?'

'It means our community. It probably meant something before, but it just carried on. We all have sewing machines at home.'

'Is it nice to come together as Wanzas?'

'It's good fun. You meet new people and stuff.'

'Why don't you go to some other *garba*?'

The girl he'd been talking to before I intruded explained. 'Because there's lots of people here our age. And it's safe and comfortable, you know who you're playing with.' Just the kind of stuff parents love to hear children repeat on their own.

Every one of the Wanza youngsters I spoke to through the evening knew their tailoring origins. I was tempted immediately to settle to a neat conclusion: that a sense of caste continues among the young. But what else could I expect to hear at a Wanza *garba*? And what of all the Wanza youngsters who had gone to non-caste *garba*s, or not gone to *garba* at all?

There couldn't be that many of those. *Garba* evenings were being held by the Wanza Samaj (UK), the Vanza Mandal (East London), the Vanza Community of South London, and there are Vanza communities in Leicester and in other towns. Given there were just a few thousand Wanza families in Britain, most Wanza families would turn up at some *garba* or other. The young were very visibly with them here, and I thought it a safe guess that they had not deserted their families in Leicester.

This hall was packed with youngsters. I'd been to the Wanza Navratri at the John Kelly School, and the young were all over, even if the per capita noise of teenagers always suggests there are more of them than there are. Taking the broad population and visible numbers, most of the Wanza young must be where their parents wanted them to be.

This didn't surprise me. I'd learnt long back to discard the lazy perception that the young today are very British, that Indian ways will pass away with the older generation. Why does everyone say that like they are the first to say it, and for the first time? And then not be right. I see far less abandonment of parents' ways among Indians in Britain than in families in India. Standard wisdom can sometimes stand quite far from truth.

Perhaps this traditionalism in the young shouldn't surprise anyone, I thought to myself in that Wanza hall. It is also true that the overwhelming proximity of a wide species of alien colours and cultures brings you closer to parents than you might otherwise have been, or that when you're surrounded by so many so very unlike your own, parents work that much harder to seduce the young to follow their way. Why else would so many young Wanzas take such pride in the tailoring skills of their forefathers?

The parents in this hall had a keen sense of their past, and they'd been working at passing it to their young. They were the middle generation between the first generation and the third, and now in the frontline of parenting in difficult new London. That their families came to Britain from India via East Africa was to others a pattern; to them it was their life story, told and retold; it only needs a new audience or a willing older one. I was the new audience this evening, and everyone was keen to get me to hear the Wanza story in Britain.

A suited Wanza around the food stall spoke to me of Hira Lal Parmar as their wise old man. It was he and his lot who had told the new Wanza parents what they were telling their children. I picked up a condensed history of the Wanza flight to Britain from conversations here and there outside the *garba* circles, there was plenty of ready memory around. Here then is a rapid chattering history of some London Wanzas:

'The Wanzas began to sail out from India to East Africa in dhows from the eighteen-nineties onwards. Nobody remembers the first Wanza to step off a dhow on East African soil, but he must have called in others.

'The Wanzas made a place for themselves sewing khanzos for native East Africans, in the style of the long gown that Arabs wear. It was not until the thirties that local Africans turned to wearing trousers and suits. The Wanzas then learnt to do those, and they were in demand again; that fashion revolution too passed through their hands. The tailors worked first under German rule in East Africa. The British came to rule after World War One. The Wanzas had no problems with either, both needed to wear tailored clothes.

'The Wanzas took fast to sewing machines when they came along, but money still wasn't good. The railway line the British began to construct between Mombassa and Nairobi in what they carved out as Kenya brought jobs, but also dangers. Many died from malaria, typhoid and other diseases. Lions often attacked workers on the railway line. A lot of them took the dhows back, or the steamer later.

'Money came finally after the end of World War Two, in the period of British rule in East Africa into the early sixties. Manufacturing was in demand, and the Wanzas began to prosper. But local African rule later brought complaints that Wanzas, like other Indians, were exploiting local people. They began to migrate to Britain in the early sixties, leading up to the exodus from Uganda in 1972.

'Clothes and manufacturing was still a big and going business in the Britain of the sixties and seventies. The Wanzas soon found enough to do, and a new prosperity that even Africa under the British could not give them. Quite a few still work in garments factories, and in the tailoring and associated businesses one way or another.

'Wanza groups in Britain began to take shape from the mid-seventies. In East Africa everyone knew everyone but here people got scattered, so societies were set up to keep Wanzas in touch, to socialise, to come to know one another, for marriages really. About eighty to ninety per cent of Wanzas marry Wanzas. They come together for the welfare of their children, so that their children know their religion, their culture, their language, and one another, so that all this can continue. And they get together so that the young may know who a Wanza is. Because you are no one if you don't know where you come from.

'Everybody is related to everyone going back generations, and that means people develop a lot of respect for one another. Or try to. It doesn't always work, there have been differences among elders, and whole Wanza societies have split. But you still look around in one another's groups to find the right Wanza for marriage.

'It is working, because the children now want to know their origins. In the seventies, youngsters didn't want to be known as Indians, now they are proud to be called Indian, and Wanza is after all only one kind of Indian. Their origins, their ways are their identity. Together you support one another, you know who you are, how you came to be who you are. Among the Wanzas fewer marriages break down because so many take place within the community. This Navratri too a few marriages were fixed up and that was by just the fourth of the nine evenings.'

Wanza societies had formed around these common memories. Navratri was going to help their commonness go down the generation line.

I remember our dhobi in Delhi like I last saw him yesterday. His bushy, expansively winged moustache was unforgettable. He always wore spotless white cotton, a simple advertisement no doubt of his skills in the washing business. He came back to mind in London after I ran into Indians who all called themselves dhobi, though none washed clothes for a living.

The Rajput Dhobi Samaj was one of the Navratri groups on Venilal's list. They would be at the Park Lane school, the list showed. I missed the hall twice up and down Park Lane, a short and winding road that leads into unexpected English greenery from crowded Wembley High Road before reconnecting with the Indian world towards Preston on the other side. The third time, Paresh Modasia from the Rajput Dhobi Samaj guided me by mobile, and I found at last the little side road that dips suddenly down to Park Lane Primary School.

I couldn't proceed far into the crowded little hall, and found myself stuck next to a handsome young Dhobi fellow watching the women at *garba*, waiting for the *dandia* to begin. He was studying something in computers, he said through some this-and-that kind of talk we got into. I said that studying computers in Britain, and coming to this hall for *dandia* because his ancestors may once have washed clothes, did not go together.

'But that is where our families come from, and our parents have taught us to respect our elders. If we have opportunities in this country it is because they worked hard and took risks and took their chances.'

'But would you marry a Dhobi girl?'

'Oh yes, absolutely.'

'Why does it matter that her forefathers should have been washermen?'

'No, it's nothing to do with that. It's just that our families all know one another, you aren't just marrying someone out of the blue, and life becomes a lot easier in similar families.'

'You mean this is not just about washing clothes, which was just the origin, it's about families knowing one another.'

'Of course.'

His reasoning sounded familiar. Work as a computer programmer if you like, but when you marry it will be to another Dhobi. It's a memory link for a group to gather around. In England, you need your own islands to live on, with your own for company, and eventually as family.

Pareshbhai came up and called me into a side room, away from the music. We sat down for our festive sweets in a corner. 'We obtained funding for the Queen's Jubilee celebrations,' he said, very Dhobi-proud. 'We used the money to hold a cultural programme, with *bhajans* and film songs. We organised Hindu prayers at the Westminster University Sports Hall, and we held an exhibition of people's experiences since they came to the UK.' The Dhobis were doing fine with some help from Her Majesty the Queen.

Far from fading, the Dhobis now had a society that was coming into its own. The Dhobi Samaj had begun to take shape only towards the end of the eighties, Pareshbhai said. 'We've been around a long time, we used to meet around Diwali and Navratri. But we felt the need to come together, because we started encouraging the young to participate in what we do.' To add to togetherness at Navratri, he said, the Dhobis now have a cricket team, and they hire a cricket ground in Hounslow that brings them together through the summer.

Pareshbhai's reasons for getting the Dhobi samaj going sounded familiar – it could be the same community leader talking everywhere. 'Now the children come, meet each other. They know who the parents are, they trace back different connections. When you find your extended families, the whole samaj becomes a family. You have togetherness, unity, support. You don't get isolated. If you have a problem, you can call one another, there's always help and support available. In a new country, the extended family can be very helpful.'

And marriages? The real question, the old question, the old reply. 'You can count on your hands the number of our youngsters who have married outside the community,' Pareshbhai said, holding up one hand. 'Our kids know us, they know one another.'

And why should this not be a good way? What if my Delhi dhobi had chanced his future on a dhow to East Africa? And become a British subject in an East African colony, then found himself in Britain where he did not have to wash clothes for a living any more, because there were other things to do. What if he then found other people of dhobi origin. Would he rather be alone in Britain or join them?

Except of course that the right girl for someone like the young Dhobi computer programmer might not be a Dhobi at all. I thought him in fact a good match for Kalpana. But he wanted a Dhobi girl, and since he was doing the Dhobi circles, Navratri wasn't going to bring those two together.

Hair Together

Someone had tried to gatecrash the hairdressers' dance party, and precautions had been taken. The hairdresser caste, the Limbachias, were at their usual hall at the community school in Queen's Park, one of those in-between zones cities have between centre and suburb.

Two bouncers and their Alsatian at the gates looked on high alert. A third chap flashed a torch in my face. Non-Limbachia, the light must have told him. Not only did I not belong to the hairdresser caste, I wasn't even Gujarati.

'I've come through the Brent Hindu Council,' I said.

'We don't have any information about you.' He was one of those smart lads with a quick manner that made him a natural for dealing with outsiders. He had a mobile phone in one hand and a walkie-talkie in the other, and who but the very responsible get to hold both?

'Could you check with the Brent Hindu Council?'

'Park outside and I'll see.'

He got on to the walkie-talkie and I went back to park round the corner. By the time I returned to the gate, he was ready to let me in.

'Sorry, we've had trouble, we have to be careful.'

'What trouble?'

'Oh, just some trouble. We took care of it.' Cool lads take care of these things and then make a show that they don't talk about them much.

Inside, about a dozen men were hanging around the foyer, very visibly the men in charge. Behind them it was *garba* time, and some scores of women had joined those swaying circles. A few men had joined in too, just to show that men never should. I stood looking at the men, then the dancing. To my embarrassment, I found myself noticing everyone's haircut. But at a party where a haircutting origin is the only thing that has brought everyone together, I excused myself. How could I not?

The word 'hairdresser' doesn't quite describe it, sounds too falsely high-streetish. 'Barber' would be a little closer to the Hindi or Gujarati word '*nai*' that more usually describes the traditional profession of the Limbachias. But 'barber' is too value-neutral, in

Britain it only describes a profession, and no translation therefore of '*nai*' who is a figure way down the caste ladder. To think of a Limbachia as '*nai*' sounded disrespectful even in thought, because attitudes drip from that word. The Gujarati *nai* was a caste apart long before hairstyles became acceptable social art, and the profession of the *nai* evolved into hairdressing, even hairstyling.

I wandered between *garba* hall and foyer, determined to get hair off my mind. Everyone at the hall had come together as people of *nai* origin, but they were not living off other people's hair any longer.

A manager in off-white kurta-pyjama was ticking off names on a list at the front desk. The checklist looked well marked, and the hall was pretty full. Many of the men in the foyer had worked at *nai* bonding for years, some most of their adult lives, to make sure the Shree Limbachia Gnathi Mandal would not weaken with time.

A young, slightly stocky Limbachia, Jitendra as he introduced himself, led me away from the foyer to the school office. Mary the caretaker, elderly, frail and bustling with corridor common sense, brought us chairs. She appeared most unexpectedly English among the Gujarati hairdressers.

Jitendra sat where he could watch a video monitor, supplied by security cameras. He had reason to, he said. A group of youngsters had turned up at the school gates and they wanted to join in the *dandia*. But they were not Limbachias and were turned away. One of them hurled a stone at the building and this led to a near scuffle at the gates. They left abusing the guards and threatening to come back in a bigger group. Jitendra was staring at the screen for signs of a fresh attack.

'Do you get a lot of trouble?' I asked.

'Sometimes. These were just some yobbers who wanted to make trouble. They wanted to come in, and we told them it is not open to all.'

'You don't let others in?'

'No. They said they will buy tickets to come in but we said we are not selling any tickets.'

'But why not let them in? It's only *dandia*.'

'But this is a Limbachia event.'

'There are some groups that sell tickets...'

'They have become greedy. They even advertise their Navratri celebrations.'

'But why are you so firm on keeping others out?'

'We want to preserve our roots, preserve our traditions. Like the Jews. Look at the Jewish example.'

'But is it happening?'

'It will take another generation for us to know if we've been successful. But our young are all with us.'

'Would you say other youngsters are being kept out because you want your young with you?'

'Yes, you could say that.'

'How many marry within the Limbachia community?'

'The last one who married outside was eighteen marriages ago.'

'And who did she marry? A Gujarati?'

'Of course. But not from our community.'

Jitendra was beginning to not like this, particularly not memories of that loss of a Limbachia girl to a non-Limbachia. He seemed more taken by the screen. 'Twenty-five per cent of our costs are on security,' he said. 'The Hindu Council helps us with some money. The rest we have to do ourselves.'

A young fellow walked into our room, followed by another.

'Who were they?' he asked. 'Were they Hindus?' And the other, 'Who were they? Were they Gujarati?' I figured that if they were non-Limbachias it would be an intrusion, if they were non-Gujarati, it would be an attack.

The two security guards now walked in. This was becoming like the control room of Fortress Limbachia. Their duty hours were over; this evening they had earned their fee.

'Can we get more security?' Jitendra asked.

'Not now, man, it's too late,' the bigger of the white guards said. 'But they'll be back. I know the type.' He was the type who always knows the type.

'Shall we alert the police?'

'Yeah, maybe we should. But I gotta go.'

So did Jitendra, and so, he made it clear, must I.

I was the outsider who had been let in, and now I had to go back outside where I belonged; I had come far enough, the others hadn't got as far as the foyer, never mind the hall. I left with a glance at the hall, the circles still going round and round in Limbachia purity.

Mahendra Solanki is famous in London's world of Limbachias as the man whose grandfather went to jail with Gandhi. That made him one of the natural founding fathers of the Limbachias in Britain. He spoke of his family history with a good deal of pride when I looked in to see him at his house in Hayes, not far from Southall.

Mahendrabhai had just returned from Luton, about forty miles north of London, from an assignment with a computer firm. His wife would join us soon, he said. I asked if she was Limbachia. Yes, he said, a little surprised at the question. Mahendrabhai could hardly have become a leader at the Shree Limbachia Gnathi Mandal without that qualification. Now he wanted marriage to work for other Limbachias, as it had for him.

'That is why we arrange so many occasions to get together,' he said, settling back on his sofa. 'The primary purpose is to make it easy for the boys and girls.'

'It's not just Navratri, then?'

'No, no. We have something happening every month. Letters are going out every month. We have cooking competitions, sponsored walks, picnics, and of course Navratri and Diwali, so many occasions in the year. Last year we had 1,200 people at our Diwali celebration.'

'That means most Limbachias in London.'

'Yes.'

'Is it all really just to arrange marriages?'

'We are not for arranged marriages, we are for arranged introductions.'

'What's the difference?'

'We only see that the young are introduced. It's up to them and their families to take it from there.'

'How many youngsters are there to introduce to one another?'

'There are about two hundred teenagers in London.'

'All this for two hundred teenagers?'

'Well, they are our future.'

'Why is it so important that they should marry among Limbachias?'

'We want our girls accepted in the family they are going into. We are concerned about our daughter, for her safety. We do not give the girl away just to the boy, she has to be accepted by the family also.'

'But what if a Limbachia girl were to marry a Lohanna boy?' I asked that one daringly, even if Lohannas were also Gujarati and Hindu.

'Our traditions are very different from the Lohannas, it would not be very easy to be accepted. So also for my sons I want Limbachia girls because it would be easy for them to adapt.'

'You mean the young are listening, they don't want to do their own thing?'

'The last marriage to a non-Limbachia was eighteen marriages ago.' Not just Mahendrabhai, not just Jitendra, the community was counting, and counting carefully.

We had paused a bit. Mrs Solanki, who had a little earlier brought us some masala tea and some sweets that are always on offer in Indian homes around Southall, had come to join us.

'The young, you know, they just love these events,' she said. 'My daughter has lots of friends at school, but she gives priority to the community. If there's a function, she doesn't want to miss out.'

'What does she like about it?'

'From childhood she has met so many children at these events. She has come to know them, they are such old friends now.'

'So for her it is not a caste issue, just meeting friends she grew up with?'

'Oh, yes.'

'But does she know that this is really a caste, that this is a caste of haircutters?'

'Yes, I have told my children that originally our people were haircutters.'

'And what did she say?'

'She said, "Oh how nice, because I want to be a beautician."'

'Are there others from the Limbachias who are still hairdressers?'

'Oh yes, we have quite a few.'

Some children of Gujarati *nais* are now London hairdressers. The rest have gone other ways, but they don't want to forget where they came from.

The Navratri spirit was spilling over into Diwali; it comes only some days later, and festival moods have a way of lasting. The auditorium that had served as the *garba* hall was now filled with chairs for the Diwali fashion show of young Limbachias. I took a chair at the back, and saw that Mahendrabhai and some others, Limbachia leaders naturally, were on stage.

They were discussing some differences between community leaders. There had been splits and disputes within the Limbachias, as there are in every Indian group; Indian founding fathers are a particularly quarrelsome lot. It sounded much the old story, with a new set of names.

Two young Limbachia girls were sitting to my left, chattering quite speedily about others in the hall. I intruded into a pause in that gossip.

'You going to be on stage?' I asked the girl next to me. She seemed dressed for it in bright red and gold.

'No, just watching,' she said.

'This is the Limbachia fashion show, isn't it? What exactly is Limbachia?'

'Our whole families, no, they believe in Limbachia Mata. There.' She pointed to the figure of Limbachia Mata in the corner of the hall by the stage. The goddess figure was in a mini-temple, with little bulbs lighting up a winding path to her feet.

'Yes, but who is she?'

'Our goddess.'

'And who are the Limbachias?'

'We come from Gujarat, and our families were hairdressers,' said the other girl in a blue *lehenga-choli* ('lenga-cholley', as she would say). It was a taught reply she had obviously grown up with.

'So you are all here because your families were hairdressers?'

'Yes, that's what our forefathers did back in Gujarat. Not everyone, like, but most. And there's some people here still do it.'

'Would you do it?'

'I like doing hair, but I wouldn't do it for a living.' We were talking right across the girl in the red.

'Isn't it funny you all should meet because your forefathers were hairdressers?'

'I suppose, if you think of it like that.'

'You don't think of it like that?'

'Everyone here's like friends, and we've been together, like, years. This hairdresser thing, right, that was in the villages in Gujarat.'

The conversation was ended by a few words in Gujarati from someone mum-like who had walked sternly up from their side. The girls left. Young girls were never going to be allowed to talk to a male stranger for long, and rightly so of course.

On stage the founding fathers had had their say and left, and their chairs had been removed. A heroic-looking host and a hostess suitably demure in a sari had replaced them, to MC the evening saying DJ-like things. From my seat at the back I began to survey hairstyles again. They looked no different from hair at any other gathering; for some reason I was disappointed that hair, which had brought everyone together, was not announcing itself in some way. That extra bit had been done to hair here or there, but that obviously happens everywhere. I saw only my eagerness to believe that all hair is special but Limbachia hair is more special than others.

The compere pair combine began to announce items, something Bollywood after something else Bollywood. Someone did a Kathak dance of sorts, others appeared in impersonations of Bollywood stars Jackie Shroff and Hrithik Roshan. A young girl stepped on to the catwalk, working hard to get her waist to gyrate to 'Shakalaka Baby' from Bombay Dreams. Her version went down well here, it couldn't have anywhere else. The Limbachia caste offered her a world to shine in. A little pull from Bollywood, and a little push from parents had made stars of young Limbachias.

The parents had begun to catch them really young. Six to eight-year-olds walked up and down the catwalk, starrily dressed by mums. Three performed a dance to 'Chura liya hai tum ne jo dil ko', that theme song of Bombay music remixed into a Bollywood number. By the Limbachias for Limbachias. They'd been pulled into caste long before they'd ever hear that word. One day it would more than likely become a world to live in and marry into. The parents were keeping watch, and keeping count.

AUNT AND AGONY

Lifeline

Who could know better than Kailash Puri that too many arriving Indians who wouldn't return, migration others call it, would never find England the dream it had appeared from Punjab. More than fifty years as agony aunt had opened up to her the cracks in home after home in what everyone speaks of as 'the Indian community' that has done so well in Britain. At home it hasn't done that well at all. Kailash Puri, Londoner from the days of the British Empire, saw the agony end of that migration story, as no one else did.

Her column in the Punjabi newspapers *Des Pardes* and *Punjab Times* brought letters week after week; some published, others that she replied to directly. How many, I asked her one of the many days I spent with her. 'Thousands,' she said. 'Thousands,' with a rotation of the wrist that suggested I should make a liberal multiplication. She's published 36 novels and short story collections in Punjabi, arising no doubt from the experiences she's encountered. Add to the books the columns, and then another ten books on sex, and she could possibly be the most writing and written to woman in Britain. Certainly, the busiest Indian woman writer in Britain by far, and the only Indian woman anywhere who's written so much on sex, the great Indian taboo.

She's lived a life of stories, stories that came to her, stories she told. Many were bedroom stories; not erotic or exciting – actual bedroom stories so often are not – but stories of fear and failure. I read many of her stories, her columns, that dug out the insides of lives that were agonisingly other than the usual picture of Indians as prospering carriers of an imported culture. If the British had wanted to limit migration from Punjab, they could have considered circulating some of her columns through the high commission in Delhi.

For some reason we never talked in her sitting room, maybe because it wasn't drawing room talk we were engaging in. That room was grand, but not right. The flowery red of the upholstery held in place by wavy wood came in the standard style of the Sikh upper classes invoking a sense of the aristocracy. Right for a woman who looks nothing if not aristocratic; she could have been the perfect Punjabi countess had Barbara Cartland migrated to Punjab to place some of her romances among the five rivers. Her black and grey hair – and for her eighty years there was a good deal of black – blended unflinchingly into a tight bun at the back. Her eyes, with a hint of blue somewhere, looked at me like they could see through me, but kindly. The blue in them marked the countess; the kindness in them made her a natural agony aunt. A naturally imposing woman, but in the kitchen a little more approachable. Besides, tea would be nearer, and kitchen conversations are so much more honest.

Kailash Puri was a lifeline particularly for Punjabis in distress. Milk and honey are remarkably cheap in Britain, but it never became the land of milk and honey of so many Punjabi dreams. When it didn't, they – women more than men – turned to Kailash Puri. Unseen behind the agony column in the local Punjabi newspapers, she was there to hold their hand.

'So what did you see?' I asked. She looked at me like I'd asked her to read out her 500-page autobiography (there was that as well). The stuff of 50 years of a column and 35 novels doesn't get told over a few cups of tea. But there is no such thing as silence over tea.

'What have I seen? What I have seen of our men here in this society, what shall I tell you?'

'Why, what is it about Indian men?'

'The man, you see, is very insecure, very cowardly, and very jealous. They are so afraid all the time that the woman will easily become friendly with someone. And they are very competitive. If she is beautiful and intelligent, and a good conversationalist, she has had it. The men mellow down a bit with age. But this happens with most men. This is the result of a modern multicultural society. A woman meets all sorts of people, she is free to leave home whenever she likes, she can be housed in a refuge home, no one will know where she is, she will be protected by law. And they all say it is because of Margaret Thatcher.'

'You mean our men are insecure and they blame Margaret Thatcher?'

'Of course, of course. They say that this Margaret Thatcher ruined our women, she gave them so much protection. Men are very unhappy about it. They say woman should just do what the man says. They say it is OK also if a woman is beaten up, it is good for her.'

'But there's not a lot of that, is there?'

'You'd be surprised.' She looked at me with some surprise that I didn't know better.

'But so many women are so independent, they are doing so well.'

'You don't know, that can be a big problem. A real big problem. Girls get promotions quickly, man does not get so much. Then he cannot stand a woman's earning power and her status. Then communication fails, meetings end, then marriage ends. Success for a woman is a big problem, a very big problem. If a woman succeeds, man is so jealous, then he cannot stand her beauty, he cannot stand her success.'

'Everyone in India thinks this is such a modern, such a progressive society, people have money, and comforts, they are doing so well...'

'Let me tell you, this lovely woman, she is married into the family of such wealthy jewellers, and she is beaten up. They lock all the rooms of the house when they leave for their business. She has access only to her own room. She sits there alone and cries, she says to me, tell him to behave or I will leave him.'

'But what do you do when something like this happens?'

'I can only talk to the woman, who has approached me.'

'But why do they keep her locked up?'

'Indians, you know, are very, very suspicious people. I know this other family. The man, he used to follow her to the market, he would tell her you are going out to meet boyfriends. One day he beat her up right in the shopping area. It was his own inferiority complex, he tried to cover his shortcomings by beating her.'

'But some of all this happens everywhere, doesn't it?'

'A lot of men who come from India to marry girls here, they beat up their wives a lot, they cannot stand the refinement of the wife. One man, he used to beat her up, and then he would tell her to tell her father that he beats her up. He said he wants her to tell the father, so that the father suffers. He used to tell her she is sleeping with white men. And this other man from India who married a girl here. He told her you are not virgin, you are used to sleeping with so many men, so why not become a prostitute. The things they say, they are crazy.'

'But the men are having affairs.'

'When a boy from here marries a girl there, again and again I see that there is another woman, he never stops seeing this other woman. That is all right, but the women can't do anything like this. You know, I know this woman in Derby. She worked in a factory on machines, she was very good. Then she started her own clothes business with her husband. They employed this

Pakistani girl. The man became very friendly with her, and he just stopped talking to his wife. He used to have such intense love for his wife, then they stopped talking. No conversations. Nights he would stay out. But she felt she must go on, because he had a lot of money.'

'And then what happened?'

'I don't know, she stopped staying in touch with me.'

'Do you see this kind of thing a lot?'

'All the time. All the time. I have seen one thing. You know, these leaders of our societies, these presidents and these general secretaries here and there, they are terrible at home, terrible. This man, he is a big leader in a gurdwara. He leaves home at eleven in the night and comes home at four, five in the morning. She (wife) says when I ask him where he goes, he fights with me. The woman is always at fault when it is a man's fault. This girl had been married two years, they never had sex because he would immediately have premature ejaculation. But the girl was blamed that the two had no relations. If the boy is lacking something, the girl is blamed, that is how marriages break.'

'Are extra-marital relations a serious problem?'

'Who is not having them? Another thing I tell you. Our men, they are very fond of white women. This girl who lives in Kent approached me, lovely girl. Her husband has a white girlfriend. And you know what, this Indian couple's daughters and the white girlfriend's daughters, they would go to the same school, same class, and they gave the same man's name as father. This woman, she says to me, how do you think I feel?'

'Everyone says men want affairs with white women, but they don't want to marry them.'

'Sometimes it is a genuine liking also. This man got transferred from London to the Midlands. There he began to have an affair with a white woman, divorced. He then came back to London. He told me he keeps thinking of her. He says he enjoys sex with the wife but can't get the other woman off his mind. So I said to him, the relationship you had with this woman, create that kind of relationship with your wife.'

One after the other these stories rolled off her memory.

'And there was this man, forty-two years old, company director, 40,000 salary, company car, everything. He was living with his wife up north, married for nineteen years. Two boys and one girl, all going to public school. Then he came to London, took house here, family also came. But he had been having an affair with a white woman there. She was divorced and had two children. He made her his secretary, gave her the company car, took her on holidays to Bermuda, St Lopez, he would not be with his family for Christmas and New Year. He told his wife, you marry someone else, I do not love you. And she said he is very English now, and he would say to her you are very backward. I want a smart woman, I want to enjoy life. He told his children their mother behaves like a middle-aged woman, I cannot enjoy life with her. Later on, he divorced her and he married the white woman.'

'It can't all be men.'

'Oh no, it isn't. This woman wrote to me, she is having an affair with a white man in her office. And then something happened, he left the office. She was so depressed, she was unwell after that, crying all the time. She would say how can I get him back to me. This other girl, she got married in India. And she would keep delaying him from coming to UK. Her parents said she should bring him here but she kept making excuses. At last her mother called me. I said let her daughter talk to me. Let her tell me what is on her mind. She said she was in love with her class-fellow since she was seventeen, they had been sleeping together, she wants to marry him. She does not love her husband, she does not want to be with him, she said she wants to be with her boyfriend. So there was no way but divorce, and this is what they did. Then she married her boyfriend.'

'You really don't see a lot of happy families.'

'Happy families? Do you know how much incest there is in our society here?'

'Incest? You mean incest within a single family?'

'No, no, I am not talking about cousins. I'm not talking about men having affairs with their sisters-in-law. Oh, that is so common here, I cannot tell you. I mean father and daughter. Brother and sister. I have seen quite a few such cases.'

'Among Indians here?'

'Oh yes, lot of cases involving father and daughter. Among Punjabis, Gujaratis, and even more among Pakistanis. Very often it is the wife who complains. There have been cases of girls as young as fifteen being raped by the father. I wrote a story based on one real case. She was young and beautiful, and the man was getting no satisfaction from his wife. The daughter, you see, she is young and beautiful. And she is around.'

'And brothers and sisters too?'

'Yes, but cases of father and daughter seem to be more common.'

'Sex seems to be creating a lot of issues. It always does, doesn't it?'

'But good sex between husband and wife should not. Here there are so many families, they do not know what to do because someone is gay or lesbian. There is this boy in a bank, very nice boy, very nice wife. Father is a doctor. But the boy, he would never talk to her after marriage, he would just stay away from her all the time, be with friends, just always move away from her. So the girl said she bought these new panties and went to him wearing them, and he said you wear a dressing gown because you will catch cold. Can you believe it? He was gay. She came to me, she told me he had never really wanted to marry her. The marriage was forced. Then it ended, and she married someone else.'

'And do you see a lot of lesbians?'

'Not that many. This woman who is lesbian came to me. Her husband brought her. She would refuse to have sex with him. But her parents had forced it. She was in a very bad way. That marriage also ended.'

'You've been writing a lot about problems when people marry outside their communities. Like about Sikh girls going with Pakistani men.' This was the hidden explosive in Sikh society.

'What can I tell you about this? I have been writing about this for thirty years now, you don't know what this is doing to our society.'

'You see this as a problem that has been going thirty years, and you say it still goes on?'

'Oh, there is now even more of this. Nobody wants to talk about it. Girls, they are being ruined. So many have told me of being raped, of being gang-raped. And there is no future for them. And nobody wants to talk about this.'

I first met Kailash Puri at her quite spectacular house in Liverpool with its even more impressive garden landscaped by her husband Gopal Singh. Neatly laid turf spread into a manicured mini-meadow around mock rocks and a fountain. That garden was an important statement for a migrant house to make in their fancy Blundellsands neighbourhood. The Puris had moved here back in 1969, they were the first Sikhs in Liverpool. That arrival, after centuries of white suburban history, created quite a stir, Gopal Singh told me on a walk around the garden. They needed to be seen as OK, and one sure way into England's social heart is through the garden. It was their green card to neighbourly acceptability.

That was their second coming to England. The first was before 1947, and in her kitchen I got to follow her through her days in London before India became independent. This I did conveniently through a copy of her lecture at a meeting hosted by the Oxford University students' union. She had dug out the copy from underneath hills of paper in another room; her filing was hardly as good as her housekeeping. The lecture told of an Indian couple in London in the days of British India.

'When I arrived in 1946 there were very few Indians in the UK. I joined my husband, a PhD from Lucknow University who came to England as a Government of India research fellow in the University of London. There were five or six students. One from UP (the northern state in India), one from Delhi, one from Bengal, one from Colombo.

'Accommodation was hard to find due to air-raid destruction during World War Two and labour difficulties. Residential places were scarce for visitors and hardly obtainable even for British people. The question of discrimination against Indians and the oft-repeated accusations that the landlady would close the door after seeing a person of black-coloured skin, hair or eyes is not difficult to understand. My husband and his friends had, with difficulty, and with their exceptionally good friendly relations, acquired four rooms in one building near Paddington in Cleveland Gardens. This was, as far as I know, the first 'little India' in England.

'There was one Indian restaurant, Shafi's, in Piccadilly and another, Veeraswamy. There were, however, two or three small places in the East End, where a plate of chicken curry and dal with *paranthas* was offered at five shillings per person (twenty shillings then to a pound). The food was heavenly but ten shillings was big money. My husband was getting three hundred and fifty pounds a year for his fellowship, of which ten to twelve pounds was spent on rent, gas and electricity every month. This was a big chunk out of our resources.

'Almost every item of food, clothing and other necessities was rationed. Everyone had a ration book. One egg per person per week, a quarter of a pound of bacon, a pound of meat, a pound of sugar, a pint of milk, a quarter of a pound of butter was on our shopping list and these had to last us for quite a time. Potatoes, dried eggs and fish were not rationed but were costly. A guinea for a fowl was a costly treat.

'There was only one Asian food store, Bombay emporium, where dal was available for ten shillings a pound. In the beginning, therefore, all we Indians would cook and eat together.

'I travelled thirteen days on *SS Princess of Scotland*. We brought some foodstuff, rice, poppadums, chutney, pickles, which went a long way. We met with British people everywhere we went, we were treated as princely. My husband used to be addressed as a "Maharaja". It was most flattering to be addressed by the shop assistants, "What can we do for the maharaja?"

'As cloth was rationed, three yards was the quota per person, per year, sufficient for a three-piece man's suit or a ladies dress. We became short of turbans and went to the rationing officer for extra coupons, and asked for twenty-four yards for four turbans. I still remember the officer turning pale at this request, and getting the first cultural shock from the Sikh maharaja. But it did not take us long to convince the officer that the turban or a sari was six yards in length. So we received extra coupons.

'There were other problems of a similar nature, but nothing damaging to our culture, religion or nationality. We were still a part of the British Empire and respected as such in the proper quarters. We had easy access to India House and officials had to look after us in many ways, although efficiency had a great deal to be desired.

'There was only one Sikh temple, Bhupendra Dharamsala on Sinclair Road in Shepherd's Bush. It was difficult to get even a dozen Hindus and Sikhs together for a Sunday gathering. Community meals were not easy because food was rationed. But I must give credit to the people living in East End who would like magic produce dal, milk, butter, and everything you needed for a meal for twenty persons. There were two other Sikhs living in London, and a Sikh doctor who used to come from Birmingham, and one or two from India House who would come off and on.

'We were invited frequently to India House meetings and functions. As negotiations for independence and transfer of power were in progress we used to see our Indian leaders – Pandit Jawaharlal Nehru, Mr Jinnah, Mr Liaquat Ali, Sardar Baldev Singh, and Mr Krishna Menon who was the life and spirit of the Indian community.

'It was only after early fifties and sixties when people came in groups with work permits and vouchers that problems started. Many came from rural backgrounds. Many had a university degree, but got work in factories or in shifts to earn extra money. Some of them had to get a loan to get here, and nearly all of them had to support families back home. They had a habit of multiplying a pound with twenty-five or even thirty to get a figure of thousands of rupees. They felt themselves rich overnight.

'Such was the attraction of coming to this financial paradise that people used all sorts of methods and means, that later became scandals, to be here. Factory work was not difficult to get, but it was hard, and coupled with the desire to find suitable accommodation near the place of work, it created social problems with the native population. The British objected to the smell of curry. See, how the problems of yesterday became today's assets.'

I asked her if she remembered anything about 15 August 1947, the day India became independent and Britain lost the biggest jewel in its crown. 'I know that the India House people announced something, did some flag-hoisting to celebrate independence. But we wanted to know something about our family because families were being uprooted. We used to get some news at the gurdwara, communication was absolutely nil.

The only way was to write letters, and then those too stopped. Wireless was there at gurdwara, we used to listen, but would not get much news, but we got to know of killings on both sides.'

Hardly a handful of Indians lived in London then, she said. 'There was a Sikh grocery shop owner by the name of Chhatwal, who had come to be called Chat-a-While because his wife was English. Only three to four persons were there. It was all very painful. We then got a radio in our bedsit, for which we paid two and a half pounds a week. But we used to hear in London about Krishna Menon, they said he lives in one room and drinks tea all day. And the Indian students, they used to eat *roti* with knife and fork. So odd.'

Kailash Puri had spoken in her lecture about discrimination, but she had other memories too. 'We used to get tired of hearing praise. They would say lovely eyes, lovely hair. When we came we were like lords, it was a very different England for us.'

The Puris returned to India in 1950 after Gopal Singh's fellowship ran out. They migrated to Nigeria in 1962 and returned to Britain in 1967. After struggling to find work for a while, Gopal Singh found the job in Liverpool in 1969. He went to work, and Kailash Puri began to write her way into lives through Punjabi newspapers.

Pakistani Threat

This wasn't the first time Kailash Puri had written about relations between Sikh girls and Pakistani men, and it might not be the last. But this time she found herself confronting two Khalistanis who came to Pakistanis' defence. As people demanding the creation of an independent country to be called Khalistan in place of Punjab, Khalistanis see Pakistan as a natural ally against India.

AUNT AND AGONY

The trouble with being a migrant was that too many unlike your own had also migrated. So when Sikhs from Jalandhar and Hoshiarpur migrated to Britain, so did Muslims from Mirpur and blacks from Jamaica. Migration multiplied the danger that the family daughter would take off with the wrong kind of guy, wrong being of course anyone who was 'other'. Among the wrongs, nothing quite as catastrophic as a Muslim girl going to bed with a Hindu or a Sikh, or a Hindu or Sikh girl with a Pakistani Muslim. Kailash Puri has been writing for years that too many Sikh girls are getting seduced by Pakistani men.

The first article followed some brief editorial comments in the *Punjab Times* published from Birmingham, that Sikh society should be alert to the dangers of such liaisons. Kailash Puri wrote the following piece in the 15 October 2003 issue under the title, 'Why the conspiracies to ruin Sikh women?'

This has not just started happening now, this agony, this destruction, this shame on Sikh society. I have been writing about this for thirty-five years. I have written about all this in '*Qaumi Ekta*', and I have written about it so many times in my monthly column '*Sejh Uljhanan*', which I wrote for twenty years. I've had many letters from India about this. But while all this is going on, our society here has been silent about it. No gurdwara or organisation ever talks about this, the injustice that is being done to Sikhs by Pakistanis. Why are they out to destroy our daughters?

This began at the end of the sixties, when Indian and Pakistani immigrants came here in waves. I wrote about this openly in *Des Pardes* in the early seventies, that our innocent girls are being misled by Pakistanis and ruined. I have met many such girls and asked them, could you not find some boys other than Pakistanis? Why did you let your lives be ruined by these 'lovers'? The replies I got threw me in deep anxiety.

There is one thing I have been losing sleep over. I was so shocked, and so agonised by it. I was very unhappy, because this question is very serious. It made my insides tremble. It was hard to tolerate what I was told. I was told that our boys are so rude, so crude, so lacking in character. I cannot understand how they can tolerate what is going on with the women. They have no shame at all. They do not know how to respect their sisters and daughters. They are so cut off from Sikh religion.

These youths of ours, they tell girls in universities that 'if you break up with me, I will blackmail you and ruin you. I will send your pictures to your husband-to-be and your in-laws, you will be ruined for ever.' My spine trembled to hear of such abuse of love and of innocent girls. Is this what a Sikh has become? Where are Sikh principles? Are these not the Sikhs of Guru Gobind Singh? No one will ever forgive them.

In schools and colleges, even where there is no co-education, girls and boys will meet. Meeting leads to friendships, friendship leads to love. Such friendships can also lead to marriage. But 95 per cent friendships are made and also broken. No one seems to have any problems about that. Then they live their life as they please. But some boys, they will not marry, and they will also not leave the friendship, and then they will see that the girl loses her reputation. What kind of injustice is this, to a friend and to a girl?

To escape all this, girls have left friendship with Hindus and Sikhs. And for Pakistanis, the doors to heaven have opened. For the girls this heaven of a few days then turns into hell. And there is then no way out of that. Poisonous letters about the Khilafa are tempting girls, and the Sikhs have taken no steps about this. All this is being done because Sikhs are doing nothing to stop it. There is no scheme in schools or colleges to prevent this. Pakistanis know what is happening, and they have become encouraged by this indifference from Sikhs.

If even now Sikhs do not take heed, then no one will ever forgive them. Destruction is upon us.

Kailash Puri followed this up with another article in *Des Pardes* a week later, initially addressing the topic that Sikh men were too involved in religious disputes amongst one another, 'throwing dirt' at one another.

I have just one question. These 'servants' of the Sikh community have taken out so many processions, they have held meetings, they have made speeches, they have burnt so many flags. This goes on all the time. On the other side, Pakistanis are misleading and cheating young Sikh women. What is going on? Why are these Sikh men not thinking of doing something when Pakistani men are tempting away, destroying, torturing their sisters and daughters? These girls will cry all their lives, and there is no one who will listen to them.

What good are these processions and meetings to the Sikh community? Or to sisters and daughters in this community? It is surprising that in the face of this cruelty, these custodians of the Sikh faith watch all this so silently, say nothing, do nothing. I know these so-called leaders whose daughters have left home because they were miserable because of their fathers, and the fathers did not say a word. They put purdah over all this, so that no one comes to know what is going on.

In one live TV debate, one Sikh councillor was also called to speak. His own daughter had disappeared from home. And despite this, he kept saying that our daughters never step out of the house. That we are joint families, we believe in arranged marriages for our daughters. I was talking about the situation these days, how so many women have to suffer, how they are tortured, how parents force them to marry against their will. And this is what the Sikh leader was saying. How could I expose the hypocrisy of a Sikh brother on television?

This face is so false, the facts are something else. Is this the way to build a strong society?

With *tan*, *man* and *dhan* [body, mind and money] Pakistanis are destroying, humiliating the girls of Sikh society. Their plan is to use all their resources to get Sikh girls to convert to Islam. They hold meetings regularly in universities. And where are our gurdwara leaders, these leaders of the Sikh community? Are they asleep? Do they not know that the community is not just shaken, it is becoming hollow.

Two letters from Khalistanis appeared the following week in *Des Pardes*, the first by Rajinder Singh Dhillon.

We see the problem before us. If Sikh women are going with Pakistanis, being led astray, leaving home, this is very worrying. Only families who have had to endure this pain will understand their problem…

She should give some proper suggestions to help these girls, not just criticise us. Suggestions for our children, in universities, what kind of vigil we should keep. How we should influence them with our culture, to help our society. We will help in every way.

The second letter was from Parminder Singh Bal.

She has talked about the issue of defending Sikh women. In this she has made all Pakistanis enemies of Sikhs, by saying that our innocent girls are being misled, and led astray by them.

But not all Muslims are enemies of Sikhs... She says our girls are being married to Pakistani Muslims, or have friendship with them. But when girls go with black men, white men or Hindus, it is the same thing. But she is quiet about the rest, why is she writing only against Muslims...

It is not just the daughters or boys of our community, we are all living in a multicultural country. According to the law, after age sixteen anyone can have a physical relationship with someone, and marry someone. People do have relationships, these are the times we live in.

If, as you say, our daughters are being forced to live in Pakistan, then tell the police and home office. If you don't want to do that, tell us. We will take some strong steps. This is a matter of law here. If there are excesses being committed against us, we know how to defend ourselves, history is witness to this.

Yes, we Khalsas do burn flags, because the Indian Union is occupying our land illegally. We will keep demanding this, according to our wisdom and our capacity. You should be happy about this, not unhappy.

To this, Puri wrote back:

When a researcher speaks of certain findings in society, they are not talking about every individual in that society. All people are not crooks and killers and thieves, or alcoholics or rapists, they do not all beat their wives. Everyone knows that we are only pointing to the irresponsible and those really at fault...

Hardly anyone would know the tragedy of women better than me. Whatever I said about Sikh girls is the truth today. The parents of such girls need to be alert... Everyone knows that I have devoted my life to studying these issues. I have been able to be a support to thousands, to the daughters, the daughters-in-law of our community. And so I will continue to do until my last breath.

Lives and Letters

I saw what Kailash Puri had meant by 'thousands and thousands' of letters. They sat in boxes, piles, folders in her cupboard. She picked one here, one there, and read them out to me at the kitchen table, taking care to leave the names out. Most letters were in Punjabi, but some from the younger ones in English. I listened like an intruder into anonymous lives.

How much of that agony came from personal relations or the lack of them and how much was a result of migration is hard to tell; pain doesn't offer distinctions for the benefit of anyone pretending sociological insights. But the letters Kailash picked up to read were all from women. When in trouble in Britain, the women behind the letters were alone; Britain had provided comforts without warmth.

From those thousands, these are just a handful of the ones in English.

I have been reading your column for four years, you are so good at solving people's problems.

In my four years here, I have not seen one day of peace and joy. I have two children, one boy and one girl. For a long time I thought that in our [Indian] society once you are married, the woman should respect her husband. That is the way happiness lies. But when the husband is not a husband, if he does not believe in his wife and gives more importance to what others say, then it is the limit. Everything is wrong outside its limits.

After living with my husband for three years, I gave birth to two children. I used to work on a sewing machine at home. Then we bought a house, but he cheated me and bought it in his sister's name. He would take my whole pay packet from me straightaway because I would be paid at home. He would take it and then beat me up. Forgive me,

I must say I did my BA from India. But now I find that I am just like dirt out here. My husband used to beat me up and push me out of the house at night. He used to say that I cannot take a penny from his earnings. I was not allowed to use the phone or write letters.

In the end I realised that divorce would be better than this. The case has been going on for a year and is about to come through. I filed for expenses because if everything is in his sister's name, what will I get? At this time I have no place to live. For a year I have been living my days and nights in agony and fear. My eyes hurt, I cry so much. I have no place to stay, so I have left my children with my husband. Can you help me?

All I get is £24 a week from social security. I do not even have money for a newspaper. Can you help me, guide me? I am from district Ludhiana. Do you know anyone I could marry? Even if he has children, I love children, I like to look after children. I am 30. If you have better advice, please tell me, so that my life can become a little happier.

I am Jat Sikh and I want to marry a Jat Sikh. I believe in the Guru Granth Sahib. Please help me… I have no one to talk to, no one can give me counsel. They just want me out of their houses, I don't know where to go and I have no money to rent a room. Only marriage can save me, life has become hell. I hope you will tell me what to do. I am sending a self-addressed envelope.

Kailash Puri said she wrote back, she couldn't remember what she wrote back to say. Some days later the woman called to say that the landlady had read Kailash's reply. The landlady seemed to have some involvement in the matter, and ordered her never to write again. Kailash never heard from the woman after that.

I hope you will not dump my letter, you write back with so much affection to all. Please do not publish my name, or my family will come to know.

I work in a clothes factory. A man gives me a lift to work. He works with me, he is handsome and single. I have become friends with him. But one day, suddenly, he took me home instead. I said, aren't we going to work? He said there is work at home. He carried me into his bedroom. I do not know what happened to me, I could not say no to him, and he began to have sex with me. I said nothing. Later he dropped me home.

Next day I went to work again but on way back I wanted to go to his house and then come home. So we have sex every day. I am married. I am afraid that my husband will come to know or that I will become pregnant. But I can't do without him either. When he touches my body I forget everything else, I forget I am married to someone else. Now I do not know what to do and what not to do. Should I leave work? I have no idea what to do. Tell me what I should do.

I am a 16-year-old girl, I am finishing my last year at school. The problem is that last year I went on a French exchange. I could not help but notice how good-looking the foreign men were, and was especially attracted to a young guy.

We became good friends which then gradually led to a close friendship. There's no one else I'd rather be with. He is coming to England to visit me, but my family does not know anything about this and would be horrified if they found out.

I need to tell them quickly as they are arranging for me to view some young Asian men with the intention of getting me married once I've turned 18. What can I do?

AUNT AND AGONY

I have a problem. I had an affair before I was married and we used to make love. Now I have been married for seven years but I still enjoy sex with other men. I enjoy drinking and the company of men. I must have sex every day. Maybe this habit is like my mother's, who has been having affairs all her life. But please tell me, is it all right to have so much sex? I can't sleep unless I have had sex. I can tell you another thing. My husband also enjoys sex with other women. I consider it just a pleasant pastime. Is this OK?

I am not happy with my husband because his family will not leave us alone. We can't do anything without them being there. It wouldn't be too bad if my husband was talking to me. He just sits there watching TV all the time, even when we have just a few minutes together. If I say anything to him or just simply put my arm around him he shouts his head off and goes off to the other room. It makes me very upset and I just want to die. We don't even sleep in the same room now, though we have only been married two years last week.

I had a very difficult school life. Everyone used to tease me because I was the only Asian in the class. Then college was the same. I just wanted to leave everything, just run away from it all. I wanted to get married since I was 13 years old. I could not wait to see what it was going to be like. Now look where it's got me.

I don't know why I changed so much since the second year at secondary school. I guess it was because at school everyone put me down. I mean, they always laughed at me, the way I talked, the way I dressed, etc. It made me feel very shy and insecure and hate myself. Now I always feel scared and unsafe. I feel people are watching me all the time and talking about me. My husband treating me this way just brings back all those bad memories. But then

215

I think to myself, if only I had the courage to stand up for myself it might have been different. For instance, if they called me 'Paki' I should have answered back instead of just sitting there and burning inside with anger. Even now if someone says anything to me that offends me I don't answer back, I just keep it inside myself and pretend it never happened.

I try to please others even if it means hurting myself. I have told my husband many times how much I miss him not sleeping in our bedroom but he just doesn't seem to care.

I'm 21, Indian and unhappy about my life. I don't want the same things as my parents want. I don't agree with arranged marriage and I'm far more independent than my mum. My parents are very stuck in their ways, very traditional. I can't go on like this. It hurts too much. I hate all the arguments and fighting.

There is no way on this earth they would ever let me do the things that are important to me, like studying and making a go of a career in teaching and, more importantly, moving in with my boyfriend of two years. They don't know about him. I love him to bits. He understands me completely.

I want to run away. It's not a decision I have taken lightly. I've actually left twice before. Once when I was 18 and again when I was nearly 20. Both times I was brought home against my will. The second time this happened, they threatened me. I was told that if I tried to leave again, I'd be found and killed. I felt awful. Since then I have tried really hard to be the obedient daughter they want but it's simply not me. I don't think I can carry on like this…

They sent me to India for several weeks because they felt I needed to clear my head and needed a heavy dose of Indian culture. [My boyfriend] and I kept in touch vial e-mail. It hurt so much. In my head we were still together. When I came back from India, I wasn't allowed to keep my mobile phone, and I wasn't allowed to use the Internet. I'd also thought a lot. I thought I'd give it one more try. To be the obedient daughter my family wanted. I didn't call or write to him. I decided it would be best if we both got on with our lives. But I still thought about him a lot.

I worked my bum off in the shop, my parents' business, to keep busy. I did a lot of house work too. I tried so much to fit in. I went to all the weddings and birthdays I was invited to… Slowly, I realised that I'm far too Westernised. I didn't want all the rules and protocol of Indian society. I really tried but I just don't fit in, I'm not happy. I'm 21 and soon they'll be pressuring me to agree to marriage. I know people who are happy to have an arranged marriage. But it's not me. I'm too strong-willed to be 'ruled over' for ever. Right now, I do what I have to, to have an easy life. I avoid arguments and confrontations.

Around six to eight months ago, I logged on to my e-mail and online pager. He is on my buddy list and we got talking. It felt wrong, like I was just looking for trouble. We chatted for a while online. He gave me his work number and told me to call him. I did, maybe around two weeks later. I still tried to keep it platonic. Then he asked me if I'd elope with him. I was blown away. I didn't say yes or no. I told him I'd think about it. I was so shocked. I let the dust settle for a couple of days. I thought and I thought and I thought. He told me he'd support any decision I made and that he loved me.

It became clearer that I could only carry on like this for so long till I implode with all the crap I don't agree with and false cheer I use to keep my family out so they don't see how much I hurt. I also realised just how much I love [my boyfriend]. He's the most beautiful person I know. If you met him you'd say the same. I don't care that he's black. I'm not bothered what people have to say. So I decided that I would elope. But I'm going to do it right. I can't afford for my family to find me. I hope you can see exactly what I'm doing now. I've not made an impulsive decision. I want a life of my own, and I know he will stick by me whatever happens. If that means my studying or working or whatever, he'll be there and I want to be with him forever.

So maybe you can advise me how I could go about changing my national insurance number. I don't want to leave any trail.

I hope you are well. I am very confused with my life since I got engaged. It's really a long story and I'll start from the beginning. I was 16 last April when me and my dad went to Pakistan along with a few of my aunties. I knew I was going to see this boy. Well this boy is my dad's sister's son and my aunt has been after me since I was 12. I knew that because we used to get letters of them asking for my *rishta* [marriage].

So last year I went Pakistan but I didn't like the boy. My parents gave me no choice. My dad said he would lose his respect even though I told him many times that I didn't like the boy. My parents were very selfish with me. I found out that many other people had asked my dad for my *rishta* but my dad had refused without even asking me.

I don't like the boy they want me to marry. He lives in a village in Pakistan, he's unqualified and can't speak English. He's very shy, and his looks, I think I'd better not write about them. He's not my type at all. All my cousins said to me do it for your dad's sake. And I thought and thought and no one would leave me alone till I said yes. So I had the engagement for my parents' sake.

Now I am back in England, engaged to the same boy I don't like. My parents are happy but they still won't let me go out where I want to or dress how I want. My background is excellent, I haven't been out with any lads and I'm a virgin. I wear salwar-kameez and I haven't cut my hair even once. I have to wear a *dupatta* on my head and I can't even talk to a boy even if it's my brother's friend. I'm sick of living like this in England. My parents still think they're in Pakistan and life at this moment is bad for me. I feel like running away or killing myself and solving the problem all together.

I have no one to share my problems with and I am dying from inside. No one has ever complained to my parents that your daughter is bad. Every one thinks I am good which I know I am. I am Muslim and I'm tied up into two cultures. Which way shall I go? The only way I can think is to kill myself so my parents can find out what it was like for me. My parents are applying for my fiancé this week. I hope the law says he should stay there. It's no use telling my parents. They don't care how I feel. All they care about is my fiancé getting here and then he will send money to Pakistan to support his poor family.

Thank you very much for reading my letter, at least you're taking some notice of my problems. I'm sending you an envelope with my work address and I hope you'll reply. I'll die but at least I won't cry.

Kailash said she always wrote back. But at some point the correspondence would drop, and she had no way of knowing what happened next. What stayed in her mind, and in mine from what I saw, were only snapshots from an unhappy album.

BRIDELESS IN WEMBLEY

Questions and Questions

What's an aunt who doesn't scold? And why shouldn't she, even if it's from the pages of *Des Pardes*? Kailash Puri was showing me some of the letters she'd received in Punjabi, and her replies to them. But this one appeared in English, just as it was written, in Kailash Puri's agony column '*Apna Aap Karey Deedar*' ('Look Within Yourself').

Question: I am Makhan. I have been in the UK for 7 years. I am 29 years of age. I have a shop with off licence. When I was my qualifications MA History of D.A.V. College Jallandhar. I work 15 hours a day 7 days a week. I have no demands or needs and I still can't get fixed up with a girl. All my family is in UK. Girls have more demands than boys. If they want marry their girl to a discent boy keep girls under control. Girls do not want to work, but want everything. Girls go to clubs and get drunk and get there virginity broken. We need a answer by next week. We want for your answer. We know you can't give a answer to this one. Give answer in Punjabi or English.

The aunt wrote back in Punjabi.

Reply: According to you, you went to D. A.V College. It is surprising that despite an MA you have made so many mistakes in your letter. In Jalandhar, Ludhiana and Amritsar, even children in the fifth grade do not make so many mistakes.

Then you say you have been in business for seven years. In seven years of working in a shop, you have not learnt a few basic things about how to conduct yourself and how to speak. But I can see from your letter what you are. When you say you cannot get fixed up with a girl, you blame girls and their parents. What you have said about 'decent' girls, keeping 'under control' and about virginity is very unfortunate. You say that you have no demands and still you have no relationship. That girls have more desires than boys. That parents do not control their daughters, that girls do not want to work but want everything, that they go to clubs and lose their virginity.

Well, relationships do not just happen on the street. Decent conduct and so many other things are important to girls. Such as the boy's abilities, his personality, his family, all these things are very important. Parents cannot give a girl away without inquiring about all these things. You must ask yourself why you are not fixed up if you have passed MA, you are young and in good business. If your demands are valid, why are the demands of girls not valid?

I agree that parents need to look after girls to make them act in a moral way. But girls too must control themselves, both girls and boys must. Books, TV, the whole atmosphere, and not just the parents, have an influence on girls and boys. Parents always warn girls against sexy kind of clothes, high skirts and dresses and all that. But how much knowledge children pick up from their parents, I cannot say. And, as for working, which world are you living in? Which woman does not work? Some may not go out to work, but they work at home. If women had not worked along with their husbands after everyone came here, the community would not have been so prosperous. The success is more than fifty per cent that of women. Even at age 60 and 70 they work to help their husbands.

Also, every club is not an alcoholics' den. It is not just a place to drink, it is not decadent merely to go to a club. Western people go routinely to clubs. They go to play table tennis, cards, squash, they go for karaoke, they go to have a drink, to socialise. You cannot stop them. So why these rules only for our girls? They should apply equally to men. Men can go to women, they can change their partners, that never becomes a blot on their character. When they marry, they suspect a girl, that she is not a virgin. They do it because they have lived like that. If she does not bleed they get angry, they forget what they have been doing in their own lives. Let me tell these so-called Romeos that the hymen can be broken without sex too. During sports like tennis and badminton. Use of Tampax can also remove the hymen, and there may not be much bleeding during the first time. The girl is not at fault. Of course, this should also not become an excuse for girls.

But see, at least I did not throw your letter in the bin.

Question: Only a few days ago I came back from hospital. I had to undergo an operation. Since I have come back, I can't stop crying. I can't sleep at night. I am in such a bad state that I cannot speak to anyone. I am not a young woman, and have grown-up children. We are a happy family. But I cannot understand what has happened to me.

In the hospital, a black doctor operated on me. He used to come to see me daily. The moment he came near me, I would come alive. I would blossom like a flower. I would wish he would just keep sitting by my side. When he held my hand I felt I have found God. My whole body, my soul felt alive. Ever since I have come home, I cannot get him off my mind. I want to run back to the hospital, look at him, listen to his voice. God knows what has happened to me, all the time I think only about him. But then I think I have everything at home. My husband and kids are all so good. Please do something for me. I am miserable. How can I go to that lovely black man?

Reply: How suddenly the spark of love appears sometimes. It is a mystery how someone can just appear and set off lightning in another person from head to toe. Like Heer–Ranjha, Soni–Mahiwal, Romeo–Juliet... these are very beautiful moments. Heer took the name of Ranjha so much that she felt she had become Ranjha. It feels like a meeting of the souls. There is no experience to match it. But now you are back home. And that lovely man is back in his home. He has no idea that a woman is longing for him like this. Remember, time is a great healer, many things resolve themselves with the passage of time. Maintain your daily routine to calm yourself down. Go for yoga. That will calm the mind and bring stability. We recommend such remedies for psychologically disturbed patients. Take daily walks, keep yourself busy. Enjoy the company of your husband and children. Slowly, thoughts of this man will become a distant fragrance, just a sweet memory.

Question: *Sat sri akal.* I have a big problem, please help me. I have four children. My son aged 23 was always a good and obedient boy. He has a good degree and I have had no problems with him. But when I told him about marriage, then his reply shook my soul. He said, 'Mum I am gay. I cannot be happy with any woman.' I am not prepared to believe that my son, who has never gone beyond home and university, could be like this. I talked to a GP too. He said it is in his mind, but there are no defects. If he tries, he can get OK. Can you help this miserable mother? Can my son be cured? I can't talk to anyone about this. Our society, our Sikh religion does not accept this. How did my child end up this way? He now has a white friend, he says he is very happy with that white boy. He talks of leaving home and going to live with him. Please tell me how I can save my son from this wrong path. He has no good future in this.

You must know what I am saying, you are like a doctor. Don't tear up this letter, please. Waiting for your reply this week. I am not giving my address, I am afraid that everyone will come to know. I just want my son to be OK. I pray to God every day, oh God, show my son the right path. I ask with folded hands, please write to me. I came to know from my son that not only he, a lot of our Sikh children are going down this path.

Signed: An unhappy mother.

Reply: Yes, I can see there is pain, much pain, deep pain. Forget treatment; no doctor or psychologist has been able to answer some of the questions you have raised. From Japan, Germany, Ludhiana, Lahore, Los Angeles, London, Arab countries, even in all Islamic countries, there have been men practising such ways for thousands of years, quietly. In Britain, such people can now live together legally. Before it came out in the open, people like this were ashamed of what they did, they used to practise their ways in hidden ways. I agree with your doctor that it is coming from his mind, and that there is nothing wrong with him. If he tries to control himself, he can be OK. But while agreeing with the doctor, I find myself disagreeing with him as well, because I have tried to understand and solve this problem among countless Asian boys and girls. There has been some success, but some people become so set in these ways that they cannot change. They don't even want to think about changing.

There is a particular reason for this. Since this community is now accepted by law and society, they do not feel the need to change. The government has lifted any shame from being gay and lesbian and this has multiplied this problem immensely. At least your son has told you this openly, but there are hundreds of Sikh children like him out there.

I feel deeply sympathetic with your unhappiness. As a mother, I can feel your pain from within. How can a mother accept something like this? These kinds of liaisons have brought hell to the home of so many white people as well, because parents naturally want their children to marry and produce grandchildren. Do not make yourself unhappy on this count any more. It will hurt, but there is so much that is unbearable which we have to bear. It is not easy to calm the mind, the heart. So, keep your routine, do your prayers. Love your son so that he keeps his relationship with you, and so you can enjoy the relationship with your son. Just to accept this defeat will be your victory.

Question: My sisters and relatives are all fair and lovely but I am dark. I don't like it, I'm ashamed of it. They all look white, and I am ugly and dark. No salwar-kameez colour suits me. I have been to many hakims for medicine to make myself fair but all of them are crooks. I have spent so many pounds but still I look the same. I am very sad and unhappy. I think you alone can help me. Please tell me how I can make myself fair. Please write to me.

Reply: What is the measure of beauty? Judges of beauty do not look just at complexion. They look at personality, height, the figure, the features, your ability at conversation, your intelligence, and so many other criteria. The colour of the skin is meaningless. Naomi Campbell is a world-famous model. Just for a few minutes of modelling she gets up to £50,000. People happily give that kind of money.

Modelling apart, this is an illusion in our society that fairness is considered beautiful, even if the features and personality are hopeless. This is just foolishness. Don't compare yourself to anyone. If someone else does, say you do not need to compare yourself to anyone else. Take this out of your mind that white is beautiful.

Question: I am a 27-year-old English Catholic woman. For three and a half years I have been seeing a Sikh man. He loves me very much and I cannot live without him. We are true soulmates. When my parents came to know, they were furious. They pressured me to leave him but this was impossible for me. They are not angry any more, but they don't want it either. My boyfriend's parents do not know about us. He said he would convince them a few weeks before we got married. I kept believing what he said but now it is a different question.

I am five and a half months pregnant and I am worried. He does not try to understand my situation. I cannot give birth to an illegitimate child. I have told him we should marry soon but now he says his parents will never accept us. They will not be able to bear this shock. If I insist, they will disown me. He does not care about my worries, he still meets me to have a good time, but he doesn't want to accept this reality. I am writing to you on the advice of my Indian friends. Please help me.

Reply: What could be the right thing to say? I have been seeing this kind of problem for ages now. What does one do? Only the two people concerned can do something.

Sometimes people come and meet me, they come a few times, and I hear complaints from both sides. I try to help in achieving family unity, love and respect. But the rules and ways of Victorian times are no longer valid in this country. Those values are buried in the past. Forget Victorian values, now you have divorce, you have one-parent families, illegitimate children. These things are happening all the time. Because boys go out with English girls, it is causing difficulties and divorces within Asian society.

The question of your Sikh boyfriend, the pregnancy, your love, his indifference, the fact that he does not have the guts to tell his parents... these are such complicated questions. On the one hand you have this irresponsible man, who enjoys the woman and then does not care about her future. And this is not just an affair, here you have soulmates. He made you pregnant after all, so the man is equally involved in it. You will have to think about the future very seriously.

One more thing. Every woman must know that a man can always run away from a physical relationship. But if a woman has an illegitimate child, it can destroy her life, her future. An Asian unmarried mother can never marry again; her parents, society, everyone curses her. I know the situation has made you unhappy. But if there is a marriage against the wishes of the family, without family and society on your side, how long will it last? Single women should know that whether a woman has friendship or a physical relationship, the woman gets a bad name. For centuries women have been told this is a mistake, a characterless thing to do. Women with illegitimate children have always been looked down upon. This is true even today.

Young women ask today, why is a woman alone held responsible? Equality exists only on paper. How many men have accepted it? This problem is not just with Indian families. Young English males also behave like this. You must uphold your self-respect, your character, your principles. Your respect is in your hands. A bad mark on your name always sticks. These things can never be washed away. Once you have got a bad name it sticks to you.

Question: Dowry demands are ruining Punjabi society here. Boys are becoming too greedy. All their life people work in factories, save money for their daughters' wedding, we do as much as we can, we don't say no. But when they hand a list, I want to die. Nor can we keep daughters at home. In this country the greed is so much that they do not hesitate to ask for details of the girl's bank account. They want thirty *tolas* [ten ounces] of gold, electrical goods, sets and pairs, Scotch whisky and brandy at receptions, these things are so common. We have had to let go three *rishtas* for our daughter because of these demands. But we are worried that we are not going to find a good family, a family that does not want dowry. Only people like you can save us from this problem. Please save society from this hell.

Reply: For the last 30 years I have been writing about dowry in newspapers here. I have delivered so many lectures on the rising demands for dowry. No one has been able to stop this problem from growing, like divorce cases or alcoholism which are on the rise. People do not address their shortcomings, they do not look critically at themselves. People do not hold any discussions or seminars on this and therefore the problem is never tackled.

Mahasweta Devi [Hindi writer] has a suggestion for escaping from this evil. She says women have to raise their voice, so why not campaign jointly against dowry? Just laws will not help. We have to put our own houses in order, and that is not happening anywhere. It does not help to condemn all men either. If you compete with men, and abuse them without any basis, the way some lesbians do, it will not help. Women must deal with this issue strongly and sensibly. Neither can live without the other. It does not help to abuse people and criticize them, that can never be the basis of a solution.

Question: I am a divorced woman of 29, and a mother of three children. I read your 'Apna Aap Kare Deedar' with great interest, and my friends read it too. But you are so grandmotherly in your replies. This will not do in England. Women will have to face up to men. Tit for tat is the only way. Think about this. This letter is from six women working in the same office in London.

Reply: Well, yes, I am your grandmother's age, but fortunately that means I can look back half a century and also see the pitfalls in the future. I have a deep connection with society, with its pains and its troubles. I see people in pain, those who cannot talk to anyone or share anything with others. They trust me, they talk to me. Many have found a new life after consulting me and they bless me for it.

I have never found tit for tat to be a solution to any problem, and it can never be a solution. Look at the way children fight with parents, and husbands and wives with one another. Good behaviour has gone to hell. People do not act human any more, they throw dirt at one another. They shut their doors on their own, they threaten to leave home and sometimes, before you know it, a married couple are talking divorce.

Our society too will soon begin to face the same insurmountable problems that English society faces. People with views similar to yours also come to me. Their situation is getting worse than that of the English. Is tit for tat all that is left to learn? Or do we need to know how to explain things to husbands and to mothers-in-law? This tit for tat attitude is going to destroy the traditions and culture of Punjabi society.

Aunt and Sex

It was back in 1970 that the article appeared in the Punjabi newspaper *Des Pardes* telling people how they should do it. It was the print equivalent of opening a nudist camp in Southall.

'People were shocked, they were shaken to the roots,' Kailash Puri said. 'They began to think, is there something we don't know? We want everything explained. Because, you see, without knowing, people can remain unsatisfied all their lives. People said, you know, birds and bees are fine but we want Kailash Puri.'

'Yes, but were people getting a kick out of it? This was what so many will call dirty stuff coming from a woman.'

'Oh, not at all. There was a stir in community, that someone has the courage and the knowledge, she can teach us. And those people who like to be holier than thou, they would keep the newspapers and books under their pillows and read them. Everyone said this is the first time we have been given any knowledge about sex. And we can read this in presence of parents and brothers and sisters, and not feel dirty, not read like thieves.'

'What did you write in that first article?'

A cutting of the article wasn't hard to find. It had appeared in *Des Pardes* on 14 June 1970 under the title 'Eternal Longing'. It read:

Human beings, animal life, plants, are all incomplete in their own ways, each is searching for fulfilment. For fulfilment you need the romantic and the physical touch, material needs are not enough. To find these, you begin to knock at doors.

We need this like we need food and sleep. Just as that longing is eternal, this longing is equally important for man and woman. Without this fulfilment, life is unbalanced.

You must understand nature. The laws of nature are pukka. This is clear, no one can doubt it. Science and psychology confirm this day after day.

Two thousand years back, during the course of religious learning, Vatsyayana wrote a book in Banaras [*Kama Sutra*] that became the book of sex not only in India but across Greece, Egypt, Europe and in other civilisations of that time. Vatsyayana gave a deep and true account of *sanjog*, of love-making.

Many scholars say you need books to learn about things like finance, but sex is natural, you don't need to take a course in sex. But Vatsyayana says no. Proper sex takes two people in a real sense. Too often the need of a man is believed to be more than that of a woman. But women must be understood. Women have their ups and downs with sexual demands and feelings, even seasons can have an effect on them. So women need sex at the time it suits them, in the way that suits them.

People all over the world think that lovemaking is a very straightforward thing. There is no problem, they say. But I can tell you that many a time this can put people through a lot of problems. This urge, it comes to a man's head like a flood. But if you think it's only a man's obsession, then it is not a true union. Only if this brings the right kind of response do you become two bodies and one flame. And that is a divine feeling.

This joy of merging into one another, of losing yourself in your partner, you can find only when there is sweetness and love for one another running through your veins. Both need to be mutually loving and caring, and then each can give joy to the other. Think of this as divine union, something pure and pious, not something to be stolen in a dirty way.

When two people are together and their physical and psychological needs are met, then they begin to enjoy themselves, then all hurdles in life can be crossed. Life can be a bed of flowers.

People think that it is easy for a man to satisfy himself. The truth is the opposite. It is never just release, it is equal giving and taking that can satisfy him.

For the sake of this love, this togetherness, this joy, and to achieve this satisfaction, a man has to proceed delicately and work hard. He should engage in foreplay with his wife, and learn to keep some control over himself. Only a man who cares for his wife's pleasure can control himself and wait until she has her orgasm.

The Masters and Johnson survey shows after looking at the case history of thousands that 50 to 75 per cent married people crave satisfaction they never get. East or West, wives and husbands hesitate about these things and they build barriers. They do not share their fantasies and desires, and so distance grows, imbalance grows.

After this article, there was no stopping. Week after week she wrote more and more on sex, and for more than twenty years. The readers, mostly from the Doaba, the land of two rivers (among the five) within Punjab where Jalandhar and Hoshiarpur stand between the Ravi and the Beas, had never known anything like this in village, town or district. And she was talking women's sexuality to them. Both *Punjab Times* and *Des Pardes* carried her column, it would have been disastrous for either not to. She was obviously getting circulation going in all sorts of ways.

She invented a new vocabulary for her Punjabi readers, offering matter-of-fact words in place of the more colourful stuff that is current. Like '*madan chhatri*' (the umbrella of joy) for the clitoris. Or '*hath rassi*' for masturbation, '*sumlangi*' for gay or lesbian, '*sikhar santok*' for orgasm. She wrote, and people wrote in week after week for years. And how could she not have addressed that size question, the one concern that keeps the schoolboy alive in every man? A surprising lot of letters came in along the lines of one that suggested that aubergines of a certain shape get sold out because men are 'gentle' men.

'I have had so many letters on this subject, so many I cannot say. People are smitten with this problem, smitten, I tell you. This rubbish about size, it used to go on and on. Men, you see, they are very strange people. And another thing I will tell you. They are not very nice. It is not very nice to think like this. After all, what are you thinking, what are you saying?'

She proceeded to set matters straight, with precision, in an article, *'Lingam: Savaalan da Savaal'* ('Penis: That Ultimate Question').

The average man takes great pride in his height and looks, a good body and shining good health. He does not just want it, he is obsessed by it.

This is especially so before his fathers or elder males in the family. But seeing them, he also begins to have doubts, he begins to think something is lacking in him. Forgetting age difference, he thinks only of one thing and starts worrying. 'Why is their thing bigger than mine?'

The strength of the penis is of tremendous importance to the male. If you think there is a problem here, it can create deep psychological problems. This fear takes over his conscious and unconscious mind. He does not have the courage to share this anxiety with anyone. But within himself he is miserable, he fears that if his penis is small, thin or weak, he may never be able to have sex. And if he does, then he fears he may not be able to get his wife pregnant. This doubt and anxiety can create psychological illness.

Writings in ancient India, in the Arab world and in China talk about this anxiety of a male comparing his penis to others he might see. He thinks the other is longer, thicker and stronger, and he asks why is his own so small and thin. But while comparing himself with others like this, men forget that everyone's height, and body are unique and different, and so also will be other parts of the body.

Also, when a man looks at his own erect penis, then it is natural that from that angle he cannot get a full idea of its size. And so it begins to look small compared to that of others. To remove such doubts from one's mind, it is good to look at the erect penis in a mirror, it gives a better idea of its size. But even so, the height, the looks, the clothes of others always looks better than one's own. This is common in the world.

Usually a man will look at a tall and strong man, and estimate the size of his penis accordingly. But Dr David Delvin says this is not necessarily so. He examined the size of 300 penises. One man's length in normal conditions was 5.5 inches even though he was only 5foot 7 inches. And a big healthy man was only 2.25 inches although he was 5foot 11 inches.

Dr Rolf Bennett, a famous sexologist says that ordinarily a penis may be three or four inches, but when erect its length can increase 100 per cent. But when it is big even under ordinary circumstances, it may extend only 75 per cent and no more. It is clear from this that when erect, the size varies from six to seven inches.

By the blessings of nature, however small and shrunken it may seem ordinarily, when aroused by a partner, it comes into its own. So there is no need to compare or copy. Because under those circumstances, no male ever gets a chance to see a male friend, unless they are homosexuals. So why do men nurse the illusion that someone else's penis is bigger than theirs? This is just suspicion coming from one's own mind. It arises from irresponsible talk, and from the advertisements of quacks that can throw a normal man into a deep well of anxiety.

Dr Philips Karanhosrzal, in her book *Sexual Sophisticate* narrates an ancient Chinese story. A Chinese king had relations with a young and beautiful woman. But he had questions about size, and so he said to her, 'Tell me what kind of penis women like. Very big? Medium? Or is it hard erection that gives a woman joy?'

The girl became shy, but how could she turn down the demand of a king? So she told him what she really thinks. She said, 'Size and erection are God's gifts to man, they are outside the body main, you can see it all. But the real question is how much satisfaction a man can give a woman during intercourse. How much does he love her? How much does he look after her? A woman is not particularly concerned whether penis is long or small, thick or thin.'

The story goes that the king then asked, 'What is difference between a hard and a soft penis?' She was a simple girl, but she replied very sensibly. 'A long penis with good circumference but which is weak and soft is inferior to a small and thin penis. But at the same time, a strong and hard one that is pushed roughly is inferior to one that is soft but moved delicately.'

I wish I could say how far the doubts of my brothers from Punjab were laid to rest by this article. But this was one article to which the response could not be measured by the number of letters. I suspect that some male readers felt silently reassured.

There were naturally going to be times when she would be attacked for her writing. As with her article on the '*Madan Chhatri*'.

Men have always explored woman's body and given all sorts of names for both the hidden and exposed parts.

Between the two thighs, there is like a jungle of hair.

The *Mansarovar* [source of holy rivers] of life is hidden here. But this also has many parts. You can see here the labia minor, or the inner lips. These are of a length of about 1.5 inches. If you look where the top lips meet, then just there is a hidden and tiny sex organ. This is the *Madan Chhatri*. Greeks called it the key. Clitoris is a Greek word; in Greek *'cles'* means key.

Sexologists say that this is very important in orgasm. You can't see it because it is hidden under those lips, and there are glands above it, of about a quarter of an inch. The clitoris can be from one-eighth of an inch to half an inch in diameter.

Since ancient times, this has been considered the female equivalent of the penis. In some parts of Africa they practice female circumcision. The upper part is cut off. They say that only after circumcision does a woman become complete. But this is rubbish, she is still a woman. The *Madan Chhatri* is not obvious like the penis. But it does transform during sex. When it is stimulated, there is a lot of blood flow, and it increases slightly in size. When this happens, it sends a very sharp message to the brain…

One angry reader did not think this should be the stuff of newspapers. He wrote to the editor:

Your newspaper is good in all respects, it takes up important matters and issues. But I cannot understand why such a sensible person like you is publishing articles like '*Madan Chhatri*'. This article is a shame upon the community.

You are a Sikh person, you are sensible. Have you forgotten what you are, to sink into such disgusting articles, which are a shame also on you as the editor? I suggest that you better stop this column straightaway.

AUNT AND AGONY

Fan mail came in to defend Kailash, but she is good at defending herself. She countered with a letter of her own.

> My works are never written only for women. This knowledge is bright like the afternoon sun. It is not one-sided, and never will be. The basis of your complaint is physical and psychological. I will write about this another time. But this subject I have written about is universal. This has always been a very important part of everyone's life. Many people are still marrying very young. Young men start imagining a woman's breasts, her thighs. Men have longed for this kind of beauty, even ignoring the needs of their wives.
>
> A man's private part feels excited just thinking of the beauty of a woman. When a man wakes his wife, he is ready but she is not. The woman is sleeping, unaware of her husband's feelings until he is upon her. And afterwards the man simply turns to the other side and does not care for her. Therefore foreplay is necessary for joy, it is necessary to be on the same wavelength. Otherwise it all becomes one-sided and selfish and just a way to treat heat. There is no togetherness, the breath of love is missing. And then the woman is blamed for everything. This is the custom.

After years of such writing, and after publishing ten books in Punjabi on sex, Kailash Puri said she did stop writing on sex, even though Punjabi editors begged her to continue. 'I did not want my epitaph to say I have written only on this', she said. But when she did write, 'there was not one aspect of sexual relations that I did not write about. I wrote to inform people in decent and plain language, never using the kind of four-letter words and cheap language so many Punjabi writers of today use. I wanted to keep the respectability of man-woman relationship that was respected by my husband and myself and by our children.'

BRIDELESS IN WEMBLEY

She said she'd like readers to see her writing on sex the way
Punjabi writer Kartar Singh Duggal saw it: '[Kailash Puri] never
wrote about sex with feelings of shame. And she made sure no
one would read her with feelings of shame either.'

HINDU WAYS

Hen-do

The tree came crashing down mere yards in front of the lady in the mauve salwar-kameez. She was just ahead of me, so I suppose we were both lucky. You'd have thought a tree that tall would give reasonable notice before turning horizontal; it was down before we knew it. It was a stormy day, a proper storm, the kind Londoners love to complain about but can't get enough of. Brits love disasters, and nothing makes their day quite like a crisis to act cool in.

The lady had parked in the same area I had picked at the bottom of the little hill below Alexandra Palace. It offers quite a view of north London, should you ever want a view of that many rows of red-tiled roofs and buses squeezing down narrow roads.

This morning it would have been a different view. Fallen branches and trees had blocked roads and extended my half-hour drive to two hours. By then all the wrong trees should have fallen, but the storm wasn't done. The tree that came down in front of the mauve lady and me made us fellow survivors, and that made conversation mandatory.

'Thank god my children are there already,' she said. We were headed to Get Connected, an educational mela for children to celebrate Diwali and to learn about Hinduism. But not enough trees had fallen to block roads, and the parking lots were packed. Hers would not be the only children to have got to Alexandra Palace and got there in good time. It's not every day that London sets up a Hindu magnet like this for children.

We stood by the tree for a bit, talking about our close escape. We counted the yards between us and the tree; these would reduce no doubt in our stories later in the good Indian way. We finally continued up the hill. Closer to the top, we joined others who had stopped to look back at the tree; there would be other escape stories, that would improve with every telling of them. By now we were a little Hindu procession walking uphill, always a good Hindu thing to do – a suburban London offering of the uphill Indian pilgrimages, even if they are just some steps up in a temple.

Survival over, we were now thinking of the mela ahead. 'When you tell the children there is a Hindu mela, they don't want to stay at home,' the mauve lady said as we walked up the last holy steps today at Alexandra Palace. 'We never forced them, they wanted to come.'

The storm was still in whistling mode as we entered Alexandra Palace. The *desi* babble within, the inevitable product of families, kids and still more kids hanging around, sounded like homecoming. But it was precision mela. The hall had been partitioned many times over, and people were wandering around the sections, each advertising a Hindu experience of some kind. This is where young visitors would get connected to Hinduism, maybe even converted to what they'd been born into. It was an attempt to convert born Hindus into believing Hindus.

I strolled up to a section marked by a handwritten poster as the 'Chill-Out Zone'. Someone was making Hinduism cool. By the side of the poster someone had stuck a large photograph of a swami in saffron with two smiling children on either side, one of them cutting a birthday cake. Words had been put in the mouth of a little girl and the swami, comic-strip style.

Girl: 'Swamiji! When *vasanas* (desires) get exhausted, then the ego is not there. Then who realises?'

Swamiji: 'There is an ant fallen inside this cake. He looks to the right and finds there is cake. On top of him and below him is cake; it is all cake-o-cake. The intellect is like the ant.'

Below the picture sat the slogan: 'Like the salt doll dropped into the ocean disappears to become the ocean, so also the ego realises that "I do not exist" and disappears to become the self.'

This was worrying. I'd hit a brick wall with my first poster. I had no idea what an ant besieged by cake should think. If figuring this kind of stuff out was being Hindu, I was hopeless. And this was a mela to connect kids to Hinduism. They might just find this harder than homework. If this sort of stuff lay within a chill-out zone, who'd get connected to what? That cake talk sounded like a recipe for getting disconnected to Hinduism. But the great thing about Hinduism is that you can shop around, no one thing is *the* thing, and I walked on in search of something simpler.

The music coming from one end of the hall sounded less intellectually challenging. *'Dola re dola re dola...'*, I heard. Reassuring Bollywood. After swamiji and his ant, I needed this. Down at that end, chairs had been laid out before a stage in a makeshift auditorium. I wasn't the only one headed that way. Parents and kids were all gathering there.

It wasn't long before the auditorium filled up. *Dola re* wasn't very Hindu, but it had got us connected. Other songs followed, but in a while the music stopped and a goddess-like figure in contemporary disguise appeared on stage, mike in hand. She wore a striking light sari, and the very big red bindi on the middle of the forehead declared style, the Hindu way. Her hair, left loose, framed her darkly as it dropped down to her hip past her whisked-almond midriff. She'd have been a strong candidate for a Miss Vedic contest in some forest clearing back in 1500 BC.

Miss Vedic made teams out of the left and the right in the make-do auditorium. 'This team is called Radha,' she said, waving her hand over the left side of the auditorium. 'And this is called Krishna. And now, guess what everyone, we are going to have a contest.' No more *Dola re*. 'OK, Who can name a Hindu god?'

Silence, and then more silence, from both Radha and Krishna. Too easy a question, who wants to answer it?

'Come on, you can tell the names of girlfriends and boyfriends, and not of your gods? Come on, who can name a Hindu god?'

One little hand went up, and a mike found him.

'David Beckham.'

'No, not David Beckham, he is not a god. Well he is to some, but not to us here, he isn't. So who can name a Hindu god?'

More silence. The Hindu quiz was not working very well.

She gave up, and listed them herself. 'Ram, Krishna, Ganesha… OK, what did Lord Chaitanya make famous?'

It was a tough one and she wasn't waiting for an answer. 'He made famous the Mahamantra: *Hare Krishna, Hare Krishna, Krishna Krishna, Hare Hare! Hare Rama, Hare Rama, Rama Rama, Hare Hare!* OK, now, loud as you can. Here you go.' She pointed her mike at the Radha team. More silence.

'Listen guys, if Lord Chaitanya came down, he'd be like, you know…'

She turned to the Krishna team. This worked, and Krishna took up the chant.

'Great, this group is going to God. And this group,' she said, turning to Radha, 'this group, is going back home.'

Miss Vedic decided to keep it simple. 'So tell me, both of you, who was Radha and who was Krishna?'

Silence.

'Hello, Hindu youth. OK, what is Hinduism? It is a religion going back to India. And OK, and what's a Hindu?'

'It lays eggs,' said a kid.

It was time for Miss Vedic to move on from the quiz, it had gone on long enough and got nowhere. She was joined by a chap wearing a long bridegroomish *sherwani*, female attention written all over him. She introduced him as DJ Technics, a student of King's College and member of the Pandav Sena, the Hindu youth movement of the Hare Krishna Hindus. He was the DJ of female Hindu dreams.

'OK, we are going to the Bengali part of India,' Miss Vedic continued, now accompanied by the promise of music to follow. 'It is very famous. It is very cultural. Most classical music comes from Bengal. Also Lord Chaitanya. But first, we will go to the Bollywood part of Bengal, then we will go to the classical side.'

Miss Vedic stepped back, and a chap in a transparent red shirt and dark trousers walked up to centre stage. He coiled himself into a stillness that announced it was about to unleash something. Two statuesque women dressed in heavily shimmering *lehenga-cholis* glided up behind. DJ Technics let a dramatic pause pass, and began.

'*Muqabala, muqabala, Laila…*' the song of challenge blasted. Red Shirt became Hrithik Roshan, the dancing dream of Bollywood, the women his skilled shadows. The dancing was good enough for real Bollywood. Now both Radha and Krishna came alive. They were competing now at dancing around their chairs. Lord Chaitanya was no challenge to this. And soon, DJ Technics would not keep the hall waiting long, '*Dola re dola re dola…*'

Dola done, Miss Vedic returned with the mike. 'OK, so now, who was the first Asian to win the Nobel Prize?'

A quick hand went up this time. 'V. S. Naipaul.'

'No, it was Rabindranath Tagore. And speak up, people, so the gods can hear.'

The classical quiz was stopped right there with a 'VIP announcement' from DJ Technics: Simon Hughes, MP from the Liberal Democrats, was here. An MP is always a candidate in waiting, and to a candidate a chance to address Hindu crowds must be mouth-watering. For Hindu groups this was the time to let British leaders know they are enough to make a difference between winners and losers in quite a few marginals. The festival was not just an event for parents and their hopefully Hindu children, but also a political matter between community leaders and political leaders. It was an advertisement for one, warning from the other.

Hughes was not about to overstay his welcome. 'There are three reasons I am here,' he said. 'One, as an MP in London who represents many Hindus and who has been to India, I have come to show my solidarity. Two, I used to be a youth leader and was so frustrated with the older leaders. It is good to see young people taking to public life. Three, I came here to see future Asian politicians and leaders, possibly a future prime minister.' The lines were scripted to draw applause, and they did.

'The Hindu community is very good at business,' Hughes added emphatically. 'They are great with fashion, art, with their culinary skills and so much more, but they have still not fulfilled their potential in terms of political leadership.' He wound up his speech now. 'Thank you for your pride in your culture. Come back next year bigger and better because we love you.' Applause again. British MPs can give these short, sharp speeches almost in one breath. And, unlike their Indian counterparts, they know when to leave a mike.

Miss Vedic now decided it was time to call off the quiz. She came down among the Radhas and Krishnas. She aimed the mike at a teenage girl on the Radha side of the aisle.

'What have you learnt about Hinduism today that you didn't know before?'

'I just got here ten minutes ago.'

'What is the song you liked best?' she asked someone on the Krishna side.

'*Vande Mataram.*' This was going to be the Krishna team's day.

'And you?'

'I liked everything.'

'And you?'

'I liked the food.'

'Yes, we Indians, we all like our Indian food, don't we? And what did you like?'

'I liked the dances.'

'And what did you come here to see?'

'To see what exactly the Hindu youth are doing.' A reply at last that she must have wanted to hear.

'Yes, that is exactly what this festival is about. Our aim is to promote Hinduism.'

Miss Vedic was done and on stage DJ Technics was getting busy again. The beat came on. Three dancers carrying huge Indian tricolour flags came dancing to a basic beat, then put the flags aside.

DJ Technics hit the domes of Alexandra Palace with the bhangra explosive '*Apana sangeet vajey, Apana sangeet…*' No more silence now, not from Krishna, not even from Radha.

On the way out I headed back for the challenge of the Chill-Out Zone to look for something more comprehensible than cakes and ants. This time I ventured past the poster into the zone within. Cool blue screens had split the area into the four sections: Air, Earth, Fire and Water. I entered Earth. A timetable by the entrance announced the programme for the afternoon: stress elimination workshop, meditation, Vedic chanting.

'We call it Chill-Out Zone because it sounds like a cool name,' said a girl at the entrance, there to say these things. 'You can sit here, meditate and reflect, gather your thoughts.' She was one of the volunteers in black T-shirts that said 'Get Connected' in yellow.

'We need that, not just entertainment,' a chap standing by her side said.

'Why are you doing all this?' I asked them. That must have been the first question they prepared for, the first they had asked themselves.

Between them they bullet-pointed the reasons pretty fast. 'A lot of the young are beginning to take a new interest in India, in Hinduism,' the guy said. 'I think it's driven by the new British interest in India. There are so many things Indian now on British television, they have so much interest in Indian music, Indian food, fashion, you name it. And so many of our own youth now, you know, want to know about their customs and their religion.'

The volunteers had been trained in all the answers, and they were waiting to be asked. The chap and his companion no doubt believed what they said, and between them they released what sounded like prepared wisdom pretty rapidly.

'This is not about providing all the answers,' the chap said. 'But we do learn a lot from our parents and we want to give something back to the youth. You see, we've been born into this amazing, amazing culture. We have so many traditions in the house, but we don't know what they symbolise, we don't know the meaning. The young now want so much to know what's going on. These things go back thousands of years. I have started to learn, I am adopting them in my daily life, and it helps so much.'

'A lot of this stuff has been in languages we don't understand,' the girl said. 'It's in high-level Sanskrit, and now there are translations available in English. A lot of this stuff is on the

Internet and that is one reason everyone's getting so interested.' Once people got interested, they would get connected, as these two no doubt were.

But the chill-out zone was for those possibly connected already, and I stepped to the kids' zone next door, a good deal busier. This is where they wanted to catch 'em young.

I ran into my fellow survivor, whose children were colouring Ramayana books on a table close to a huge flag of India pinned up on a screen. A painting exhibition had been put up over partition screens, the produce of kids trying to be Hindu and be good, which they must be told is the same thing.

Beneath the multi-coloured lettering of the prayer 'Satyam Shivam Sundaram', correctly spelled with some assistance no doubt, a kid had written: 'You should tell the truth not a lie you should tell the truth so you dont get told off you should always tell the truth.' Another had drawn a figure of the god Ganesh under the banner 'Help Ever Hurt Never'.

A poster exhibition raised the questions kids might ask. A boy on a poster asked: 'What is Hinduism all about? Why so many gods? It's all so confusing.' Another boy on another poster: 'Do I have to come on pilgrimage to India? I'm going to miss the Cup final! What makes India so special?' A girl's poster asked: 'Today in school we learnt about evolution. What do Hindus believe? What happens at death? Does this affect how we treat others, including animals?' Another offered advice on 'How 2 respect your parents'.

A partition screen listed the seven matas, mothers, we all need to respect. 'Desa Meta is where you live as a citizen, so your desa mata is UK.' And there is Bharat Mata, 'the ancestral country, in this case it might be India'. And there is Bhoomi Mata (Earth), Deha Mata (mother), Matru Mata (mother tongue 'never to be abandoned'), Veda Mata (spiritual heritage) and Go Mata (sacred cow). If a kid could remember four of the seven, that kid would go back a more knowing Hindu than I've been all these years.

But perhaps the kids were learning something they were not being taught. It seemed like message enough that hundreds of kids were there, and as Hindu kids. They didn't have to make sense of cakes and ants and learn all seven matas by heart. And it didn't matter that what got them going was Bollywood. The fun was the hook, the Hindu message could have been what clever people call subliminal.

Bollywood now made its way to this zone. My tree-spared companion's kids must have seen it coming. They'd coloured gods enough in the Ramayana books, and were now abandoning them quickly to gather around a girl in a Get Connected T-shirt. With a flourish she switched on '*Laija Laija…*' on a CD player, and launched into a dance. Now this was fun, and it seemed OK by all seven matas.

Priti had such a striking presence the second time I met her that I was surprised all I could remember of her from our first meeting at the Oadby racecourse in Leicester was her blue leather shoes. A passing shoe fetish, who knows?

We'd agreed to meet at the eats stalls, but if two people can meet exactly as planned at a mela, either something's not right with them or the mela's not doing its thing. Priti had done a great deal to get the Get Connected mela together in Leicester. After Alexandra Palace, Leicester wanted to Get Connected, and Priti and her gang obliged. It can't be easy to get a mela, or Hindus, together, and if she didn't turn up then she must have had more momentous matters on hand than a chat with me.

We met later at the Sanatan Mandir in Leicester. The temple was about as clear a statement as anyone could make that this would be a business meeting, not a date. That date business was neither on my mind nor hers, but in Leicester a meeting very quickly becomes a date in other people's minds. Pack thousands of Indian families into houses strung together around a central street, and people will come to know people; residents will become that rare thing in modern cities – a community. And what's a community without an expanse of sustaining gossip?

Priti led me to a prayer hall next to the mandir. Some *masis* and *kakas*, the usual Gujarati words for elderly women and men, had just vacated the hall. We sat ourselves on a bench patronised by *kakas* who can't sit cross-legged on the floor, because *masis* invariably can.

Priti looked confident and radiant. She had all the grit and grace of an Indian woman who spends an efficient day at work and then floors men with her effervescence in an evening sari. This evening she wore a black jacket and trousers because she'd come straight from work.

'Your e-mail says NHS,' I said. 'Is that National Hindu Students?'

'No, it's the National Health Service,' she said. 'I work for NHS.'

That was in her non-Hindu mode. But why would she have a Hindu mode at all? I couldn't figure out why a British Indian girl and others like her would spend months fixing a mela to connect young Hindus to Hinduism, and to one another. There was always so much else to do, with or without boyfriends or girlfriends.

'What did you do to make this event happen?' I asked.

'We are a committee of young professionals. We have site managers, architects, all under the age of thirty, and we did professional high-quality presentations on the Get Connected agenda at all the temples. The feedback we got from the temples at first was, these young people, what are they going to do, what do they actually know? We were looking for temples to sponsor us, to help us financially. The temples gave us a very small fraction of our overall budget. We struggled to raise the money.'

'And what was your total budget?'

'All in all £45,000.'

'Where did the rest come from?'

'Some businessmen sponsored us.'

'What did the temples say?'

'I found it very annoying when I had to go and say at different temples that you don't see what these youngsters have in them, why can't you see these are the people of tomorrow? It's all very well to have these massive big buildings and these extensions done to them, but what is the point when young people will not attend these temples? You're here today but you're not tomorrow. The youngsters are not just going to come and take their shoes off and come into the mandir, because they don't know what it's all about.'

'What makes you think your event made a difference?'

'I've got living examples of what was happening after our event. After the two days of the event we asked for some volunteers to stay behind. So many young people came to help out. Then a few of us said that to thank God let's all go for the *arti*. And then all these young people, who didn't know the first thing about doing these prayers were all here at this temple. We said, wow, this is so good. It was all just amazing. So if there was one religious person there, it almost started to become a mentoring, peer education kind of thing. And they were saying to one another, you go hang around in bars, why don't you come to the mandir. It wasn't coming from me. It was young people networking. And they were talking amongst themselves.'

'You mean if you can talk Hinduism in their language, they're waiting to come?'

'Oh, absolutely, absolutely. There were doing it on their own, it wasn't coming from the displays, it wasn't coming from the workshops.'

'And you, have you always been a pukka Hindu?'

'I picked this up later. I was born and brought up in this country. I didn't even see India till I was eighteen. But I've always had this thing that India is where I originate from, I am always Indian. I was Indian because I knew I was different to all the other white kids in my class. Being Indian made me special. I was Indian when I came home. And then I was Hindu because I would go to the mandir on a Sunday.'

'How did you become so much of a Hindu?'

'I think I was fifteen. It was 1988, and I went along to a recital by Morari Bapu. That was the first time he came to do a discourse from the Ramayana for the youngsters. A lot of young people went along, because it was summer holidays, no one had anything to do, and they were targeting young people. Lots of young people, in fact most kids from my school went along. I went along just because I had nothing better to do. It was on our school grounds. That Ram *katha* (that unique Indian blend of sermon and recital) changed our lives, it opened us up to Hinduism. It was in Gujarati. Lots of people didn't understand it, I didn't understand it fully. The funny thing is that on the last day of the *katha*, young kids of the age of four, five, six, who didn't understand a word of what Morari Bapu was saying, they were all crying, saying, oh my god, the *katha* is now finished. So many people still talk about that *katha*. Something had happened to make them want to progress in the Hindu way of life.'

'Did you get picked on by others, that Hinduism is this and that, that you worship a monkey god and things like that?'

'Oh yes, all the time when I was at school. I still get it. I get it at work. I was organising this Get Connected, and we were exposed to a lot of media. My work people would say what is this you're doing, what's all this about idol worshipping. Last week I'd gone for my cousin's wedding, I had *mehndi* on my hands, and they said, what's all that, have you been writing with orange pen on your hands? No, I said, this is traditional.

You know, there are people out there who still lack knowledge. And I know from the white people who attended this event, because we were asking for feedback. I know some people said they learnt a lot about Hinduism: that we have only one God, really, when they thought we had thousands of gods. We said, yes, we have thousands of different *roops* of God – forms of God – but there is only one God. They started to relate to that.'

'Was there a lot of this when you were growing up?'

'Oh, yes, sure. When we first moved to Leicester, and I was a kid, we were living in the area of Rushymead. And when we moved there, Rushymead was predominantly all white. So when we used to go out and play, all the kids were all white. And we used to be called Pakis and all kinds of names. That you smell of curry, and why are you coming out, and all kinds of racist remarks. Then, as time passed, Rushymead and Belgrave and Leicester all became predominantly Hindu. Now there are only two white families living in my street. Everybody else is Indian. So we kind of took over.'

'Feels better now?'

'I feel at home. These two white families on our street are actually very friendly, they are very accommodating, they are very pleasant to meet in the street and say hello, good morning, how are you. They don't have no problems. Like for example when it's Diwali, every house has *diyas* lit up, and these white families, they don't say anything to us, they help us celebrate, and we take food to their house. And they enjoy it.'

This is the kind of thing I heard from a lot of youngsters again and again, in Leicester, in London, everywhere. Not from all, though. There's a partition among the Indian young. There are some who'll go out to immerse themselves into the English way, won't speak their parents' language, won't even eat Indian food. Maybe I'm biased because of my own irredeemable immersion in ways Indian, but I could argue that Indians who present themselves as differently coloured cultural Brits are a minority. Just count the youngsters at Navratri, and there can't be that many others left.

I doubt that many who came to these events – and there have been others – got connected to Hinduism just through what they heard. What mattered is that they came and others came; that they made the connection, and as Hindus.

Krishna's Army

We were an army, of a couple of thousand or so, and we had a general of our own. 'He's the *senapati*,' a chap by my side said as our army began to march out from Russell Square.

Like me, he hadn't joined the march yet, and he looked lost between joining and watching. The force had just begun to emerge onto Southampton Row. The *senapati*, our general, a slim guy under a red baseball cap that his followers wouldn't miss, was also watching from our pavement. 'Great turnout,' I said. 'Could have been better,' he replied. He introduced himself as Arjun Ruparelia. He had taken a moment off from shouting commands over his hand-held hailer to talk to me, and I was pleased with this attention from the leader.

But the real leaders were rightly the three big Indian gods Krishna, Ram and Hanuman, and they were leading the procession. Hanuman carried a mighty mace – his *gada* – and Krishna was naturally blue all over. A bunch of tourists – Japanese, who else – on an open double-decker bus from The Original London Sightseeing Tour now stranded on Russel Square must have had a better view of the gods on the street than most others. This was the first bus the police had stopped for the procession, and the Japanese were clicking busily away at a sight no London promotional pamphlet had promised.

I squeezed through to the start of the procession to walk in the company of Ram, Hanuman and Krishna. Underneath the blue paint on her face, Krishna was a petite girl of sixteen or so. She'd worked on the blue. Her arms, and her legs down to her feet below her knee-length red and yellow half-sari, were all Krishna-blue. On her head she wore a shining crown held in place by a firm rubber band, and she'd done her face up with bright bridal dots around her eyes; not what anybody said the original Krishna did, but girls must have their privileges. In her left hand she held a foot-high brass Hanuman with a long red tail.

To her left was the plumpish Hanuman himself. The one outsiders would disparage as the Indian monkey-god. He had not attached a tail to himself, but rounded lines around his mouth, and the bright silver *gada* he carried over his shoulder said it all. On the other side to Krishna's right marched Ram, wearing mostly red, with a long bow wrapped in silver foil slung over his shoulder. He was a tall chap, and wore his crown with becoming ease over a shoulder-length wig that came curling down in the accepted style of the Vedic forests Ram had inhabited for 14 years of self-imposed exile from his kingdom.

I shadowed the three gods down the pavement on Southampton Row, walking alongside an elderly man with very youthful vigour. We both stopped near a crossing to look back at the tail of the procession, still hidden somewhere in Russell Square. 'This is wonderful, just wonderful,' he said. 'I am eighty-four. I never thought I would live to see this day.'

It was the day of the big protest against an order to stop public worship at the Hare Krishna mandir in Letchmore Heath village, just north of London. Some local people had complained against the crowds the public worship brought through the village, and their complaint had been upheld by the local Hertsmere County council.

Letchmore Heath is a nice quiet village and the village pub is its heart. It's the place to gather for the village gossip underneath the mock wooden beams pretending to hold up that old roof. There must have been months of it when ex-Beatle George Harrison bought the estate next door. The trouble arose after George Harrison donated the estate to the Hare Krishna people. Bhaktivedanta Manor, as it then came to be known, became a local pilgrimage centre, particularly on Janamashtami, when thousands of cars brought tens of thousands of Hindus through the little village all through the night to celebrate the birth of Krishna.

Pilgrimage to Hindus was traffic to the village. But it did more than ruffle the English way of life for that and some other festive nights through the year; it divided the village. Some people thought traffic on a few nights a year acceptable. Others did not, and they took a stand for the English way of life in what became quickly a stand-off between old England and post-immigration Britain. They complained to the local Hertsmere council, and prevailed. The council ordered a halt to public worship at the temple.

The council ruled that Bhaktivedanta Manor had been approved as a centre for religious learning, not a place for public worship. But that ruling did nothing to stop the Hindu cars driving in on Janamashtami. Of all birthdays, no one was going to miss Krishna's. They still came in thousands to the blue god's birthday bash, and they came to make a point about themselves in today's Britain.

This march was another protest against the council order. My fellow walker, Bal Mukund Parikh as he introduced himself, thought it wonderful that so many Hindus had found something to complain about, something to fight for. What else would have brought a couple of thousand young Hindus out together on the streets of London?

The youngsters had set up an 'army', and called it the Pandav Sena, after the army of the good guys in the ancient Hindu epic Mahabharat. The army behind the *senapati* on Southampton

Row was that Pandav Sena, backed by irregular forces of the interested. This was a local village matter no more. If some in Letchmore Heath had gone beyond a village matter to raise the spirit of old England, then the Pandav Sena was marking a Hindu foothold in Britain.

Had the temple been left alone, the young Hindus would likely never have thought much of it, or of any other temple. This was no metaphysical awakening, no spontaneous rediscovery of Vedic texts. In defending their space they found themselves defending their religion. The longer the council maintained its ban, the more Hindu became the youngsters determined to break the ban. No parent could, just for the sake of Hinduism, have persuaded a Ram, Krishna and Hanuman onto Southampton Row, and then convinced a couple of thousand others to follow. Young Hindus had mobilised their own army, a *senapati*, and the gods themselves to lead it. No more was Hanuman a strange figure to be hidden from white friends, no more a secret between you and your parents. This Hanuman appeared to be leading everyone through the heart of London.

For one silly moment I thought it would be sacrilegious to go talk to the gods. Then, to erase my embarrassment over that thought, I had to. So I said 'hi' to Krishna, and she said 'hi'; her name was Anita Halai, and she went to school in London; as Krishna, she was having a great day out. Her parents followed the Swaminarayan sect, she said. But she had strong enough convictions at 16, or whatever, to follow Krishna and not Swaminarayan. It was a bold decision. The Swaminarayans, a relatively new sect of Hindus, make Krishna a lesser predecessor of the nineteenth-century Sahjanand Swami, who they consider God himself, Bhagwan Swaminarayan. At the celebrated Swaminarayan temple in Neasden, Krishna is only a small figure to the side of Sahjanand Swami. For a daughter in a Swaminarayan family to follow Krishna, and now to become Krishna, was a religious coup of sorts for the Hare Krishna temple.

The Neasden temple had not worked for her. 'They separate males and females there,' she said. 'And that's a lot of Gujarati which I don't understand. But I'm not against the Swaminarayans. I think Hindus should get together, right.' She wanted the two as cousins, not rivals. She had some pretty firm views on religion.

We were walking now through the crossing by Holborn tube station, the police were making sure we had right of way. I could hardly have dreamt that I could one day walk past that tube station with a real blue Krishna by my side, as the police halted traffic to make way for us. Krishna looked remarkably unselfconscious. Her mind was on the battle, not the traffic. 'We must fight for the temple. Everybody only goes to the temple, they don't really do anything.'

Hanuman on my left walked quietly, looking a little bored. After a bit, I told him that. 'I came because this other guy couldn't come,' he said. 'Then this other guy called me, and he was like desperate because this other guy couldn't come. But to tell you the truth, I'd rather be home right now.' After a pause, he said, 'Maybe it's not so bad because at least everybody's taking pictures of me.'

I asked if the *gada* he was carrying was heavy. 'No, not really,' he said, and offered it to me. I suggested it would be more appropriate for him to keep carrying it.

We were approaching Bush House at the end of Kingsway, with India House next door. The procession was going to loop around behind Australia House onto the Strand. I decided on the shortcut. I said bye to the gods and found some time to watch the parade.

Right behind the gods two lads carried a large six by four foot picture of Krishna and Radha, his female companion in a mischievous yet holy way. Then came the rest, marching, singing, waving banners. 'RAPE of Religion' said one banner, with 'rape' in bold red letters. Below the slogan a picture showed a woman being dragged away by policemen outside Parliament House, a Hindu flag saying 'Om' in her hand. That had happened at another demonstration in support of the temple. Below her picture sat the caption: 'She's not your mother... but she could be. This is what they're doing to Hinduism. What are you doing about it? If you're not on our side, you're on theirs.' 'IT'S TIME TO RUMBLE! RISE & WAKE UP BEFORE IT'S TOO LATE!' cried another banner held up by two girls making fists every now and then of their little Gujarati hands. The banner warned also of a 'future proposal to ban wearing of turbans.' The closure of the temple was 'the final twist in our backs, while we stand and watch!' Another poster carried a call from the original Krishna: '*Mam anusmara yudh ca* ... Remember me and fight – Bhagvad Gita 8.7'.

I'd never have thought this lot would ever be seen in anything like a Krishna army if I'd seen them somewhere else. Not the chap in the deep blue sweatshirt with 'Armani Jeans' printed on it, with a saffron sash around his waist, under the placard 'BRITISH HINDUS FEEL RAPED'. Or the girl in glasses in maroon salwar-kameez with the banner 'UNOFFICIAL APARTHEID ALIVE IN UK'. Not the tall guy in the loose T-shirt with 'BRITISH BORN, BRITISH RIGHTS' on his placard. Or the tall girl in the green T-shirt that was never going to descend to belt level with 'REMEMBER ME AND FIGHT'. The chap with gold ear rings and denim jacket with a coke bottle in one pocket, with 'WHEREVER THERE IS KRISHNA, THERE IS VICTORY', and 'NO TEMPLE NO VOTE' above the girl in the flimsy white dress approaching transparency.

A bunch of about thirty girls came by shouting louder than most. 'We-want-jus-tice, when-do-we-want-it, NAAOW!' The *sena* was marching to different songs. '*Ram ji ki sena chaleee...*'

– that was a bunch of gym-going guys. Two girls holding a banner '*Ram sena*, Woolwych', came leading another lot. One of them was dressed in tight jeans, suede shoes and a loose orange T-shirt, the other in a long blue skirt and particularly high-heeled leather boots, her hair tied back with a saffron scarf. This was a very Londoner-looking Hindu army.

Up at the traffic island outside Bush House where I was standing, the *senapati* had detached himself from the army and walked right back in the direction of India House, and so had Krishna. 'We have to tell India something,' Senapati told me as I stepped up to meet him. 'We're going to present a petition.' They crossed the road, and I walked along.

Krishna in her golden crown, her pocket Hanuman still in her blue hand, Senapati and I walked up to the front door of India House. We came up against a glass door, locked, with another glass door behind which also looked very locked. Behind the doors three men were sitting around in idle talk, obviously security staff who had the place to themselves on a Sunday.

One man walked up behind a glass panel. He looked too annoyed by the intrusion to bother with the shape and colour of the intruder. Years of government service had come to sit on his face, and they would never leave. But to Krishna and Senapati he was Mr India.

'Yes. What you want?' he said. Why do you want anything here, that is.

'Open the door. We want to give you something,' Senapati said.

'What you want to give?'

'Open the door, we'll give it to you.'

'We cannot open door just like that.'

'Listen, man. Just open the door, we want to give you something. We want to give it to India, you know, to In-dia.'

'That is all right but we cannot open the door.'

'Oh please, come on man, we have something for In-dia.'

Mr India was now joined by another member of the Sunday chat society. A tall chap in a green sleeveless sweater, he knew what to do with this, he did with all situations.

'First you tell me how have you come in here,' he said to Krishna. It surprised me that he too seemed not to notice Krishna's colour and crown.

Krishna looked at us, then back at the chaps behind the glass. She was losing her cool. 'Come on, you silly idiots,' she said in a low voice, not for them to hear.

'Look, can you take this for India?' Senapati was trying again.

'How we can just take anything?' The man in green was now going to do the talking.

'I don't know how, but you'd better do it.'

'But who are you?'

'Look, we're British citizens, right, but we're Indian, you know what I mean. We feel Indian. We're, like, with the Indian government.'

'But how you have come in here?'

Krishna produced a little camera from somewhere and started to take a picture.

'No! No camera! How you have brought camera here? Leave it out.'

Now Krishna spoke. 'Look, we want to give you this petition, right. We want a picture giving it to you, OK?'

'No, not OK. No camera. You just go out.'

'But you've got to help us.'

'This is Gorment of India office. Anyone can take pictures?'

'What is your name?'

'Why I should tell my name?'

By now the third man had appeared behind the glass. He had been staring suspiciously at the Hanuman in Krishna's hands.

Senapati saw where the third man was looking. 'We are not going to give you Him.'

'All right but what do you want to give?' Third man wanted to end all this.

Senapati waved a black folder. The petition was inside.

'All right, you can pass it from here.' He pointed to a slot in the glass.

Senapati tried, but the folder was too big. It wouldn't go in straight and it wouldn't go in folded either.

'All right, you can leave it outside. We will pick it up afterwards.'

'But what is your name?' Senapati said.

'Why do you want to know my name?'

'Because I'd like to know who I've given it to.'

'You can say you gave it to duty officer.'

'But can you come to the door? We want a picture of us handing it over. We told them we would take a picture of handing it over.'

'No! No camera!' The man in green was angry again.

And so now was Senapati. 'India is messed up, man. Better get your government sorted out.'

'You just leave this and go.'

'Look, we're Indians. You are Indians. You're not respecting we Indians, man. You know, you're really not respecting us.'

The first man had been staring at me as I took notes.

'What you are writing? Why you are writing?'

Before I could say something, Krishna raised her camera.

'Look!' he said. 'Inside Gorment of India office, never take picture. Never do it.'

'Where are your Vedic principles?' said Senapati.

'All right. You just leave it outside and go.'

'I'm not giving this in, man,' Senapati said. 'I'm not giving this here.'

Senapati walked out, carrying the undelivered folder. 'Bloody mad,' Senapati said. 'They're in no way representative of our culture. I'm going to give this directly to India.' Krishna and I followed him out. India of all countries had snubbed Krishna of all gods.

I looked at the petition as we caught up with the procession on the Strand. It was printed in ornate type:

To the Most Revered Governors of Bharatbhumi,
Namaste, Jai Sri Krishna.

We the undersigned, hereby wish to petition the government of Bharatbhumi, India, that as residents of Great Britain, we are in need of your assistance to maintain our cultural heritage. We feel that not only is it your duty but also an obligation which you must fulfil. You hold the position of representing our Saintly Raj Rishis who ruled according to our traditional Vedic principles. In order to uphold our rich heritage of 5,000 years we insist that you take the necessary action to assist our plea.

We may not be responsible for our heritage but we are responsible for the future. Our future depends on our past – our heritage. The British government have taken plans to ban us from all worship at the home of our cultural heritage – the Hare Krishna temple outside London. We call upon you to preserve our culture and act as the responsible heads of the state that you are and uphold Sanatan Dharma.

We hope that due consideration of our plea is taken.

Yours in the service of Sanatan Dharma, British Hindu Students Movement, Pandav Sena, Ram Sena, National Hindu Students Forum and all other British Hindus.

I completed the march up to Trafalgar Square almost guiltily. As an Indian, I wished India had received the *senapati* better. But the march ended happily enough and victory balloons went up before everyone went on their way. Hanuman finally laid the *gada* aside and went home as Nitin Patel. Krishna was Anita Hilai again.

Victory was theirs, later. Step by step the message went home to the government. A national Hindu uprising could not be handled by local zoning wisdom any more, the government decided. The dispute over public worship being allowed at Bhaktivedanta Manor was taken out of the hands of the local council and referred to the Department of the Environment. The Hare Krishna lot offered a solution. They would build a new access road to the temple from the opposite side of Letchmore Heath. The plan was finally approved. Money poured in, the new access road was built. The Hindu way, the English way, both had their way.

Shakha

This sort of gathering, every liberal says, would be the Hindu counter to Islamic fundamentalism. It was the Shakha called at Heathland School in Hounslow by the Hindu Swayamsevak Singh, the HSS, the British wing of the RSS, the Rashtriya Swayamsevak Sangh in India. And RSS has long been a name for Hindu extremism. But not terrorism; they don't bomb people and trains and planes. But extreme is a bad word, and to the declared liberal, the RSS is bad, and so therefore is its British cousin. And it has imported the *shakha* tradition from India, a camp-like gathering designed to put discipline and steel into Hinduism.

The HSS was celebrating the birth anniversary of the RSS founder Dr Keshav Baliram Hedgewar, and *swayamsevaks* and *sevikas* as the Sangh members are called, would be here from many of the weekly *shakhas* held around London.

As it happened, I got to park right by the ground taken up by the *sevikas*. A group of girls in white salwar-kameezes were lifting dumb-bells to commands from their leader's whistle.

A gaze-arresting leader, she had the tangy good looks that go with a heightened awareness of males. And here she was in a male kind of role, it was OK to say that to myself, no feminists listening to my thoughts in the car. And she had adapted her very feminine dress for it. The *dupatta*, that modesty scarf that customarily dips down from the shoulders over a dress to cloak any silhouetting of breasts, descended in a narrow and disciplined diagonal line to lock itself into a tight waistband over her *kameez*, failing spectacularly to do the intended job along the way. It signalled modesty with a mission. Besides, loose *dupattas* and lifting dumb-bells don't go together. I watched her a while from the car, if someone had said ogled, I wouldn't contest it. Her commanding ways had me hooked. She was in complete charge of herself and the other *sevikas*. She became a little more interesting for being a little intimidating, it was the kind of appeal a good-looking policewoman carries.

Not everyone in the group lifting dumb-bells was in white. A fair number of girls had arrived in their Sunday usual, more everyone's idea of young Asian women in London. They would change if and when they saw the light. The girls in white were the *sevikas*, the others tasters of *sevika* ways.

Behind the dumb-bell girls, another group of *sevikas* was twirling six-foot sticks to commands from their leader. Not a skill a London woman can use much, but no doubt they were told it was meaningful for the mind. Further up, another group was split into teams where one team sat in a row with neighbours facing opposite ways. But one of the team would be on the run, with one from the other team chasing. You could transfer the run to another from the team who had their back to you, unless of course the one chasing caught up with you first. As more and more got caught the row would diminish and eventually vanish. This was the more acceptably girlish *kho-kho*. Everyone looked like they were playing with a purpose other than the playing of the game.

I walked past the girls' ground to the *sevaks*, the males who had occupied the ground further up. 'Move on, mite,' the captain-looking chap in the middle of a bunch was shouting, quite a Londoner in the cause. He was making room for himself in a chain of six. They linked arms, called in a seventh teammate, and closed themselves in a circle around him, facing outward. The other team of six charged at the circle, yelling '*Har Har Mahadev*' that unmistakable slogan of Hindu muscle. '*Jai Bajrang Ki*,' the chaps in the circle of six shouted in equally Hindu invocation of the mighty god Hanuman. The Mahadevs were charging to get at the chap the Bajrangs were protecting.

The teams clashed. The captain, a thin chap, probably quite gentle outside the circle, was kicking and pushing wildly at the Mahadevs. After some grabbing and pulling – just the kind of thing good Hindu boys are otherwise taught never to do – the circle collapsed. The Mahadev team dragged their prey away. Next round they would close a circle around him to face the charge of the Bajrangs.

'It's a game called *sher-bakri* (lion-goat),' said a man who had walked up to my side. He was elderly, but in youthful white trousers and white T-shirt with a saffron lion printed over the T-shirt pocket. 'It is a very good game for developing the character.' He smiled approvingly at the boys, moving his head in turn from the *sher* to the *bakri* side. 'It is so difficult to stop myself from joining them.' But he was there to show others the way. Many of these teams were one *shakha* versus another, he said. So there were teams from the Harrow weekly *shakha*, from Slough, from Wembley and other places in the 'south-west zone' of Britain's *shakhas*.

The boys charged at one another for a bit and then my companion decided to call the games to a close. 'Come on, we are going to start our meeting now,' he said. He shouted some instruction, and the boys disappeared to their changing rooms, while he and I walked to an indoor basketball court, picked up our blue mats from a side and headed for a discussion circle on the floor. We were waiting for some others, and there was time for a few introductions.

Someone announced Narain Swaroop Sharma, elected MP from the Jan Sangh party in 1967, long before the Jan Sangh grew into an equally Hindu but government-ready BJP. The pioneer in India had later migrated; and here he would always be a star. I wandered over to another group readying their blue mats, and ran into Ramanbhai Khatru, whom I'd met at several BJP events. He was looking around the basketball court, pleased with the turnout. 'One day we will win,' he said. Ramanbhai had retired some years ago after repairing watches in north London. He has been a *shakha* regular for years, he said. Another familiar face was Dina Nath Bahl, a herbal doctor who was 72 but looked hardly 50. He told me he'd been a Sangh member since his days in Rawalpindi in Pakistan before the partition of India. He was also a pandit. 'But I don't do marriages any more. So many marriages break up, it is so sad.'

We soon sat down on our blue mat circle, and the meeting began. 'We are not useless,' a member was saying to his neighbour as he moved into cross-legged position. 'We are just used less.' Through some talk of this and that, my guide at *sher-bakri* made his point a little louder than the rest. 'You see, even after the *domraja* dinner they do not realise what has happened.'

'*Domraja* dinner?' I asked. 'What is this *domraja* dinner?' I had given away my ignorance too early, announced myself as alien among my own.

But RSS men have disciplined themselves to be patient with the ignorant Hindu. 'Of course you will not know,' he replied. 'Even in India the English language press has not reported it.'

A man in the circle brought out a copy of *Panchjanya*, the RSS newspaper. The banner headline in Hindi called that dinner the 'revolution of the century'. He explained the revolution. Brahmin sadhus and *sants* (saints) from Varanasi had gone to dinner with the low-caste Sanjit Chaudhry, the *'domraja'* who manages the cremation *ghats* of Varanasi. *Panchjanya* had a picture of the dinner with the caption 'unbelievable sight'. The caption named Mahant Avaidhya Nath of Gorakhpur, Vishwa Hindu Parishad leader Ashok Singhal and former police chief of Uttar Pradesh Sri Chand Dixit, all upper-caste Hindus, among the dinner guests. This was the first time that the sadhus and *sants* of Varanasi had visited the *ghat*, where the cremation and then body disposal was handled by low-caste Hindus. Thousands of people had lined the roads of Varanasi to witness their journey. Long-haired sadhus in saffron would sit on the floor of a Harijan's house in Varanasi in dinner diplomacy that would transform Hindu society. The dinner had been proposed at a 'religion parliament' by Vinay Katyaar, head of the militant Bajrang Dal, and everyone else agreed to join.

At the dinner, *Panchjanya* reported, the *domraja*'s mother handed out *gulab jamuns* to the *sants*, and the *sants* ate them happily. Given the caste identity of those doing the serving and those doing the eating, this was news. It was revolutionary that Hindus were having dinner with Hindus, that some Hindu leaders had their *gulab jamuns* that evening where they had never had *gulab jamuns* before. With them were dissolving the differences across a caste divide that spanned centuries.

I sat unexcited over this revolution. Because if this was revolution, it was not the first. Now and then, here and there, some Brahmin sadhu has shared a symbolic meal with some lower-caste people. It was going to take more than a cross-caste transfer of *gulab jamuns* to change Hindu society.

The meal had answered half the *roti–beti* (literally, dinner–daughter) test, because only if families can share both do they really bond. But that dinner was the far easier half. The revolution had achieved all of one meal by way of *roti*.

But *beti*? Would any of the Brahmins be happy to hand over their daughter, or the daughter of a less celibate associate, in marriage to the *domraja*'s son? Or to another of those low-caste workers who make a living off corpses and their remains at the cremation ghats? That would be revolutionary.

My lack of enthusiasm must have showed. 'You people from the English language press of India, you are worse than the English language press of England.' This was aimed at me, it came from a somber-looking man in wide glasses set within a thick frame. Those kind of glasses always add weight to words, and I felt the accusation that much more. He looked at me piercingly, like he was looking through me and not liking what he saw. 'You do what you want, don't do what you don't want, but we will win.'

Someone who'd been introduced as an arrival from a Birmingham *shakha* eased the hostility. He suggested they should forget about me, but look around to see how little the Sangh, Hindus in fact, are recognised in Britain. 'We are the largest community here and we are the least understood. Just Asians, that is what we are. How many Hindus are in jail? Less than fifty. How many Muslims? Go and count, go and ask the Home Office. And for these people, everybody is an Asian. We are not Asians, we are British Hindus. We must tell them that.'

More such views arose from the circle and grew into a chorus. 'We are one in six in the world, we have tremendous assets, but when we have problems we are marginalised,' said one. 'What is wrong?' another member asked. 'Are Hindus too mild, are they not sufficiently empowered?' And another: 'We cannot consolidate our position as a powerful, influential community because we are divided. That is the main cause of our undoing. Hegdewar said we must meet regularly to overcome this. The days are not very far when the youth can take up techniques we have learnt here.' Anger relieved by occasional hope flowed on another half hour or so.

By then the elders had talked, the young had done their exercises after the games. The *sevikas* were now walking into our basketball court to one side, the *sevaks* to another. Our circle made way for them.

A sharp whistle ended the chatter. It came from the skipper. He was standing at one end of the court, facing the gathering. Very captain-looking. Chest out, stomach in, arms straight to the sides, hands tightened into fists, stern profile, crew cut. He could have been on the cover of a regimental magazine, the new recruit bristling with promise. I pitied the enemy who'd run into him.

Some of the elders took their chairs on stage, by the side of the chief guest, police officer Alan Hamilton. Once they were settled, the captain launched those moves that are to the Sangh the stuff of discipline, and to outsiders military stuff. He marched to a side of the basketball court, stopped, spun around, clicked his heels, and blew the whistle again. Five *sevaks* and two *sevikas* ran up to take positions facing the RSS flag on stage. The captain took two smart steps to the flag and halted. He took one step on, and one of the seven took position where he had halted. Six halts later, all seven were in place behind him. The whistle sounded again, and everyone fell in place behind the top seven. A few hundred babbling youths had been ordered within minutes into seven neat rows.

Another *sevak* marched up to the captain's side, very earnest behind his glasses, very much the thinking lieutenant type. He asked permission to unfurl the RSS flag. Permission granted. On another command a few hundred hands went into namaste and heads were bowed simultaneously. To more commands, prayers were recited. The captain ordered everyone to attention, then stand at ease, then into cross-legged sitting on the floor to listen to the chief guest.

'I have never, never, and I absolutely mean that, I have never, never seen such discipline among the youth in Britain,'

Hamilton said. As a police officer he must know youth in Britain as a world of football louts, bullying gangs, neighbourhood quarrels, fights in the pub, teenage sex as common as blue jeans, pregnancies, of helpless parents watching all this if they hadn't already turned away. Where else would Hamilton find this kind of London youth?

Discipline was relaxed after the meeting, and it was a relief to see everyone ease into such normal activity as eating samosas. The HSS crowd began to look more like usual Indians.

I spotted little Bharati by an eats table; she had taken position in her straight line some minutes back with a push from her parents. Her father was a member of the HSS, or the Sangh *parivar*, the name for that larger family, as it is sometimes called. But she seemed pleased, not just pushed to be there.

'I've been going to the *shakha* since I was three,' she said. That gave her eight years experience as a *sevika*.

'Is that because you are a Hindu?' I asked. 'Can you be Hindu without going to the *shakha*?'

'Hinduism is, right, like different things, and there are so many gods and in the end only one God. There's not like only one way to worship that one God.'

'Is that why you come to the *shakha*?'

'I find the games fun, I make friends.'

'Do you know anything about India?'

'There has to be, like, a Ram Mandir. That was the birthplace of Ram and building a mosque over it was not very clever. Then they broke it down, and then arresting the leaders was a bit stupid. It was done only to please Muslims.'

'So you would like a BJP government?'

'The BJP should win elections but the Muslims, they vote all together, and there are some Congress Hindus who are traitors.

The Hindus are scared because the Muslims are rough and do these bombings. The Muslims are scared because the BJP is powerful.'

A cup of tea later I wandered over to Brijesh. He was 19, and he'd just started to study law at King's College. We got talking about growing up a Hindu in Britain. Like when he was 12, he said.

'It was really hard then. It was so hard to say what Hinduism is, who you are. A twelve-year-old in India may not understand either but he does not have to explain.'

Brijesh recalled the many 'points of attack' – idol worship, the caste system, the many and strange gods. 'You can't try to answer all this, you can only tell the other chap to get lost, if you have the confidence.' And confidence in being a Hindu was something he didn't have. 'I was very confused at the time. There was so much that was strange and wishy-washy, it was so hard to explain. It was all so incomprehensible, it genuinely was.'

But Brijesh had now found some ready answers. 'I can tell people today that we do not worship the idol, it is only a point of focus, a symbol to enable concentration, to bring out ideas of devotion. An idol is like the pole in pole vault jumping, you use it to get to the top, then dispense with it.' And he had found answers for questions from other religions – the Christians have their cross, the Muslims their Kaba. 'Ours is a more elaborate, more complex symbolism. When we worship Ganesh, obviously it does not mean God has an elephant head. It is symbolic.'

'But you don't sound very confident about your own answers.'

'There are so many twists and turns, there are no direct answers. That intellectual reasoning is not there. I feel I want to give reasoned answers to all those questions, but it's frustrating. If only it had been a monolithic faith. Too many rituals, too few answers, that's where Hinduism has come unstuck.'

He had run into everyone's problem. You can tell children they're Hindu, you can try to tell them they must be proud to be Hindu, but nobody can quite tell them what it is to be Hindu.

He knew he couldn't talk to a red-cheeked teenager in England about some deeply philosophical, wonderfully diverse, all-embracing faith. Ganesh was to him a god with an elephant's head, and that was just weird. The many-armed goddess Durga riding a tiger is bizarre, a god Krishna who is a blue-coloured baby that grows up to acquire many girlfriends is a holy playboy, and that makes no sense. And if these are the figures Brijesh would pray to, how much more un-British could he get? A 12-year-old Hindu in Britain can be quite a loser. He's the British Hindu who doesn't know how British he is, and who doesn't know what Hindu is.

But it was OK at the *shakha*. You didn't have to explain yourself to anyone. There were things to do, and the others, who were like you, did not ask questions. The parents were all there, and so many grown-ups around couldn't all be wrong. The Sangh had recognised the pangs of growing up Hindu in Britain, and reproduced the Indian *shakhas* here at least partly as a way out. A *shakha* offered collective routine as an answer to complexity, at least for now. The philosophy at London's suburban *shakhas* was not to be too philosophic. Respect Hindu philosophy, leave it alone, and get on with a togetherness bound by discipline and common purpose. Those questions and answers can go on for ever.

Just being together was enough. These bonds would strengthen Hindu society, and a whining immigrant minority badly needed that strength. The rest, the complexity, could be dealt with privately, and later. Pray to God personally, but be protected while you pray. You can't abandon yourself to meditation if you're under attack. Hindus have been attacked too often, they have lost for too long. Hinduism needs muscle to protect Hindus – and its own metaphysics. Here you don't sit around interpreting symbols, you play *kho-kho*. You salute the saffron flag. You do what you must when the whistle blows. That was Hindu enough, for now.

The captain turned out to be Rajesh. He had much on his hands at the *shakha*, but we caught up later for a cup of coffee at an Italian place on Kingsway, just across from the London School of Economics where he was studying.

Over cappuccinos, as usual never hot enough, he told me what the *shakha*, the temple, meant to him.

'I was taken to the *shakha* by my father,' he said. He was then just a kid. 'I have been going ever since, on weekends. I just can't think of life without the *shakha*.'

'And why not?'

Rajesh stirred his cappuccino, and made a little clearing between the foam and his young moustache. 'Because that is me, a Hindu. My Hindu identity is for me a matter of self-preservation.'

'But why do you have to be Hindu to preserve yourself? And if Hindu is what you want to be, why a *shakha*?'

'Because a *shakha* is where you meet others like yourself. For many of them it's a sense of rejection that brings them in. In a temple, at a *shakha*, you may not know the meaning of the Sanskrit words, but at least you don't get rejected.'

Shakha began to sound like a club for besieged Hindu boys. You didn't have to be fired by ideology, just attracted by a desire for normalcy. The *shakha* was the weekend Hindu hideaway. Hegdewar's ideas were working in Britain in ways he never could have anticipated. Because you don't even have to be very Hindu to want to be there. At a *shakha* boys can be boys. Outside they might just be brown Asians worshipping strange gods.

Rajesh told me he had set up a Hindu society at LSE. He spoke of it as among the more useful things he's ever done, almost like setting up a shadow *shakha*.

'But why set up a Hindu society at LSE?'

'It really gets to you when you get to the university. That's when you get your choices, that's when you make your decisions about who you're with and where and when. You can go to a rock 'n' roll club, you can go to a white pub, and it can be a bit awkward, you can come away thinking this is not the place for me. Or you can think the disco is the place for you on Saturday night and a *shakha* the place to be on Sunday morning.'

Rajesh told me he goes dancing almost as often as he goes to the *shakha*. 'You have to, if you want to be with the girls.' But he will not give up the *shakha*, he said. 'Going to the *shakha* gives me confidence. You go once a week and charge your batteries. It really makes you feel assertive. It's the entire programme; our salute the *bodh pranam*, the queues, all the exercises to the commands of your leader, singing together, playing together. They all work for me, at different times in different areas. It's so magnetic, I can't describe it. It's an experience you have to feel, and you want it again and again. It's a *nasha*, real intoxication.'

Rajesh was silent for some time, looking into the rain outside. We were by ourselves near the window; it was quiet in the cafe. The waitresses had taken up a table not far from us; ours was a world very far from theirs.

Rajesh looked at them too. 'I have many white friends and Muslim friends but there are some things they just don't understand.'

'Like what?'

'Like marriage, and I don't mean just arranged marriages and love marriages. At my age you start thinking about marriage, what you think the wife should be like. I can talk to a few friends at the *shakha*, I can't talk to anyone else.'

'So what do you think about marriage? Don't you want to marry some sexy *sevika*? Maybe all *sevaks* should marry *sevikas*.'

'No, no, each should marry someone else, that way you can bring more people into the *parivar*.'

But he also knew that these things don't always work that well. 'So many *sevaks*, you know, their wives are fed up because the men put everything into the Sangh. One *sevak* from Leicester went to Paris to help set up a *shakha*, and his wife didn't even know he'd gone. Now that can be a problem.'

Some Sundays later I drove up to my nearest *shakha*. The HSS tool hire shop on Kenton Road couldn't have been more conveniently placed, or named. 'Just take the turning opposite HSS,' Anil Pota who heads the Overseas Friends of the BJP told me. That road would take me a couple of hundred yards down to St Gregor's School, and this was where the Sunday *shakha* was held.

Pota had been very welcoming, and had sounded very *shakha*-proud when I ran into him at a temple in Kenton some days earlier. 'We have about sixty to seventy shakhas every weekend in Britain,' he had told me as we sat chatting in his BMW – one of those new things more squat than sleek. 'We have an attendance of about 1,200 every week, and most of them are youngsters.' He suggested I should come and see for myself.

His directions were precise, and he seemed right about the youngsters. It was a happy little group on the paved basketball court in the school grounds, on a golden Sunday morning. The twenty or so chaps had split into *kho-kho* teams, it was a fun start to a day like that.

It was a while before I spotted the older *sevaks*. They were walking around the basketball court in threes and fours. Their pace was rather purposeful. They walked very straight and made sharp right turns with a focussed look. This was disciplined patrolling, no Sunday stroll.

Quite suddenly a whistle stopped the *kho-kho*. A team leader in blue T-shirt issued orders in Sanskrit. The teams launched now into *kabaddi*, a 30-second foray into enemy camp where you touch one of the others or more and return to base, unless they managed to hold you back. The switch from *kho-kho* to *kabaddi* was awkward, like a badly done cut from one film scene to another.

The *kabaddi* ended as abruptly as the *kho-kho* on another command from the leader, the *sanghchalak*. A football was brought out from the boot of a *sevak*'s Ford. Not standard at a RSS *shakha* in India, but the HSS was adapting to local conditions since football is what gets young boys going. There were other signs of respect to local conditions; no one wore khaki shorts, uniform of sorts at *shakhas* in India.

One group of the elderly who had completed their clockwise round of the basketball court had stopped, and I walked up to join them.

'You must have seen the new book,' an elderly *sevak* was saying. 'Hindus will become a minority in India in two hundred years.' He paused, seemed to approve of the silence around him, and added, 'The Muslims will become the majority.'

The silence was never going to last after this remark. Many-sided wisdom sprouted.

'But it may not happen. You see, as education spreads among the Muslims, they will stop having so many children.'

'*Arrey*, what education, bhai. What education they will get from the madrasahs?'

'But really, in two hundred years they will be majority?'

'Yes, the book explains this. I forget the name, but you must read it. It has explained very nicely.'

'But you know you cannot say about two hundred years.

These people, they just draw a graph, and they just show a line going up. But graphs do not go like that. They go up and down, and then again up and down.' The *sevak* holding out this hope made his point waving a finger up and down in the direction of Kenton Road.

'But one thing I tell you. Indian Muslims are not for Pakistan. They have seen what has happened to Indian Muslims who went to Karachi.'

'*Arrey* bhai, you tell me this. When these killings happen in Kashmir, how many of these Muslim leaders speak out? They keep talking about this moderate leadership. Why doesn't the moderate leadership speak out?'

'Do you know about the Christians? Have you heard about the Christians in Kashmir? They are saying the hair at Hazratbal belonged to Christ.'

'Yes, Christ went to Kashmir. Those twelve years when he went missing, he was in Kashmir.'

'But they are not able to convert anybody in Kashmir.'

'These British are such fools. But how did they manage to rule us?'

'Because we are bigger fools.'

'You know they said Sir, Sir, Sir and they took over the country.'

'And even now in India people say Sir, Sir, Sir.'

'You see, between Muslims and Christians it's a different matter. But the Muslim leadership never speaks out about killing of Hindus in Kashmir.'

'They are scared, that is why. I don't know why they are scared.'

'But you see how America will deal with them now.'

'Oh, I am not sure at all about America's way of dealing with these things.'

'Next they will go for Syria, then Libya, then Iran. But why they never talk about Pakistan?'

'They will go for North Korea.' But no one seemed very interested in North Korea, even if Americans went after it.

This was more or less standard *shakha*-speak, and it continued a while. The other *sevaks* had by now stopped and were talking in their own circles. And again, suddenly, the *sanghchalak* issued an order in Sanskrit, and conversation halted. He gave commands, and those brought us all into a circle. More commands followed, all in Sanskrit, and we did as commanded. 'Attention! Stand at ease! Attention! Right turn! Left turn!'

Another order, and we all sat down in the circle. An assistant of the *sanghchalak* distributed a sheet with the words of a song written on it in Hindi and Gujarati, with a translation in English.

He began to sing it. He sang well, and everyone repeated over a range of comfortably few notes so as not to challenge a non-singer.

Jai Bhavani, Jai Shivarai...
Raksha kee is bhoomi ki,
Nyaya, neeti, adarshon ke...

The translation read:

Victory to Bhavani (Durga), Victory to Shivaji!
Shivaji protected this land as well as law, order and ideals.
He awakened the spirit of Dharma.
You are the inspirer of the youths.
You are the icon of humanity.
You were a man of sterling character.
Let us hail victory to Shivaji.
Let us hail in Jija Mata.
Let us hail victory to valour.

Not everyone repeated the lines on cue, simple as the tune was. The *sanghchalak* had a word to say about this. Get it right next time, he warned, and gave further precise instructions.

HINDU WAYS

The *shakha* was drawing to a close. We formed two straight rows. Again we were called to attention a couple of times. On order, the two men right at the back took a step to their right, and marched past us to the front. Another sidestep to the left and they were at the head of the rows. On order, they about-turned and inspected the rows. The chap before me was considered to be a couple of inches too far out to the left, and he was ordered in line. I couldn't see the chap giving the orders for our row, so I must have been all right. Another order from the *sanghchalak*, and the two men marched back to the back of the rows. It was their job to straighten us out, and they had.

They about-turned again. A good deal of brisk marching followed. The leaders marched towards one another, away from one another, towards us, away from us. Another order, and we brought our hands together in a namaskar. Very ordered, and a little abrupt, quite different from the laid-back folding of hands I'd been brought up on.

A second group song began. I stood a little embarrassed by my silence. I'd never heard this song before. In my silence I figured I heard the approval of Indian secularists. I hadn't expected to hear it on a basketball court in north-west London.

SUMMER GURUS

Grounded Bapu

Morari Bapu is something India produces and Britain never: a holy celebrity.

One way to tell was the long queue of devotees I was overtaking on the lawns of the Grim's Dyke Hotel just north of London. Morari Bapu was giving audience to devotees at the far end of the lawn; I was jumping the queue, under propulsion from a busy volunteer, because I was going to interview him. That queue was a picture of well-populated devotion, but if Morari Bapu's feet were easy to touch, or even sight, who'd bother? Difficulties in access always feed true devotion.

I was privileged to have got far enough to be right before him now. At the *kathas*, where so many thousands come to listen, he is only a slight figure in the distance, blown up on screen. For the first time I was seeing his familiar good looks up close, the squarish, well-formed face sanctified by a red tilak. His still black hair receded in distinguished contrast to a very white beard. A folded black shawl made a shelf of his right shoulder as usual, above his customary white vest. That look never changed.

It was never going to be easy to get him to talk to me after I asked just the wrong question.

'Why did you do a *katha* on board a Jumbo jet?'

SUMMER GURUS

A businessman had told me that he and some of his friends had chartered a Boeing 747 in order to listen to Morari Bapu's religious discourse mid-air. The seating had been rearranged to give him centre stage on the 747, with passenger-devotees all around. The *katha* began when the aircraft reached 35,000 feet or so, and continued hours, unless perhaps interrupted by bad weather. It was an unusual location for a religious sermon, and I had to ask Morari Bapu why he'd thought it necessary.

Sitting on a *jhoola*, Morari Bapu contined to nod occasionally to bowing devotees before answering. I must have asked his least favourite question, and he did not look pleased. The question meant, among other things, that I was not particularly devoted to him.

'It is our ancient Hindu tradition to do *parikrama* of holy places,' he replied. 'Where you find a holy place, you will see people will walk around it many times. What is more holy than our Mother Earth? So when we did our *katha* on the aeroplane, we were doing a *parikrama* of our Mother Earth.'

'And is that the reason you did a *katha* also on a ship?' Because another summer his devotees had hired a cruise liner in order to listen to him that way.

'Yes. But then I simply go wherever my devotees make arrangements. My only interest is to do my *katha*, and to explain the Ramayan to anyone who comes to listen.'

The look he sent past me made sure the minder ended the conversation. What might have been an interview was reduced to a two-question intrusion into a holy exchange of bowing and nodding. The queuing fans clearly presented a far more pleasing sight to Bapu.

I made it back past them, unescorted this time. The quick chat had given me new status among the many Gujaratis on the lawns, in the queue and outside of it. When an Indian jumps a queue, he isn't rude, he's important. And I'd not only had *darshan* of Bapu, I'd spoken to him.

BRIDELESS IN WEMBLEY

Darshan is a thing unknown in the West. You don't meet holy men, you're not given audience with them, you only can have *darshan* of them. The privilege of queuing and bowing, and if you're lucky, getting acknowledged in glance. The blessing of placing yourself in the potential line of the holy one, the privilege if you can manage it, or pay for it, of being just near. The devotees in this queue never got as far as a close-up *darshan* of Morari Bapu that my aborted interview had inadvertently given me. They were bowing more to his wooden sandals, the *khuraons*, placed on the ground below the Bapu on the *jhoola*. Wooden footwear is the surest announcement of gurudom, but there was tradition behind bowing to those. Ram's *khuraons* sat on his throne 14 years through his exile in the forests to symbolise the absent king, because his brother Bharat could not bear to occupy the throne in Ram's absence. After that *khuraons* would become standard footwear for a guru; they would be an announcement of godliness. That Morari Bapu's *katha* was always on the Ramayan, the story of god Ram himself, must give his *khuraons* particular legitimacy. On the God-via-guru path, Morari Bapu had built himself into the most popular means to access Ram, and earned himself the right to more Ram-like ways than other gurus.

Devotees were still pouring out of cars to join the queue as I headed back to the parking lot. Some crusty white folk were making their way to the bar within the hotel in pursuit of old local traditions that lead to particular watering holes. But they were far outnumbered by the Gujus headed for *darshan* of Bapu. Post-immigration Britain had taken over around Grim's Dyke quite spectacularly. Grim's Dyke had adapted very well to new Indian conditions. It had made space under a tree for the *jhoola* Morari Bapu is so known to love. The grounds already offered pleasing pathways now put to previously unsuspected use for those long queues around the castle-like walls of Grim's Dyke, which were wrapped in ivy below red-topped turrets. The hotel was built deliberately in the style of something out of a fairy tale. But old England has faded here under new Gujarati Britain.

The likes of the whites headed for the bar would never turn the other way, not even for a Christian Morari Bapu. In a land where nobody listens to anybody any more, Morari Bapu draws tens of thousands. Fans or devotees, they listen all day, day after day, usually the ten days at a time that his *katha* lasts, within huge marquees set up in parks, or often the 11,000-seat Wembley arena. Multiply such numbers many times to count in people watching *kathas* broadcast live on local Indian channels. An off-duty priest at Grim's Dyke must ask where good Christians have gone.

I'd like to see the day good Christians hire a jumbo jet just to listen to a sermon from the Archbishop of Canterbury mid-air. I found myself thinking up headlines for that story. 'For Christ's Sake'. Compared to headlines in *The Sun*, no doubt this would be polite.

Morari Bapu was coming for a *katha* again in the summer and Manubhai Madhwani was going to tell us all about it. Manubhai Madhwani, or Moneybhai Madhwani as some like to call him, is one of those businessmen who made Morari *kathas* happen. This was his summer to present Morari Bapu, and a little more. He'd invited the media to a press conference to tell us about it.

I stepped up to the Edwardian I Room at St James's Court Hotel, later renamed Crowne Plaza St James, a close neighbour of Buckingham Palace. Moneybhai, balding, portly and a little sage in that successful way, was receiving us at the door. By his side was his younger brother Mayur Madhwani, the one who had gone off, legally, with the Bollywood actress Mumtaz, every man's love of the seventies. That made Mayur celebrity-looking too, assisted by hair with those grey streaks that always looks distinguished for some reason, an eye-of-the-beholder hang-up. The hosts received us in front of posters slightly taller than them announcing a 'Festival of Spiritual Unity' named 'Samabhav', to be held at Roundwood Park. It would be a festival to highlight the unity of the spiritual essence of all religions. The Indian businessman is always at worrying ease with things spiritual.

The Madhwani byline was a rather prominent feature of the announcement. Two video monitors of the forty-inch plasma kind were installed high in Edwardian I. One flashed pictures of the Kakira Sugar Works in Uganda, reworked into success by the Madhwanis after the wasting days of Idi Amin. It showed fields, factories, happy workers, cared for workers, workers who said 'Kakira, we salute you!' The second monitor featured Morari Bapu doing a Ram *katha*. This would be a festival of spiritual unity, with Morari Bapu as hero, as held up by Madhwani.

Further into the room a young lady was handing out copies of the group brochure. Kakira was obviously the star of the Madhwani success. A presumably happy worker – Hira Singh, almost certainly a Punjabi – had written an ode to Kakira, proudly published in the brochure:

Ah! Kakira sugar is ever so sweet
So say one and all whoever we meet
As we merrily walk down the street.

But everything that fed the success story was not so sweet. The magazine told us about the Nile Breweries that the family lost during the Idi Amin exodus, and got back in 1992. Now 'a full rehabilitation has been implemented to improve the production and quality of beer'. And the company had launched a new brand of beer in Tanzania with 'a higher alcohol content to cater for the specific group of people who love to have a strong beer'. Beer wouldn't be served at the *katha*, but beer could help serve a *katha*.

The press conference began and Manubhai took over from the monitors. 'We are businessmen,' he said in his halting but weighty way. 'And increasingly it falls to us to be responsible for the kind of world we live in and the kind of world we leave to our children. Without unity, without finding the way to allow all of us to live in peace and understanding, the legacy we leave our children will be a world of polarised peoples. Far from uniting today we see more than ever a world divided, a world divided by dogma. Our faiths must now unite us, not continue to divide us. My family give thanks for once more having the opportunity and the resources to serve our fellow human beings.'

If a festival like this can at all bring spiritual unity, why not have it in Uganda or India where it is needed more, someone asked. 'It is needed more here,' Madhwani said. 'We have made this country our home, but what have we done for our children? We will reserve a special area for the youth at this *katha*.' More noble aims were announced. At the back, the monitors were repeating their stories, the business on one, the *katha* on the other. The stuff of one monitor would pay for the content of the other, the blessings from the other would further the success of the first. Spirits sometimes can supply spiritualism.

With Harlesden and Neasden as neighbours, Roundwood Park could not have sat in a more uncelebrated location. Neasden did not become a metaphor for the nondescript in *Private Eye* for nothing. In the snob game of addresses, Harlesden and

Neasden take courage to admit to. But Roundwood Park would be fine for a *katha*. Any place that is gettable to from north-west London in 15 minutes is fine for gathering Indians.

With Indian-carrying cars to front and back for company, I crawled along Harlesden Road and then Longstone Avenue down to Roundwood Park, which now stood out for its huge white marquee. The parking lot in the park itself was packed. This was VIP parking, you could tell from the number of Mercedes Benzes with 'RAM' featuring in their number plates. After what's paid for a Merc, this must be a minor additional investment, an appropriate extra for God, who after all made the wealth for the Merc possible.

I had to drive past the privileged parking to plain London roads. I found a slot after the usual spot-the-space contest, and walked up to the park and then the marquee through that Mercedes car park. A Merc is usually the clearest statement of wealth there is in the Indian world, and Indian businessmen like to make some things very clear. But there were some Jaguars, BMWs and a couple of Rolls around too. At this festival of spiritual unity, the one unifying factor in the parking lot was the price tags of those cars. Out in the forests Ram had presumably led a hard life; here in this English park he could command a pretty expensive fleet of cars. I didn't need to step into the marquee to figure that well-tyred devotees would have all the front seats. They were dressed for devotion as I saw them stepping out of the cars and into the marquee through the VIP entrance. The preferred wardrobe for the day was something Indian in off-white silk for the men, boutique saffron for women. I walked round to the other entrance.

The *katha* marquee was 500 feet long and 90 feet wide. All those square feet weren't enough. The chairs inside were all taken, and so was the space on the floor. Devotees had spilled over to the outside of the marquee on the non-VIP side. The latecomers outside were lucky that rain had not been forecast.

The *katha* had begun. Morari Bapu was on what had been done up as a spiritual throne, a much satined and cushioned podium, with a halo done in silver arching high up behind him, in the middle of the marquee. Preachers from other religions – Christians, Muslims, Jains, Sikhs, Buddhists – took these positions on the sides, all equally lower than Morari Bapu. They had no silver halos. Morari Bapu had been set up to be more spiritually equal than others. This did not seem encouraging of spiritual unity, but the others seemed to sit comfortably in their seats below him, and if they didn't like it, they didn't show it.

Morari Bapu began to sing in his low, somewhat husky voice: '*Sita Ram, Sita Ram…*' The thousands sang his lines after him. Gently he took the pitch higher and higher. The rest followed as far up as they could. He speeded up, and so did the rest.

He could sing of course, but the marquee was not overflowing with devotees to hear him sing. Everyone was waiting to listen to his views on the Ramayana and on the world. He must have something to say if so many had turned up to listen.

It was at a later Ram *katha*, this one held at Wembley arena, that I caught up with some of his crowd-pulling magnets. And figured also why the Merc number plates said Ram and not some abbreviation of Krishna. Ram is obviously more number plate friendly. But Morari Bapu is celebrated emphatically and only for his Ram *kathas*. Other businessmen import summer *kathas* on the Gita, that text from the Mahabharat, the other big Hindu epic besides the Ramayan, but it wouldn't be Morari Bapu doing those. Businessmen are happy for blessings from any god, but they do have their favourites.

Story and song will always pull crowds, but Morari Bapu was not drawing crowds just as religious storyteller or singer. He was making us feel good about ourselves. 'It is not so bad to sin,' he was saying. 'People are good, it's just that sometimes the times are bad. So we do what we do. We make mistakes. And who does not go wrong now and then? Do you know, I once got a Diwali card from J. Krishnamurthi, you know the famous philosopher. In that he had written to me, "Please sin a lot, and best wishes for Diwali". So you see, we all sin. But it is not good to do the same sin again and again.'

In fact it would, he said, be a sin not to sin. 'If you take the name of God, your sins will be wiped out, even if you have committed many. And if you don't, then God will ask, why did you do no wrong? Did you doubt my power to forgive you? At least you should have tested my compassion, my ability to forgive.' As a Morari Bapu follower, I would be doing God a favour by sinning because God's powers to forgive would otherwise be wasted. We could all believe this and go back from this *katha* quite happy with ourselves.

Morari Bapu offered evidence from the Ramayana of the need to sin in order to establish God's power to forgive. 'You know the story of Ahalya, the woman who sinned. She was turned into stone. But she would come back to life again if Ram were to touch her and bless her. Ram came and blessed her, and she became human again. *'Yuhin koi mil gaya tha, sarey raah chaltey chaltey…'* From Bollywood, the song, that one day the singer met someone she really liked. Also Ahalya's song? If you like; if not, never mind. Everyone who knew the song, and many did, joined in.

'But don't forget, it was not just she who was waiting for Ram to come and forgive her. Ram too was waiting to bless her and redeem her… If you accept you have sinned, it will all go away. Say to God, we are your children. If children go wrong, it is the mother's fault. If we go wrong, then God has gone wrong, we can say; God, you are responsible. But if you believe, you will be redeemed, like Ahalya. So if you go wrong, don't be angry with yourself, don't feel guilty. Say I am human,

I have gone wrong, so what? And if anyone says anything, say you have this from God and from your guru.'

Divine Ambassador

The men bowed deep before the figure on the throne as they marched past the high point of their procession at Piccadilly Circus. On that elevated throne, Parmukh Swami, elderly, portly and gentle, was everything you'd want to look up to in a holy Hindu figure. The round face with the round red tilak over a sparse white beard could have walked out of a regular Hindu calendar.

Up on his throne-like sofa chair installed many heads above head height at Piccadilly Circus, Parmukh Swami Maharaj was a manifestation of God to the thousands marching past him; God, not just guru. Because the men, and these were only men filing past at the moment, were Hindus of a kind, as every Hindu is a Hindu of a kind, far more than any Christian or Muslim is a kind of Christian or Muslim. These were relatively new converts from one kind of Hindu to another. They were followers of the nineteenth-century Gujarat preacher Sahjanand Swami, who came to be known among his followers as Bhagwan Swaminarayan, as God himself, the final stage of a holy evolutionary process in which the god Krishna was only a predecessor now many stages back. That made the Hindus walking up Piccadilly the Swaminarayan Hindus, and since there are enough Hindus around for ever more divisions, these were not just the Swaminarayan kind of Hindus, but a certain kind of Swaminarayans. The sort who believe that Bhagwan Swaminarayan always maintains a living ambassador in this world, currently Parmukh Swami Maharaj.

That faith determined Parmukh Swami's elevation. It meant he could survey his followers below, and they could look up to him, as they should. But for someone so tied into celibacy that he must not look at women, or even think of them, his only company at eye level was Eros, London's dubious god of erotic love. The unintended neighbourliness could hardly have been on the mind of the Swaminarayan followers. This was a procession to celebrate the opening of the spectacular temple at Neasden, and Parmukh Swami would bless it from the heart of London, and be seen there doing so. Eros just happened to be around.

A Rolls parked by the base of the Eros statue announced that Parmukh Swami's ride to Piccadilly Circus had also been quite special. It's the only time I've seen a car parked inside Piccadilly Circus, or an elevated throne in there for that matter. Some negotiations with Westminster council and the police, and no doubt persuasion from higher-ups must have gone into that.

From his height, Parmukh Swami would have seen the long march all the way down Piccadilly. The men who had formed the first half of the procession had almost moved on, and soon the women came marching by. The male–female division of the procession, as within the hall at the Neasden temple, was as strict as any Islamic division in such matters. Now the women were bowing and looking up to him, many with hands folded as well, all the show of reverence anyone could produce. It was all right for the women to look at Parmukh Swami but by the commands of the faith not at all right for him to look back at them. I watched particularly to see exactly how he would look away, or perhaps look in their direction. He did, more than once, seeing no doubt only that the procession had turned female.

It was a victory march. London had just got its now famous Swaminarayan temple at Neasden that had added 3,000-year old Vedic architecture to the London skyline and Hindu history to Britain's. The Hindu image in Britain was being lifted by architecture and edifice as never before, and London should know.

SUMMER GURUS

Bands led the procession, playing Western and victorious sounding marching tunes. A pick-up van dressed like a lion carried a life-size image of Sahjanand Swami. Figures of his associates accompanied him. Other floats, dressed like birds mostly, followed with images of Parmukh Swami's predecessors; they had been living incarnations of Sahjanand Swami in their time. I thought London was being given a *darshan* of the gods. A devotee corrected me: London was not getting to see the gods, the gods were getting to see London. The gods were being shown the city they were moving into. They would see London, and bless it.

Parmukh Swami later went to greater heights than Eros level at Piccadilly Circus to bless London. He took off in a white helicopter from the grounds of the Swaminarayan school next to the temple and showered petals on the city. On his return the Rolls that had driven him inside Piccadilly Circus took him from the school grounds to the temple. He entered the temple over an elaborately decorated pattern of fresh flowers, the *rangoli* assembled with painstaking labour, blessed to be scattered by his feet.

And did Parmukh Swami think he was God's messenger on earth? He has never said so. He speaks of himself only as the servant of Bhagwan Swaminarayan. To make the point, a miniature figure of Bhagwan Swaminarayan cast in spiritual-looking splendour on a little tray is carried by a sadhu before Parmukh Swami wherever he goes. The point is made simply and visibly; the two go together; you do not worship one without the other.

Parmukh Swami has been far from uncooperative with the eagerness to treat him as God, apparently unassuming as he is in his manner and in his language. The royal treatment is usually an idea of the godly and, on one of his birthdays, when he was visiting London, he appeared as holy royalty in a chariot pulled by devotees dressed in orange bridegroom-like uniforms. Other volunteers in blue and yellow ceremonial dress and turbans did the *garba* dance before the advancing chariot within the Neasden temple. Parmukh Swami did not appear an unwilling passenger.

His followers believe he is in exclusive communion with God. And he alone could consecrate the deities at the Neasden temple. He whispered words that only he could, to summon deities out of stone, to turn a building into a temple. With a brush dipped in honey he opened the eyes of the images to the devotees before them. He and he alone could talk to both God and man, and to women too; as long as they sat behind the men, and he could speak without looking.

Set away from the rest on stage amidst erected ideas of magnificence, Parmukh Swami speaks with unexpected simplicity. His words are recorded and sold at the temple bookstore in CDs and DVDs that each add to the spiritual heritage, and to a sense of Bhagwan Swaminarayan's godliness, and his own by association.

'Rushab Dev did well to give this teaching to his children. You have to learn seriously from this kind of teaching. Parents teach their children, guide them. If the child listens to them, the child does well. If the child does not follow their advice, the child becomes unhappy. But these days nobody likes to be told what to do. Today's children will say "nonsense". But our culture was that of the children of Rushab Dev. On his advice Bharat gave up his rule.' Simple stories, but it didn't really matter what he said; his words became divine in the listening if not the speaking.

To Hindus who've grown up with ideas of Ram and Krishna as the inevitable Hindu gods, Hinduism of the Swaminarayan kind is unacceptable, even upstart faith. Ram and Krishna are to them the timeless Hindu gods; they see the nineteenth-century preacher Sahjanand Swamy as too recent, among other things, to be considered God himself, as he is by his followers.

The layout of the gods within the Swaminarayan temple announces the differences, and if your beliefs are emphatic one way or the other, a civil war among Hindus, and even within the Swaminarayan faith.

A small figure of Ganesha, the bountiful god, stands to one side, across from Hanuman, Ram's powerful ally in the fight against the evil Raavan, each in tiny shrines of their own. Further ahead, and to a side again, the quite small Ram and Sita stand to the left, with Shankar, more familiar as Shiv, the god of destruction and consequently creation, with his companion Parvati facing them from the wall opposite. All these gods are situated as only the sideshow. No doubt non-Swaminarayan Hindus, and non-Hindus who visit the spectacular temple, are invited to believe that Bhagwan Swaminarayan is the real Bhagwan.

London is home to several other Swaminarayan splinters, since Parmukh Swami personifies Swaminarayan only to some Swaminarayans. Muktajivandas Swami started his own sect that came to be called the Swaminarayan Gadi. He came to London in 1970 and led a procession from Hyde Park to Trafalgar Square, much the route taken by the procession to mark the Neasden temple. The Parmukh Swami march was no doubt a statement also how much farther the Parmukh Swami people have gone down that path, how many more they are, how much more they have, and have built.

Another sect, the Muktajivan group, bought a church hall in Golders Green in 1981 but only a relatively small group gathers there now. The Amdavad group of the Swaminarayan faith back in India have their own temple in Willesden Green, through the autonomous Swaminarayan temple in Bhuj in Gujarat. This is not very far from the Neasden temple. Swaminarayan followers from Kutch in the north of Gujarat have their separate temple just off Kenton Road in north-west London, and early in 2007 another Swaminarayan temple came up in Stanmore.

At these other temples the Swaminarayans worship Bhagwan Swaminarayan directly, not through Parmukh Swami or anyone Parmukh-Swami-like. They believe Swaminarayan left no living lineage through which he may be manifest. But the followers who believe in that special spiritual relationship between Swaminarayan and Parmukh Swami have the more spectacular address. A good deal more money has gone into a belief that provides a god by your side who can talk to you. Access to God seems more comfortable through someone you could talk to.

With elections coming up, no one was surprised to see so many candidates queueing on stage for blessings from Swami Hariprasad, another god to another kind of Swaminarayans. If the British hope to contest elections from an Indian area, in time they would seek blessings from an Indian god.

Hariprasad's followers have nothing like the Parmukh Swami temple at Neasden, and they had hired Brent town hall to receive the swami's blessings. When enough Gujaratis have a statement to make, it will appear one day or other at Brent Town Hall. It's the Trafalgar Square of the London Gujarati. It's the place to show Indian commitment to a cause, to a party, to a belief. In one of its quieter statements, it's seen Indian gurudom grow, particularly in the early stages of a guru's visiting successes. When you don't have a temple for your guru, there's always Brent Town Hall. A drive to the hall is often local pilgrimage, and this was just one of several evenings where I had driven to Brent Temple.

The hall was divided into a front and a back half, men in front, naturally, since this was a Swaminarayan event. The safety rule on keeping aisles clear, observed usually quite firmly, had been broken by a large sofa chair placed in the aisle between the front rows. This was where Hariprasad swamiji would sit for some time in informal majesty before ascending the throne on stage.

What do you call those things if not thrones? To say chair, seat, sofa or such-like would be disrespectfully inadequate for that huge red and gold, yes, throne, set up on stage, with crimson cushions rising high around an expansively cushioned seat. A beige and red arch in Vedic looking papier mâché formed the backdrop. An image of Swaminarayan marked the focal point in the almost stage-size arch right above the throne. The throne, the sofa chair on the aisle before it, the rest of us in the packed hall, we were all waiting for Hariprasadji.

He wasn't late, the holy never are. All you can ever do is to blame organisers for inviting people early. But Satish Chatwani, the man responsible for bringing Hariprasadji there, was too rich to be blamed for anything. When someone with that many hotels keeps you waiting, it's his privilege and your problem.

'He is thirty million,' my neighbour whispered conspiratorially. Chatwani, that is. So many *The Sunday Times* millionaire lists later, the guessed wealth has come to be like a surname, because the rich simply are their money. Mittal two billion, Chatwani thirty million, never mind whether one has exactly those billions or the other just that many millions. But it was a lot anyway, and we couldn't complain about waiting, because he was rich and we were Indian. So we listened to the *bhajan* music setting the holy mood, and had neighbours around our seats tell us about others' neighbours on other seats while we waited for Chatwani. This was his show, his saint.

In time the VIP guests, a collection of local British politicians among them, were swiped off the front rows to receive Hariprasad swamiji at the entrance. A *dholak* beat led him in. He walked down the aisle, naturally between women on both sides at first, and naturally looking neither left nor right. At the end of that straight looking walk he sat down a minute on the aisle sofa, I had no idea why, before he ascended the stage.

Swamiji settled comfortably on his throne, elbows on cushions; he was familiar with elevated comforts, he'd been there before, much of his life really. He took off his turban – probably made with as much cloth as a Sikh turban, but flat as tarmac on top. A lesser swami who had followed him closely took charge of the turban and seated himself at Hariprasad's feet with gingerly reverence. He was the honoured slave, the proud shadow, blessed to be of service to God at such close range. Hariprasadji sat there surveying us, with a flower-like halo behind his now bare head.

Chatwani appeared in a dark safari suit to conduct the holy evening from a mike by the side of the throne. He clearly polished his good looks a great deal. He had a manner of speaking the Indian rich sometimes have; it's the tone of men with far more experience getting listened to than listening. He now introduced the god before us.

'Bhagwan Swaminarayan ensured the presence of a continued manifestation of the self, and therefore is ever present through a succession of God-related saints,' he said. 'He embodies the absolute spirit of God, and that becomes seemingly known in his behaviour, as you will see today. God is obedient to him, God moves as he wishes. He has conquered all stubbornness, envy, ego. Worship him, and god is worshipped. God cannot live without him. By his *darshan*, you have *darshan* of God.'

The white guests up front wore, I thought, that polite look that multiculturalism demands so often these days, though the look is a little more transparent than most white people think. Chatwani had promised *darshan*, and here it was, on offer now to male VIPs in the front rows. One by one they took the side steps to queue up on stage. Chatwani had a long male list to read out. Local MPs Tony McNulty and Barry Gardiner, then contesting Labour candidate for Brent East Robert Evans, members of the Hindu Council, businessmen, local councillors from Brent and Harrow. About fifty in all. We the rest had only distant *darshan* of Hariprasad and, in witnessing the queue, of the who's who of north-west London.

The rich queuing on stage stood to get richer. The MPs, or the aspiring MPs that all the councillors from Brent and Harrow were, looked blessed just to be seen to queue up by a thousand or so vote-carrying devotees. This kind of visibility was blessing enough for anyone in politics; anything divine would be a bonus. Blessings are always safe to go for, you never know which one might actually work.

Robert Evans was carefully introduced as a member of the European Parliament, and not the aspiring parliamentary candidate from Brent East that he then was. 'It's an enormous delight to have such a large audience,' Evans said. 'A rare privilege. I can't remember the last time I went to a meeting and people were standing on the side.' The spillover to the side after all the chairs had been taken must make a candidate's mouth water that much more. Evans made a grand show on stage of oneness with the devotee-voters. He bowed, knelt, folded his hands before swamiji, did about everything an official devotee of the swami would do. But he did not win the election.

The swamiji himself, 'the sadhu lost in love of God' as he was finally reintroduced, delivered a fairly earthly speech. About Nehru, Gandhi, about 132 pure saints in India and how 'not a fraction of a drop of their blood is impure.' Coming from God, it was pretty disappointing stuff. But it must be my fault for not thinking him God, and being therefore an unholy and inadequate listener.

The capacity to deliver speeches and to listen to them in at least outward patience must be the most travelling of Indian habits. Just when you think a speaker has run out of words, there are more, just when you think the event has run out of speakers, there are more. Here, the speeches lasted about three hours. Eventually the speakers to one side of the hall failed; the speakers couldn't take the speakers any more.

An Indian abroad is far more ready to receive God than the average Indian in India, Swami Satyanandmitra was saying. 'I could never have imagined this kind of popularity of our religion when I came here first in 1976,' he told me. He was on his annual visit to London, the visits having been at least annual since he set up his own centre in Harrow where the driving test centre used to be, just behind the civic centre.

Like Swami Hariprasad, Satyanandmitraji had a follower sitting on the floor by his side. Satyanandmitraji and I chatted at sofa level in the American-size house of a devotee in Pinner just north of Harrow. 'In 1976 I did not even think I would come here again and again,' he said. 'But people just began to say you must come every year.' Britain may or may not get an Indian summer, but it gets a more and more Hindu summer every year.

Swami Satyanandmitra, a comfortably elderly sadhu, lives mostly in Hardwar but has charitable institutions all around India and abroad. He had a devoted following in East Africa, and as they migrated to Britain, his summer flights changed path too. He likes this moneyed flock, he was saying, because their money makes them more religion-ready. 'This happens everywhere. As people progress economically, they begin to believe more and more in religion. In 1976 people had just come from Uganda and from other countries in Africa. They were busy just trying to get settled. In poverty, you see, people turn to religion out of fear. When you are well off then you make a proper choice. So it becomes important for good people to come here and give them direction.'

SUMMER GURUS

'So do rich Indians outside India become better Hindus?'

'It may be, because the conditions are such. People here are more dedicated. Either they don't want to know or, if they do, they want to take something good from it, they want some knowledge. Who was Ram, who was Krishna, who was Rana Pratap? Why do we keep pigtails, why do we ring bells, why do we go to a temple, why do we say "Om"? There's a lot of reasoning. In India nobody cares. Others are going, so we are going. It is herd instinct.'

'But is there such a difference between practising Hinduism in Britain and in India?'

'You see people here have fewer practical difficulties. Here you don't hear of corruption. You do not need to pay a bribe for a train reservation, for going to a hospital. This whole problem of bribes, this has really shaken the belief of people. As long as there is poverty and corruption in India, India cannot become a truly religious country. How much can you expect from a poor man? That he should be honest? When ministers get caught in corruption, he asks why should I alone remain honest?'

'So you need money and comforts for true religion.'

'Absolutely, you cannot do without that. You cannot be religious on an empty stomach. Ram and *roti* must go together.'

'But what is getting so many of the youngsters here so involved with Hinduism?'

'When people of other religions get aggressive about their religion, then the youths of other religions say we should also get assertive about our religion. So this is psychological. Christianity and Islam are spreading very fast on the basis of their money and their strength. So youths from other religions will want their own *utsav*, their *garba*, their *raas*, Janamashtami, Ram Navmi, anniversaries of their mahatmas. This is good, because it keeps the festivals going, and preserves our traditions.'

'So do we have other religions to thank for this new interest in Hinduism?'

'Youths see other religions. But when they see Hindu philosophy, it touches their hearts more. I do not criticise the philosophical background of other religions, but they do not have anything like yoga and meditation. When our youths sit for meditation, when they go for yoga, for vegetarianism, they find it is of great benefit. These things calm our minds, clear away our tensions. When we express faith in our God, in our religion, it cuts down our depression as well. So one says to another it has helped. These days no one will follow religion just for some later salvation, they want to see it doing some good for them here and now.'

Bedroom

And then there was the case of this guru.

Clearly, to the policewoman who took notes as the Gujarati woman spoke, this was just another case, this one recorded as a case alleging rape by a holy Indian.

This is most of what the policewoman recorded, barring the names of those concerned:

I am the above named person. I am a Hindu woman. I have been married for 23 years. We have three sons, aged 22, 15 and 13. We have another property on the same street and live within extended family.

Last year I came into contact with Gulabnath Bapu. I chose to have him as my guru. He has other followers in England. It is an honour to have Bapu stay at the house. He moves at various addresses during his stay in the UK. As guru he expects his followers to observe certain rules and they are as follows: 1) to be vegetarian, 2) not to drink alcohol, 3) not to see a person of opposite sex with bad intentions (commit adultery), 4) not to tell lies or steal.

Since meeting him for the first time around spring time last year I had met him personally again, worshipped him and abided by the rules set by him.

Around the beginning of May 2002 he had been staying somewhere nearby when my brother-in-law invited him to stay at our house which was considered a great honour for our family. Bapu accepted the invitation and came over to stay with us on 13 May 2002. During this time I acted as his *sevak*, which means taking care of his requirements – washing his clothes, preparing food for him. During his stay he had his own bedroom with one double bed, chest of drawers, a computer and a coffee table.

The house we live in is a three-storey house. On the first floor there is a bathroom and three bedrooms and one bedroom on the second floor. The bedroom I share with my husband is at the end of the hallway, next to it is a children's bedroom, next to that was Bapu's bedroom and adjacent to that was the bathroom.

I usually get up at about six o'clock in the morning and normally I am the first person to get up.

On Friday 17 May I got up and had a bath at around 6 a.m. When I came out of the bathroom Bapu opened his bedroom door, he was wearing a saffron coloured linen dhoti, and a tunic top, also in saffron colour. It is quite common for Bapu to wear saffron coloured clothing. I was wearing a full-length nightdress, a bra and no knickers, I was on my way back into my bedroom when Bapu's door opened. He put his arm around me and guided me back into his bedroom.

Once inside the bedroom he embraced me and kissed me on the lips, he did not use any force. I was very shocked at what he was doing. He sat me down on the edge of the bed and pushed me backwards so I was lying across the bed. My legs were hanging down beside the bed. He pulled my nightdress up using one of his hands and with the other he inserted his penis into my vagina. To do that he did not have to remove any of his clothes. He would have to just pull his clothes (dhoti) to either side to enable him to expose his genitals.

I felt like I had gone into a sort of trance. I felt I was not able to do anything. He was on top of me for about a minute. He then ejaculated inside me. He did not use any protection. Whilst he was on top of me with his penis inside me, he spoke quietly. He said the children must not wake up. He seemed anxious that I might make a noise and wake up other people in the house.

While this was happening I remained still and silent, I had my eyes closed, and I did not attempt to push him away. I was so shocked at what was happening.

The other people in the house at that time were my husband and two sons who were sleeping in our bedroom. In the bedroom next to Bapu's were two other boys. Upstairs on the second floor was my other son.

After Bapu had ejaculated, he withdrew his penis. I got up from the bed. I then straightened my nightdress and said to Bapu, 'I will get your coffee.' I went downstairs and cleaned my teeth in the kitchen as normal. I got Bapu's coffee and returned to his bedroom. I left the door open. Bapu was sitting on the bed. I put his coffee on the coffee table, I sat on the floor opposite Bapu about six feet away from him, I stared at him. He did not speak. I said, 'Who do I call my guru now?'

He replied that he was still my guru because when I chose him as my guru it meant I pledged my 'body', 'soul' and 'wealth' to him. I told him that my guru should not have done what you have just done. He further said that I should keep him in my heart and look upon him as being my guru. We sat there for about fifteen minutes whilst he had his coffee. I got up and went into the bathroom, washed myself and went into my bedroom where my husband and children were still asleep.

I felt a little bit discomfort on the outside of my vagina area where I applied Sudacrem. I got dressed for work and woke my husband up. By now it was about 7.30 a.m. My husband went into the bathroom and I went downstairs and had a cup of tea whilst he got ready. We left the house at around 7.45 a.m., my husband drove me to work, which is only about five minutes drive from my home address. As soon as I left the house I broke down and it was as if I had suddenly realised what had happened. I started crying. I could not stop and continued to cry throughout the journey to work. My husband asked me a number of times what the matter was, but I was not able to say anything.

Throughout the day I continued to cry at work and my colleagues asked me what was wrong. I did not tell anybody what had happened.

At about 5 p.m. on the same day my husband picked me up from work. He again asked me why I had been crying in the morning. I asked him to take me to the park near Waitrose. I did not want to go back to the house because there would be too many people there. My husband parked the car in the car park opposite the nursery. I told my husband that Bapu had raped me that morning, my husband did not believe me initially. I think the reason for not believing was because it was unbelievable that Bapu would do something like this. I suggested that we should inform my husband's elder brother.

I went back to my home address with my husband, he went into the house and returned with his brother. We all then went to the park. My husband informed him what had happened, he was very shocked and said now it had happened anyway, we shall have to deal with it as best we can handle. I was crying. It was decided that I would not be alone with Bapu at any time.

My husband's brother was concerned about other female members of the family and how they can be protected from Bapu. It was decided that my sister-in-law will attend to Bapu's needs along with her mother. By this time it was getting late and we were expecting a lot of people to arrive at our house at 9 p.m. The people were coming to our house to honour Bapu, pray and sing. During the evening we were all very busy with the guests and nothing more was discussed about the incident for the rest of the evening.

On Saturday I went to work at 8 a.m. At around 2 p.m. I telephoned a family friend. I asked him how I could get Bapu to leave without upsetting him as I was worried that he would curse me and the family. He assured me that Bapu would not do anything like that and nothing bad would happen if I asked him to leave. He did not ask what my reasons were for wanting him to leave.

I finished work at 4 p.m. and returned home. On the same day, Saturday, early evening, my sister-in-law asked me what the matter was as she felt something was not quite right. I told her what had happened on Friday morning with Bapu.

On Friday and Saturday night I slept at the other house a few doors away, so that I was away from Bapu.

On Sunday Bapu said he was going to stay at other follower's house where he wanted to be dropped off. He asked my husband and brother-in-law where he wanted to be dropped off. He asked that his clothes he had taken off that morning to be washed and forwarded to him at the address where he was staying.

After Sunday morning I did not see him or speak to him again. Sometime during the following week he telephoned our house and spoke to my sister-in-law. He asked why myself and my husband had been cold towards him. She pretended to know nothing about the reason. Bapu told her that my husband and I had asked him for £1,000 and that he had refused. He also told her not to mention that telephone conversation to anyone including her husband. She went straight to her husband and told him about the telephone call. I can say that neither my husband nor I have ever asked for any money from Bapu.

On 26 May 2002 a friend came to visit someone we know. He informed that friend about what had happened to me with Bapu. At that time it was disclosed that his 12-year-old daughter had made an allegation that Bapu had sexually assaulted her. We discussed everything and my husband and I decided that Bapu must not get away with what he was doing, that is the reason for us to come to the police station today to report it.

Since the rape I have had sexual intercourse with my husband every night since Monday 20 May to 26 May 2002. This is normal sexual activities for me and my husband. I did not have sex on Friday 17 May and Saturday 18 May and Sunday 19 May 2002 because Friday was the day of rape and Saturday I slept at the other house. On Sunday I chose not to have sex. Since the rape I have not experienced any discomfort during sexual intercourse with my husband. We do not use any protection when I have sexual intercourse with my husband as I have had a coil fitted.

After the rape I have washed all the clothing I was wearing and the bedding from Bapu's bed has been washed too.

It has been over a week since the rape but I still feel anger within. If he came in front of me I feel like killing him. I will attend court to give evidence if required.

She did. When the case came to trial, the jury ruled that Bapu was not guilty of rape. All eyes in the court room were on him as he walked up to his solicitor. He took off his his garland of holy beads and put it around him. Who could have done more for him?

LONDON LEATHER

Red Caps

No shop looks like it can sell a new religion, but Ravi Trimmings, Gurdev Das Luggah's thread-and-buttons store on Katherine Road in East London was about the unlikeliest of the lot.

Luggah, tall, dark and with suggestions of a handsome past, looked the failed fighter. He was talking thread with a customer in a hijab as I stepped in. He nodded in my direction, and I waited. Threads out of the way, he would tell me about the new holy book he had prepared for the Ravidassias.

The Ravidassias, many of them Punjabis, I had just discovered to be families caste-bound to work with leather and animal hides, which meant usually the shoemaking profession. This was seen as dirty work, and those who did it unclean; they became untouchable to Hindus who would never handle leather this way – they were born, they believe, for higher things. For that work with *chamra*, leather, they had come through abusive association over centuries to be called the *chamaars*.

Over the years, the people marked out as *chamaars* struggled to find another name for themselves that wouldn't carry abusive associations. A consensus formed over the name Ravidassias, from Ravi Das, a fourteenth-century preacher who was a shoemaker by profession, and so also derided as *chamaar*. But he was also revered as preacher, and so became a model of acceptability. In naming themselves after him, the *chamaars* would now be defined self-respectfully by their own, not abusively by others.

The Ravidassias had found a foothold in the Sikh holy book, the Guru Granth Sahib, by way of some verses of Guru Ravi Das included among thousands of others. On that inclusion those abused as *chamaars* hung hopes of their own elevation. If the Guru Granth Sahib could find room for those verses from Guru Ravi Das, surely Sikh society too could find a place as Ravidassias for those stigmatised as *chamaars*? Or so the Ravidassias thought.

Trouble arose with the very title: was he 'Guru' Ravi Das or not? To his followers he was, but he is not counted among the ten Sikh gurus. The Sikhs therefore consider him a *bhagat*, a devotee, and deny him the title of guru.

Luggah had decided to fix this problem in his own way. Guru Ravi Das had written very much more than the few verses included in the Guru Granth Sahib. Rather than place a magnifying lens over those few to proclaim acceptability, Luggah had compiled all the verses by Ravi Das he could find into a separate holy book for the Ravidassias. He had introduced this as the book of worship – alongside the Guru Granth Sahib – at the Ravidassia centre on Carlyle Road in East London. Here Ravidassias listened to recitals wearing red caps, to mark themselves as followers of the new book. Luggah was building up the exclusiveness of the excluded, and he wanted it to show.

Customer-free finally, Luggah led me to the office at the back of the shop, a darkish retreat from the front counter. He positioned himself to keep an eye out for customers, and I took a small, straight chair across from a mountain of buttons. They were a pink that made me nervous. I was thinking what London might look like if these buttons attached themselves to cloth and went public; it's usually too unadventurous for that kind of pink.

'I was the first cloth manufacturer in this whole area,' he said, after taking a phone call in a Punjabi untouched by Britain. 'I was also the first wholesaler in this whole area.' But the first decent turnover of buttons in a certain part of London, and a deceased manufacturing business, were not the firsts he really wanted to boast. Anyone can sell buttons, not everyone can put together a brand new holy book for a new religion. He left buttons behind and turned to the book.

'It took me twenty-two years to put the new holy book together,' he said. 'I began work on it in 1965 after coming here from Jalandhar in 1963.' He paused and then reached out to a filing cabinet by the table to pull out the result of his efforts, a Bible-sized book wrapped in red cloth within a polythene wrap. Luggah removed the wrapping reverentially. The title read: *Shri Guru Sikhya Sahib*.

'The Guru Granth Sahib has only forty *shlokas* of Guru Ravi Das ji Maharaj. This one,' he said, raising it a respectful few inches towards his forehead, 'has more than one thousand two hundred.'

'Where did you get the material?'

'Every year I went back to India to collect material. Every time I found new books on Guru Ravi Das ji Maharaj, new literature. I wrote letters, I was interviewing people. If I found material, I wanted it all.'

'And how did you find the time?'

'I did most of the work when I was working in a rubber factory in London, in my first fifteen years in London.'

'But did no one else try to do this in India?'

'Yes, Sant Hira Das, he is from Phagwara, he has made a place there. He wrote *Ravi Das Deep*, that is pure history. I got that, then I researched it and put it into the form of *shlokas*. Then I developed it into *bani*, in the music of the ragas, in the way

309

of the *bani* of the Guru Granth Sahib.' So the text was in the form of religious verse, the *shlokas*, and the manner of recital the *bani*, as with the Guru Granth Sahib.

'And you have read the Guru Granth Sahib?'

'Oh yes, for thirty-four years I used to read from Guru Granth Sahib as a priest. It is a great work. We have no quarrel with it. All we are saying is that now we have our own separate book of the teachings of Guru Ravi Das ji Maharaj. Let them follow their book, we will follow our book.'

'And when did you publish the book?'

'I completed the study in 1987. Then I placed it before the committee at the temple on Carlyle Road, I mean the good ones among them. These were from the Ravidassia Sartaj Committee UK at the temple – all sensible people, intellectuals, thinkers. So the committee had the book printed in 1991–92. So now we have a book.'

'What will you do with it?'

'Our people will know now that they are Ravidassias.'

'But they were Ravidassias before.'

'But because they believed in the Guru Granth Sahib they were seen as Sikhs.'

'Why do Ravidassias want to be separate at all?'

'You must hear sometimes what they call us. They call us *chamaar*, *choora*, *nai*.' Shoemaker, sweeper, barber… caste professions that became words of abuse.

'Why do your group always wear red caps?'

'Guru Ravi Das himself had said that our colour must be *majeethia* – red – and so we had the red caps.'

The airman style red caps I saw at the Ravidassia centre on Carlyle Road were the more colourful part of a whole new set of rituals. *Bhajans* composed for the new religion played out loud in the prayer hall, some to the tune of familiar film songs. Ravidassia men were here called 'Chaudhary' and the women 'Chaudharain'. The congregation at Carlyle Road was required to place a statue of Guru Ravi Das at the head of the hall. There wasn't a statue yet, so they were using a portrait of Guru Ravi Das instead.

But these rituals were to be seen only at this Ravidassia centre among the many in Britain. Enough Ravidassias had migrated to Britain from Punjab, and done well enough to set up several centres of their own. The biggest by far is in Birmingham, down Soho Road in Handsworth. Another big centre is the one down Western Avenue in Southall. The Ravidassias had set up more than twenty centres all over Europe, one now in Rome, and another in Paris. But these centres all had the Guru Granth Sahib as their only holy book, though some rituals were distinct from Sikh rituals.

Prayers in this form continued for some time at the Carlyle Road centre. But a religion that required you to walk around in red caps did not go down very well in that part of East London, even if most followers would take their caps off before stepping onto Carlyle Road itself or on to the busy Romford Road to the side. They wouldn't work either as style or as religious announcement. Attendance at the centre declined. Many Ravidassias who were regulars at the centre took up other premises to meet and pray – with the Guru Granth Sahib as the holy book, rather than Luggah's compilation. Legal disputes followed. Eventually the Luggah group lost control of the centre after a court order.

Luggah made enemies at least partly because he declared himself a *sant*. In a booklet circulated to promote his new religion, he spoke of himself as 'Sant Gurudev Dass Luggah'.

'How did you come to call yourself a *sant*?' I asked.

'You see "*sant*" is not a proper word. We don't have a proper word so far for people who conduct prayers. Hindus say *pujari*, Sikhs say *giani*. I am just a simple man. I am not here to sit on chairs and have my picture taken. But who is a *sant*? Sometimes a *sant* was just a beggar. Sometimes they were people who were worshipped. Some were *sants* because they were lost in their own world. There are different types of *sants*. We say *sant* because we have no real name yet for a preacher.'

This was heretical to Sikhs, and unacceptable to most Ravidassias. More than the Sikhs, Luggah felt betrayed by the other Ravidassias. 'They know nothing about the Ravidassia mission. They follow a different type of policy, and they made themselves the majority. They wanted to have the Guru Granth Sahib back in the prayer hall. They did a propaganda against us. They wanted committee by election. We said we will have committee by selection because that is our constitution. You tell me, religion is always by preaching by the learned. It is not by vote. Religion is not a parliament. We said we will not allow vote. They took us to court.' That ended the Red Cap reign at the Carlyle Road centre. Now Luggah's group meets at rented premises in the neighbourhood.

Carlyle Road was blocked up ahead by a white limousine. But I found some reluctant respect for the driver who had brought it down a road where mere normal cars struggle to squeeze through the parking on both sides.

The limo had stopped outside the Shri Guru Ravidassia hall and released a very Bangladeshi bride in the company of bridesmaids who shone only a few sequins less than her in the bright afternoon sun. The wedding guests were headed for the Ravidassia hall, by the side of the Ravidassia centre.

Like the limo, the Ravidassia centre stood out, this one a distinct pink amidst the usual red-brick look of a British suburban street. It was the pink of one of Luggah's buttons over the facade. Painted perhaps during the days of the Red Caps.

I stepped past groups of young Bangladeshis who had taken hands-in-pocket position outside; if you're male, young and cool, you don't walk into wedding halls with your family. I was going to the centre to meet Bali, a member of the new committee at the Carlyle Road centre. The Luggah group had by now been ousted, and the Guru Granth Sahib no more had the company of Luggah's holy book in the prayer hall.

I ran into Bali at the entrance. 'These are Bangladeshis, you know,' he said with a glance towards the outside. 'Most of the people who rent our hall are Bangladeshis. We hardly have Indians hiring our hall. They have too much money.' Also, for too many Indians, this would be the hall of the untouchables.

I followed Bali into a sitting room that looked more like a storeroom at the back of the centre. He was balding in a sporty sort of way and said everything with passion. 'You should hear the way some of them say "Ravidassia",' he said as we sat down. 'They say it like we are *chamaars*.' That of course was always going to be the problem; people would just translate Ravidassia into *chamaar*. You'd be Ravidassia to yourself, but *chamaar* to others.

'Look at us here. We are the Ravidassia gurdwara. Isn't it strange that believing in the same book, reading from the same book, we should have separate gurdwaras? These white people, they may be English or Welsh or Irish, who cares, they can go to the same church. But we people, we unravel identities like you peel onions.'

Bali ran his mind over all the gurdwaras in the neighbourhood he does not go to. The gurdwaras, as the temples of the Sikhs, were meant like Sikhism itself to have evolved away from the Hindu caste system. But Bali was drawing a caste map of gurdwaras. 'There is the one in Barking, ninety-five per cent Jats, there is Rosebury gurdwara, one at Goodmayes, the Santan da gurdwara, the one on Neville Road – they are the carpenters, you know – and the Upton Lane gurdwara, the Namdharis. But you see if you have caste-based gurdwaras, then Sikhism is not the same any more. The spirit of Guru Nanak's message, it is all gone.'

The Ravidassias were separate from the Sikhs, but that didn't make the Sikhs all one. The Jats from the farming background traditionally go to their chosen gurdwaras. The Ramgarhias, mainly carpenters but also others like blacksmiths and masons, have their separate gurdwaras. So do the Namdharis, who believe Guru Gobind Singh was not the last of the Sikh gurus but was followed by a succession of living gurus – this lot was separated by belief more than caste. Bali doesn't go to any of these gurdwaras and they certainly will not come to this one.

'If all are equal, why do you have community-based gurdwaras?' he went on. 'The Ravidassias, the people in the leather trade, were a depressed, downtrodden people in India. We were looked down upon by the Jat Sikhs. And here same thing goes on. When they need donations to set up a gurdwara, they take from all of us. When it is established, they say, "Why are you here?"'

He was talking a little like Luggah here. They had both seen and suffered the same attitude but they believed in different ways of dealing with it. Bali thought the problem with the Sikhs no reason to distance himself from the holy book, the Guru Granth Sahib.

'The Guru Granth Sahib has been around for four or five hundred years. And our guru is also in it. We could not have the book written by Luggah in its place. So we got hold of the Guru Granth and we removed the other book. You see, whatever the logic of the new book, there was never any spiritual attraction to it. A religious book, it needs large numbers of people with it. It needs time. It needs history. And what did we have? One book published by one man with some approval from a few more. But most people were not interested, they just did not want to bow before it. You see, it had no roots.'

But it did have roots, I argued. It had the verses from Guru Ravidassia, it had brought together other compilations, it had brought together other teachings of Guru Ravidassia. Why was that not good enough?

'Because there is no suffering behind it,' Bali said. 'A religion needs suffering. Think of the suffering of the fifth Guru. Sikhism really picked up only after that. And after that also it took a few centuries to develop. You cannot win respect, you cannot win following unless you have suffered. You cannot just make a religion in a drawing room.'

Luggah had laboured for 23 years, but he had not suffered. An annual flight to Delhi did not add up to suffering. Or even the painstaking compilation of teachings, and then adapting them to the style of the Guru Granth Sahib. If this was scholarship, then scholarship can still only produce a book, not a holy book.

'We do not say that is a bad book. But read that book at home, read it from another platform. Not where Guru Granth Sahib is kept. Tell me, could you replace the Ramayana by just something else? It is most difficult to get people together over something like this.'

Partition

Gianiji ran into the old divisions soon, he said, after arriving in Britain. Enough Sikhs had come in before him to set up a gurdwara at Shepherd's Bush. A Sikh Cultural Society was also in place at the gurdwara. Everyone went there, and so did Gianiji – for a while. 'Then some things started happening that were not right. The same old things. We did not think they would happen in London.'

We were sitting, six or seven of us, around Gianiji in the little library-office at the Ravidassia Bhavan in Southall, their religious and community centre. The others around the table were all Ravidassias; they knew the stories, they'd heard them, told them, over years. Now everyone was gathered to listen, and tell, again.

The prayers upstairs were done, we'd had our tea and pakoras in the *langar* hall, the food hall next door. It was only late Sunday morning; home and lunch were far, and a bore, and this was talk-time. The library, a cheerful, many-sided little room with windows all around, was just the place for a chat like this.

'What we wanted did not happen, what we did not want started to happen,' Gianiji said. As Gianiji, the learned one, his beard was necessarily long and pointed, but it stood out the more because he was otherwise a diminutive man. He had just begun to speak but others joined in, like many voices with one memory. Everyone had much to say, because what did happen was not one thing but one thing after another. The past came crowding in on us around the table.

The togetherness at Shepherd's Bush did not last long, they were saying. That gurdwara was quite far from Southall. In the early sixties, they began to meet at a home-gurdwara at 11 Beaconsfield Road in Southall. Then they built a small gurdwara at The Green. And then, finally, the gurdwara at Havelock Road, now rebuilt into a spectacular structure.

'We all used to go to Beaconsfield Road, then The Green, then Havelock Road.' This was the stocky man who sat to my right; he ran a shop in Southall. Getting everyone's name was not necessary, I'd been told, and I didn't push. Names were a sensitive matter here, I discovered later. 'But you see, in the *prabandhak* committee of that gurdwara, they started developing an attitude. When anyone from the Ravidassia community would have a wedding, they would make one kind of arrangement. When it was someone from the Jat community, it would be another kind of arrangement. And it was something else for the Ramgarhias.

'Those members from the prabandhak committee, they told us if you are not satisfied, go and build your own gurdwara. They told Ramgarhias same thing. So the Ramgarhias bought a laundry on Oswald Road and made their own gurdwara there. We were also being treated badly. And that is why the other gurdwaras came up. That is why you have now separate gurdwara for Jats in Southall, separate for Ramgarhias, and now we have our own.'

It was the Jats who were responsible, said the frail and elderly man from the far end of the table, his face creased with long bitterness. 'You see, they would not let any of us join the executive committee. We felt the need for something of our own.' So rebellion rose within the Sikh Cultural Society, with Gianiji in the forefront. 'I said to our people, if they cannot include us with any honour and respect, then let us quit. Some people stopped going to the gurdwara. If they wanted help to do a wedding, I was there for them; we used to do it somewhere else.'

'When our numbers were small, our difficulties were less,' said a man opposite, much the old-fashioned gentleman in a tie. 'We had small jobs, very little money. When more and more people came, the numbers grew, the needs became greater. People started thinking of other things. That was the problem, when you come from one society, one country, and still people are not treated like equal.'

They never were equal in India, and the time had come to be not equal in Britain. It had to happen, the shop owner said. 'We came from the same land, from the same culture, how could we change suddenly? Today so many years later we are still back there, if you ask me. You think it is any different now? Where are they sitting and where are we sitting? We always think of background, this one here, that one there, nothing can stop it. Same thing is happening today, never mind if people are educated and living in England.'

I asked if it was any particular incident that had turned them away from the gurdwara at Havelock Road. 'Oh yes,' he said, in a voice that seemed to come from the past. 'I remember that day, it was so cold. There was so much snow. I had taken my family to the gurdwara at Havelock Road, it was the birthday of Guru Ravi Das ji Maharaj. But what did I see in the gurdwara? Nothing. They had done nothing for our guru's birthday. That was the day that ignited everything for us, that was the day that we said we have to have our own separate organisation, our own separate place. We raised money and we bought 25 Park Avenue, which is a bungalow. There were some restrictions, but it was all right, it was a stepping stone to this place we have now.'

There was silence. Everyone seemed to be thinking of that turning point, that turning away point. It was also the beginning of a coming together, away from the others. At the bungalow meetings they raised funds to buy a scouts' hut, which they built into this bhavan.

But it seemed obvious that their assertion of independence had brought confirmation of the very separateness they had been fighting and, who knows, fleeing. They weren't now being pushed out of the mainstream of Punjabi life, they were edging away on their own. Guru Ravi Das had moved towards inclusion, his followers were now inviting exclusion. Surely, the minute you turned into the Ravidassia Bhavan from Western Avenue, you marked yourself by your caste? I shared these thoughts, with some hesitation. Didn't they want to be included in the larger society rather than stand away as Ravidassias?

'Let me tell you,' said the gentleman across the table. 'Yes, that is how it should be. But we have not reached that point yet. We don't know when we will reach it. That may come, that may come, that may come, but we don't see it yet, it is far beyond our sight.' He didn't sound like he thought it would come, ever.

'I will tell you how this happened,' he continued. 'It was thrust upon us. It is still thrust upon us. You ask me about my caste, I tell you I don't give a damn about the caste system. I don't know why people cling to it. But what to do? We said, all right, if this is going to be thrust upon us, then let us become somebody. Let us get united, let us show these people, that all right, you have thrown us on the scrap heap, now we are going to show you that we are human beings, we have the brains, we have the education, we have the organisational skills, we can promote our society in such a way that it can stand up, you know, in the whole system of this country.'

'But when you set up as a different group, you only stand out,' I repeated.

'It has given us a sense of pride, of achievement. Because we are telling our brothers that, look, you cannot just throw us on the scrap heap, you cannot just throw us on the rubbish heap. We are human beings, we are a part of your society, we want to have the same honour, same respect, same place in the society, and we are trying to become capable of it.'

'You mean six hundred years after Guru Ravi Das, you are fighting the same battle, here in London?'

'This is what I call enigma. See? Enigma. Even after proven things, even after Guru Ravi Das proved this wrong, our society clings to it. Why? I don't know.'

The youngest member of our group, so far about the quietest, now loosened his scarf and spoke up. 'It is like being British,' he said. 'You think just having a British passport makes me British? No matter if you are first generation or third generation, whatever generation, you can have a British passport, European passport, but that does not make you British, it does not make you European.' That too was a caste-like system, he was saying, that no Indian could change. He was a man straddling two caste systems.

'You see, here I have my brown colour. And discrimination is here just like there is in the caste system. You will always be portrayed under this Asian banner. But when I am Ravidassia, I am not just Asian. At least I know who I am. And my children, born here, they all have British passports, but they do not think they are British. And I do not expect some British person, some English person to classify me as British just because I have a British passport. So I have to know who I am because I cannot be British and I cannot only be Asian. I must know where I belong, where my ancestors come from.'

'And have you told your children this?'

'Basically I bring them to the gurdwara, I have educated them who their guru is, what our guru's teachings are, what caste we are, it is very important to be a member of this community, so that I know which community and which caste I belong to, so that I can portray the same benefit and the same identity to my children. So I have told them where they belong and which is their caste.'

'But what is all this about which caste anyone comes from? Can't you just forget it and move on? Just be, you know, just people.'

The shop owner to my right spoke to me with the deliberate kindness reserved for the naïve. 'You know something, if we had let them put us where they wanted, if we had been scared of them, if we had agreed to some of the things they wanted, our identity would have been finished. From being in a situation where we were told you can't do this and can't do that, we are in a stage where we can stay in our own community, our strength is intact. They respect strength, I tell you. Now those very people who never used to care about us, now they come and consult us on some things. Because we are come to foreign land, they say we can deal with some things if we are one. So today we have own voice, own strength. Why? You think their thinking has changed? No. Because we have maintained our identity. If we had remained the way we were, we would not have been valued.'

The others might hear in Ravidassia only a new name for the old. But the Ravidassias were re-creating themselves to themselves, overwriting stigma with independence. Their breaking away from the old Southall gurdwara to set up their own bhavan became for them an opportunity for a new self-acceptance.

Views on this were piling fast onto the table now. A turbaned Ravidassia – he must think himself Sikh as well – who had joined us a little later, said separateness was wonderful, because memories of togetherness were painful. 'You know, I was a student of DAV College, Jalandhar. And what did I see? At the shop they would leave the change on the counter. They would not give it to me because he might touch my hand, because I am untouchable.' From being untouchable in the wider world, as the *chamaars* were thought to be, it was far better to have a world of your own where no one was untouchable to anyone else. I was a little surprised at myself for figuring out this late that morning that I was sitting with people who were considered by so many to be untouchables.

'Nobody says we will not touch you because you are untouchable, but the attitude, it just showed in their attitude,' a sober and grandfatherly looking man joined in to say. 'They thought they were the highest, they show it, you can feel it, you can go anywhere but you feel it, the attitude is there, that we are the untouchables.'

A solicitor, the youngest in the group, young enough for denims and a hint of the Southall Jamaican accent, brought up memories of growing up in his village in Punjab. 'The shopkeeper in our village, he was a Brahmin, and when I went to give him ten paisa, he would move his hand away if we ever tried to put it in his hand. There was a tin next to him, we would have to put the money on the tin, and he used to pick up the money from the tin, and then he used to wipe the tin because it had been touched by a Shudra, because I am of the lowest caste, you see. That's something that really sticks in my mind.'

BRIDELESS IN WEMBLEY

The turbaned Ravidassia recalled those days like they were yesterday. 'The difficulties I faced in society, I do not forget. I only used to ask a question, I am human being like any other, I belong to same society, brought up in same environment, in the same place, why the hell I am looked down upon? Why hurdles are put in my way for human achievements in society. I have right to education, I have right to form an association, I have rights which are rights declared fundamental rights of human being. Why those rights are denied to me? It is a funny old world.

'And when I came here same things happened. Now by inventing our organisation we have achieved one thing. We move freely with one another, nobody looks down on anyone. And we have removed that inferiority complex, we have placed our people at par with others. We should not have to do this. But this is the way the world is, the way it works, our society works.'

The solicitor narrated a story of a Sikh woman and her Ravidassia husband who split up after 20 years of marriage. 'After all this time she turns around and tells him to get lost, she says I don't want anything to do with a Ravidassian, I don't want anything to do with a *chamaar*, to put it bluntly. This is after twenty odd years or so. And her son, her son refuses to accept him as the father because he says I cannot possibly be a *chamaar*'s son.'

There was power in these stories because the characters, the experiences seemed interchangeable – he today, me tomorrow, it was him, it could have been me. Every individual's story became the story of a community, a collective experience lodged into group memory.

This was only one side of the divorce story, but that was not the issue here, the telling of it was, because it spoke of a way of living where the distant and the merely possible begin to feel actual. At meeting after meeting, in conversation after conversation with Ravidassias in Southall, in Bedford, in East London, Birmingham, I heard much the same story again.

'Tell me, do you know who your father is?' Gianiji, who had been quiet for a while, asked me. He was answering my question about forgetting Ravidassia roots and moving on. 'Every child grows up and asks, who is my father? The mother will have to tell the child who the father is. So in our birth we know who we are. For all of us together, who is our father? Always somebody from one caste. And you know they always ask when the children have grown up. They always ask when it is time to marry. Who is the father?'

It had to be this, finally. That you don't have the option to stop being Ravidassia. You might just get away with it at a school among very different others. But marriages between Ravidassias and Jats or Ramgarhias would be impossible to arrange. Take away the odd love story between some Ravidassia and non-Ravidassia, and the rest just had to look to marry within the caste. Whether this group, any group, exists at all, will depend on how many marriages take place within it.

'But are most marriages taking place within the community?'

'Yes, at least eighty per cent,' someone at the table said.

'It must be ninety-nine per cent,' came another voice.

'No it is one hundred per cent,' said the gentleman-looking man. 'You see, that is why we need the centre, that is why we need the hall here. It is not just for birthdays and festivals, all our weddings take place here.'

'You should have seen the weddings at the Havelock Road gurdwara,' the shop owner said. 'If we could not celebrate the birthday of Guru Ravi Das ji there, you think they would let us have the wedding the way we like? There was one, I remember, and they were in such a hurry, and they spoke so fast that no one could understand what they were saying. Tell me, marriage is a big thing, you would like someone in your family to be married like that?'

'If they had not treated us badly,' the gentleman said, 'maybe we would not have felt the need to build one, the Ramgarhias would not have felt the need to build their own gurdwara. But now we have a centre point, for all our gatherings, for our weddings. And now this place, this hall here, is just not enough for our needs. And you know, that attitude of theirs, that attitude was the foundation stone for our gurdwara.'

It was uneasy triumph. Because everyone at the table knew it was a pity that it had been necessary in the first place. The final triumph could only be the demolition of what they had created because one day nobody would notice a need for such separation.

Barker Shoes

A shoe can carry so much more than the person in it. Just about everything the Ravidassias were facing really came down to shoes. Only Indians get that way about shoes, leather shoes anyway. A shoe is by now not just footwear, it's a metaphor for hurting by humiliating.

When Sikh religious leaders at the Akal Takht have wanted to punish a Sikh for straying from the Sikh path, they have ordered him to clean shoes, and to be seen to do so before cameras to heap on the humiliation. Punjabi abuse is rich with shoes. The contempt for *chamaars* must go back at least as far as that tradition of leaving shoes outside temples, and later gurdwaras.

England looks at its shoes differently. So did a Punjabi friend managing the factory for Barker Shoes in Earls Barton village who I'd looked in to see after a meeting with a group of Ravidassias in Bedford. My friend was no Ravidassia, this was a modern-day acquisition. An Indian company had taken over the old British shoe firm. The factory was closed for the day, but he took me through their website.

Like Guru Ravi Das, the nineteenth-century Englishman Arthur Barker spent a good deal of his life making shoes. Their written stories on offer on the website began somewhat the same way, too. 'Guru Ravi Das was born in a humble family...' And from Barker Shoes, 'The foundation stone of the Barker brand was laid in a humble cottage in the heart of England's shoe manufacturing industry in 1880, by an enterprising Northamptonshire bootmaker.' The similarities ended of course at the beginning. It was possible in England not to be ashamed of the leather link. Barker did not start off a new religion, among other things he probably didn't need to.

I read through the Barker boast. 'Arthur Barker was a skilled craftsman and natural innovator... Barker invested in factory premises at the turn of the century, later securing contracts to supply the British army with boots during the World War One... the Barker brand went from strength to strength as Arthur's three sons joined the family business, taking the brand into new markets and territories... For over a century, the Barker brand name has epitomised fine quality English footwear... with each pair individually hand-cut and matched from the finest leathers.'

Arthur's three sons were born into the leather business and proudly took it further, but an inheritance that could be a matter of pride in one country was cause for shame in the other. Most Ravidassias who migrated to Britain have nothing to do with leather, but they are still fighting off that *'chamaar'* label.

I'd driven on to Earls Barton after an evening with Des Raj Mehmi's family in Bedford. I'd heard that Bedford too had seen a Southall kind of partition between the Ravidassias and the Sikhs, and that this was a caste issue and not another of those quarrels mandatory in Indian organisations.

Des Raj Mehmi had other matters on his mind when I turned up. The Ravidassias were angry, he said, over the incident at Talhan in Punjab where a portrait of Guru Ravi Das was said to have been torn down by some Jat Sikhs during a quarrel. Ravidassia and Sikh groups had fought, the police were called in, and a Ravidassia, Vijay Kumar, died in police firing. Mehmi had led a Ravidassia protest outside the Indian High Commission in London. A memorandum was handed over to the Indian High Commission, and he showed me a copy. 'The Jats refused to sell milk to them, engage them for work in their fields, prevent them from easing in the fields, normal practice in villages, and forcing them to defecate in public by the side of the village roads,' the protest letter said.

Mehmi and I had met at a petrol station by the outskirts of tiny Kempston and I'd followed his gold-coloured Mercedes home. Another car carrying his friends and relatives followed me, and our little Ravidassia motorcade made it soon enough despite the unexpectedly heavy traffic the little town outside Bedford had managed to produce. We added up to quite a meeting in the drawing room, largely on the strength of a joint family. 'The Mehmi family, you see,' Mehmi said, 'is quite something.' Through the evening the Mehmi wives brought us Coke, biscuits, tea, pakoras, Bombay mix, salad, beer, whisky, dal, chappati, pulao, alu, raita, chicken curry. Nothing special. In a Punjabi household all this is the gastronomic equivalent of breathing normally.

Only, the conversation was not normal. Talhan was the trigger. It linked past with present, and Jalandhar with London and Bedford. The Talhan incident had become only a more extreme extension of the experiences of British Ravidassias with Jat Sikhs in Britain. Exclusion was the painful commonality. The story of Guru Ravi Das himself, those memories of growing up in India as marked people, the disputes with the Sikh gurdwara management in London in the sixties, now the tearing down of a portrait of Guru Ravi Das by Jats in Talhan, it all felt like a single unbroken experience, always waiting to happen before it actually did.

Before anyone knew it, we'd moved from the troubles in Talhan to those in Bedford, and from those of migrants to those of British-born children.

A young turbaned Ravidassia said his son had come home with stories, so it was not just the elders. 'These boys were getting together, they had made some kebabs, and the sauce was in one plate. Then someone said he is a *chamaar*'s son, get him another plate for the sauce. But good thing the host said no, he said we are all one, either we eat from the same plate or we don't eat.'

The parents around the room all said their children brought home similar stories. 'The children come home and say they are teased, they are called *chamaars*, they are humiliated,' Des Raj said. 'What do we explain, what do we say? They ask us that we believe in the same book, why we go to separate gurdwaras? What do we tell them? They ask us, who are we? My kids have asked me that. They say, daddy, what's wrong with us? Why are we untouchable? My boy, he says to me I am smart, I am young, I am well-spoken, I have a smart car. Why am I untouchable? He says the whites never say that to us. What do I tell him?'

Here in Bedford, as in Southall, no one thought it would come to this when they landed. The early migrants all got together to set up a single gurdwara at Queen's Park. And then came the attitudes, and the inevitable split: the Ravidassias their way, the Ramgarhias theirs, away from the Jats.

'We wrote a letter to the Ramgarhia gurdwara and to the Queen's Park gurdwara that we are taking out a Nagar Kirtan [holy procession] on the birthday of Guru Ravi Das ji,' Mehmi said. 'The Ramgarhia people said all right, no problem. Queen's Park also said welcome. When we took out the procession they gave us respect.' This sounded fine, but there had to be a but. 'They wrote back to us, and they called us "Ravi Das Bhavan". You see, they never write to us with the proper name of our bhavan, which is Shri Guru Ravi Das Bhavan. They will not speak of Guru Ravi Das ji as guru, or even as a *bhagat*. They just wrote, Ravi Das Bhavan. There is no respect in this.'

Dinner was now being served, but with bitterness in the air. 'Do you see what this means?' said Mehmi. 'They have accepted white people, they have accepted black people, but not their own people. To white people they will say "Mister", they will say "Sir", but they cannot show respect to a guru of their own people, whose teachings are included in their holy book. We fought against the British, Shaheed Bhagat Singh was from our same land, Shaheed Udham Singh was from our land. And they can show respect to those people who our people fought against, but not to us.'

Sikhs accept white people more than fellow Punjabis even when it comes to marriage, Mehmi said. 'It is all right for a girl from a Jat family to marry a white person but not one of us.'

Sikh-Ravidassia marriages were said to have had hellish consequences. 'It happened recently,' said Mehmi's wife, who had come in to take a break from the demands of the kitchen. 'This boy, one of our boys, such a good job in the railways, he married this Jat Sikh girl who was already divorced and had a child also. But the girl's *bhua* refused to come for the marriage, and so no other member from the family came. And the girl's side never gave a party for the marriage, the boy side had to do the party.'

The marriages that have taken place between the two communities have rarely succeeded, Mehmi said. 'The couple have always suffered, because the other family can never stop thinking of the boy or girl as a *chamaar*. And this is England in the twenty-first century. This is what we are dealing with.'

Name and Shame

'What is a *chamaar*?' I asked a 15-year-old girl at the Ravidassia Bhavan in Southall.

'Some people who are Sikh,' she said, 'they classify *chamaar* as a very low caste. But I don't believe that, because if you're in Britain everyone's the same caste, unless you're rich or whatever.'

'Has anyone called you a *chamaar*?'

'At our school we had a fight, they were saying to me that oh, you are a low-caste or whatever. It happened a year ago. It's still going on now.'

'Who said that to you?'

'I go to a girls' school, there's that bitchiness, that oh, you are low caste. Because their parents haven't taught them, that's what I believe, their parents haven't taught them about our religion. If they don't want to know, they can think their own thing. But they should learn.'

'And what's going on now?'

'Just the same thing. They keep saying it.'

'But how do they know who is who?'

'They can always tell from the surnames.'

I asked a 17-year-old boy the same thing.

'They always say you are a *chamaar*, you are this, you are that.'

'Give me an example.'

'One time is like, you know, you're all going out with a group and you meet someone and they started talking, *chamaar*, low caste, he shouldn't hang around with us because he is a *chamaar*, low caste like. I tell them, mate, I'm a *chamaar*, what's wrong with that? I said, I'm a human being, what's the difference? And they didn't say nothing. They just shut up, like.'

The surname left nowhere to hide. 'In India surnames are like a language,' I remembered a Ravidassia saying. 'You just pick up a language.'

So one way to escape the stigma would be to change the name. This was common, a Ravidassia solicitor I'd met earlier told me (many Ravidassias spoke to me only after I agreed not to use their names). 'The Ravidassians, those who lived where the majority of people were Sikhs, they would have names which say Singh. Where the majority were Hindus, they would have names like Ram Rakha, Rakha Ram, you know, Ram would appear. Where there were Muslims it would be names like Allah Rakha, you see, so Ravidassian community, they did not have an identity themselves because they were not able to have one.'

A change of name would help find a job. 'Those days if you were a Ravidassian it was not easy to join the army, and most of them adopted the name Singh and, you know, kept long hair and wore a turban. My uncle was one of those, so by keeping the name Singh he was able to join the army. So many have the name Das, and Das means slave, and so, as people realised they could change, they began to change names.'

'Ravidassia' is itself a name only now in the making. Gandhi had called them Harijans. 'Why Harijans?' a Ravidassia had argued. 'It means children of God, right? Why do I have to be a child of God? Why can't I be the child of my parents, like everyone else? How did Gandhi dare to call us Harijans?' Whoever wanted to be called kindly by another name so you could be saved from your own?

At the Ravidassia Bhavan in Birmingham, the biggest British centre of the Ravidassias by far, a member of the management said he had pushed hard for 'Ravidassia' to be adopted as the official name. 'Our community in the past was given many names by politicians, like Gandhi said Harijans, some others and so on, I said, so, enough of this rubbish, we are all educated now, let's simplify this one to Ravidassia community.'

That meant circulating new literature about Guru Ravi Das, even if it did not come formally from some new red book. Everyone tells the story of how the Brahmins made fun of Ravi Das once because he did not wear a *janau*. So Guru Ravi Das ripped open his heart and revealed a shining *janau* within. Everyone tells the story like they believe it and like you would be showing caste prejudice if you didn't. The story made Ravi Das more Brahmin than the Brahmins; no one was arguing yet that he did not have to be Brahmin-like at all. The Ravidassias were finding stories of triumph because those were the stories they needed.

Independence meant the establishment of their own little world in which a new collective memory could be created. The unhappy story with the Sikhs and their gurdwara was being replaced by happy stories involving only their own, told to themselves. It had become necessary to wrap old legends in new wonder, to 'touch up' the actual past in much the same way as individuals 'improve' their biographies. As with therapy for an individual, they sought to build a new life story for the group.

'I see that you are proud of Guru Ravi Das and you are fighting for your rights,' I said to a Ravidassia businessman. 'But is there also sometimes a feeling of embarrassment, maybe even shame over these origins, and all those experiences of rejection?'

The question made him furious. 'Ashamed? Why should we be ashamed? Those people who have been doing this to us, they should be ashamed of what they are doing. What wrong have we done?' I apologised for the hurt caused. But we did not meet again.

People who would drop decency with someone they saw as a *chamaar* were of course guilty, and of course they should be ashamed of themselves. The one so judged, or so seen, would have done nothing to be guilty about; but that does not by itself wipe out feelings of shame. You don't have to do anything to be ashamed of in order to feel shame. It's like rape. The rapist ought to feel the guilt, but whether he does or not, the victim feels the shame. Thousands of prisoners have lived with feelings of shame in concentration camps, having done nothing to be guilty about or be ashamed of. Guilt over causing hurt is rarely a lasting problem; getting hurt always is.

As it was with Tolstoy's Levin: 'There had been in his past, as in every man's, actions recognised by him as bad, for which his conscience ought to have tormented him; but the memory of these evil actions was far from causing him so much suffering as these trivial humiliating reminiscences. These wounds never healed.' J. Alfred Prufrock too could have been a Ravidassia.

'And I have known the eyes already, known them all –
The eyes that fix you in a formulated phrase…'

Every time I met Ravidassias, the one thing I felt I could never talk about was leather. The thought felt like kicking into a wound that never heals, particularly when they were making such efforts to cover up that wound.

Bollywood

Nehru's Footsteps

Mum was pushing her seven-year-old daughter gently towards her first Bollywood exam. 'Go *beta*, don't be nervous,' mum said, with a close hug. The little one was still looking unhappily at the dance floor as mum wished away the nerves. Bollywood dancing was fine, but exams are always serious. But they were the only way Honey Kalaria could make sure the Indian young would learn, and they must if they want a social future in Indian Britain.

The dancing exam was being held in the Methodist Church hall in Finchley in north London. Diva Entertainments, run by Honey Kalaria, hired the hall once a week for her Bollywood dance classes; the hall saw more people that one day than any other. If the priest at the church could ever have drawn as many youngsters as Honey, Britain would be another country.

A teacher in jeans with silver things all around her ears and wrists was lining up the children in two rows of about seven or eight each. Two other teachers sat at desks with registers open before them to write the marks; this really was quite a serious exam. I admired the kids braving it out there, and felt for the one who couldn't bring herself to step in.

In a moment a respectful hush settled over the babbling kids. They looked around, the teachers looked up towards a slightly overpainted woman in jeans and a bright orange T-shirt who came bouncing into the room in a strong announcement of youthful energy. Honey Kalaria, who else?

She was on the floor in no time. 'OK,' she said, with a sharp clap, and the attention was instantly all on her. She let forth a string of cheery nothings. The kids eased up, and the nervous one found the strength to abandon mum and join the others on the floor. 'What are those sparkling things up in the sky?' Honey asked brightly. They answered together. See, that's what they would get in class, she said, stars, not marks.

She was going to prepare them for the exam. A nod to a teacher, and the song began, '*Bole churiyaan, bole kangana…*', ('My bangles speak my love'). The five-to-seven-year-olds knew just what to do. They rose in a posture of tip-toed teasing, and threw at the teachers the come-on looks they'd been taught all term. One way and another Bollywood women only make dancing moves to invite the lover to make his. The teasing is built into the dance, and it was only right that kids should begin to learn it. Honey offered a final refresher. 'From the neck, from the head, one-two-three, round and round, very very good, one-two-three…' The children began to gyrate hips that weren't there in the direction of a lover who wasn't either.

Honey stopped the music. And what would they get stars for, she asked. The answer came in a chorus with every finger of Honey's hand that went up: Smiles; Energy; Sharp Moves; Timing; Classical Hands. As Honey figured, the five things, for a start anyway, that add up to Bollywood dancing.

The exam began, and the kids had a go at putting them all together on their own. Not everyone was managing, and particularly not the seven-year-old last in. I saw a sinking look appear on her mum's face, over which she was working at painting an encouraging smile. Mum and daughter both looked relieved when it ended. The kids made their way back to the gallery where I sat with a lone dad and several mums.

The mums now took over. 'My girl, you know,' said one, 'she is so good, I tell you, she watches films all the time. Every new film she has to watch. She is six but she can teach me.' 'She used to be a classical Kathak dancer,' another mum was saying about hers. 'But she didn't like it. You know all that instrumental and classical, so boring. So she moved to this. Bit more interesting, no?'

Mums sound so much the same. 'This one gets nervous in a crowd. But at home, I tell you, she's so good.' 'My one is so fond of Bollywood dances and I am so fond of her. She is just dancing in front of TV everyday. She watches every film.' In this mums' gallery every kid was out-achieving every other.

The mum nearest to me was quiet, a bit stuck with lone dad and me. I asked her what had brought her and her daughter to Honey. 'I just love films, you know. She also. You know, we enjoy the music. And it helps to practise language also. And in this country it is a form of socialising. We go out as family to other families, then kids have something to do. Otherwise, you know, in this country for girls there are too many distractions when they grow up. We don't like that. This way, they get together in a cultural sense, you know, and have fun.' She seemed convinced her daughter would dance her way to goodness.

'It's nice to go to the films and learn this dancing,' said an unseen mum behind us who joined in, as mums do. 'When we came here, there was not that much of our culture. These days we feel so confident to talk about it.'

'OK.' The command from the silvered teacher rose sharp above the talk. She was getting the next class into place for the exam for the bigger students, the teenagers and twenty-somethings. The floor had filled up rapidly, and so had our gallery. If this had been a bus, someone would have been asked to get off.

Honey took over from the teacher to rehearse this lot. 'Come on, let's have a "U" with the bottom, nice and neat "U".' The thirty-five or forty girls, and two or three boys in the class, followed Honey's U-turns to *'Keh do na, keh do na, you are my sonia…'* (Tell me, aren't you my beautiful one), the syllabus for this class. Honey led them through the song step by step, through one teasing swing after another. She showed them what to do, and showed us in the gallery why she is quite the star teacher for Bollywood dancing in Britain. 'To-the-left and to-the-right and nice-and-neat and punch-punch-punch and *keh do na, keh do na…* Come on, you want the eyes on you at the next party, don't you?' After a pause, she asked, 'And who wants to be in Bollywood films?' I couldn't spot a hand that wasn't up. These must be among the world's most eager extras.

As the two teachers at the desk judged teenage hips, Honey and I had time for a chat. We strolled over to the room behind the church hall, past a separate class for bhangra. 'That's mostly for older people because it's slow,' she said. 'Bollywood dancing, that's really fast.'

Honey looked very camera-ready as we sat down, and I felt I let her down because I didn't have one.

'I have offers already from the US to start dance academies there.' She knew what she wanted to deliver, and she wasn't wasting time. 'Five years from now, I will have franchises worldwide. There will be two hundred branches the world over.' The success in London looked humble before her ambitions. In true Bollywood style, she wouldn't take all the credit. 'I'm grateful to God,' she said, with a quick glance at the ceiling.

'Why has this whole Bollywood thing picked up so much now?'

'Some years back, parents were not very encouraging. Nowadays a lot of parents want their children involved. It's now accepted for kids to take part in Bollywood shows.'

'Why is that?'

'It's good for health, fitness, you make new friends, you gain more confidence. It's a good, enjoyable hobby. It gets them off the streets, so much better than going to a club.'

'Do Indian kids particularly gain confidence from this?'

'Dance is very psychological, a lot of it is in the mind. When you learn to let go in your mind, the body follows. Here children build dancing skills, choreography skills, then parents come to see. Some kids are not very confident, they don't open up. We encourage them, and they begin to open up, they begin to feel good. I can make anyone dance who says they can't, I guarantee that.'

'And how many kids get taken into Bollywood films?'

'I was privileged to give my students a chance to work in *Kabhi Khushi Kabhi Gham*. I had nine hundred artists who took part in *K3G*. Dancers, other roles. For *Mohabbatein* we provided three hundred artists including twenty, thirty dancers. One little boy was first offered a role in *K3G*. But then they took the other one.'

'So you're sort of Britain's Bollywood studio?'

'If you come from India, you don't have to bring all these people. It cuts costs, works both ways. And people here have an opportunity to use their skills for Bollywood films, stage shows.'

'How do you teach so many?'

'I train teachers. Once they are up to a level, I let my assistants take over. I go to a class once every two, three weeks.'

'When did you begin yourself?'

'I came here from Malawi in the eighties. I was dancing to Bollywood songs when I was thirteen, when nobody was doing it. But even then I was quite a lot in demand. They call me Bollywood's ambassador to Britain.'

'Never thought of moving to Bollywood yourself?'

'Now that I have set up the academy, I can't leave it and go, or they won't trust you afterwards. I want people to know that we're here to stay.'

'And the kids here, you see them going more and more the Bollywood way?'

'Oh yes, yes. You wait; you haven't seen anything yet.'

We chatted on a bit. But the one thing that stuck in my mind was that she could make anyone dance. That included me. What if she taught me to dance like a dream and I became so good that I could partner her at a party? These were just the fantasies she had turned into business. Honey could make you shine, star-like, at parties, and then, who knows, even in Bollywood. She would get you noticed, at parties, on stage, on screen, somewhere. Bollywood offered the dreams, Honey the technique to make them come true, at least as party dancer if not as Bollywood star. She would teach you to shine safely among your own. She had brought parents and kids to the same side.

The mums are counting their blessings, and Honey her success. A few years back, she began teaching just 22 students. Now, she has well over a thousand at something like £75 a term, three terms in a year. And that's not counting the money from her shows and from the extras offered whenever Bollywood came visiting and in need. Nice work if you can get it.

It was the big evening when all that education would go public, in the five Honey commandments, in hip movement, in making eyes at that notional someone, in teasing meaning out of timing. Honey's students from her 'academies' in Finchley, Harrow and Ilford who'd been training for a year or more would compete at the big show at Acton town hall. It was time to show off.

As an Indian I knew my way to the hall, quite a centre now for Indian events. The hall had been smart once. It was built when Britain still looked back to a sense of the grand, expressed usually as rounded lines with ornate interruptions here and there. But its doors open now to people quite different from those it was intended for. The days never come when you might see a few hundred white British mums head out, cameras in hand, to watch their kids do a Michael Jackson, but when little Nitesh is doing a Hrithik Roshan, you can count for everyone like him on mum with possibly two aunts and some cousins thrown in.

Diva Entertainments had prepared a poster exhibition in the foyer upstairs. One poster presenting an impish and animated Honey standing with a bunch of teenagers welcomed visitors. 'Fans drawn like bees to see dancing queen,' said the bold lettering across it. Another picture of Honey and her dancers was pasted on another poster with the caption, 'Honey with her lucky, lucky sprogs.' 'Opportunity to be a star' said one, and another listed just what Honey could do to make that happen: 'Dialogue Delivery, Emotion, Voice Projection, Observational Skills, Mime, Impersonation, Diction, Hindi Language, Body Language and much, much more...' Like, for example, 'Dance, Bhangra, Catwalk Modelling, Singing and Keep Fit.'

Honey's students 'have already had opportunities to work in Bollywood films, TV productions, stage shows, pop videos and next to superstars', a board by the collage of posters said. Bollywood stars Amitabh Bachchan and Govinda appeared with Honey in a photograph, the picture of contacts in high places. Another notice on the board said Honey's shows were on offer for 'Festivals, Melas and Corporate Events.' There was even a money-back guarantee from Diva Entertainments for making a Bollywood dancer of you; the bit that might have been of interest to me had I joined.

I walked into the packed hall. Only a few seats at the back were still vacant. Digi-cam carrying mums were lining the hall in scores all the way along both sides. Guest after guest at home would be shown the impressive steps their young were taking, and some day they could look back on their own early steps.

The show began. Lights. Mums' cameras. Action. Two large Indian flags danced onto the stage to a disco version of the nationalist Indian song, 'Vande Mataram'. Bollywood is India, and Honey was saying it loud; the first dancer of the evening was the Indian flag. Britain was incidental here, Honey was doing more to connect British Indian youth to India than those hundreds of sedative speeches by Indian high commissioners who come, blabber and go. The dance ended with one flag held the wrong way up. But these girls were British too, and we all knew they meant well.

The toddlers followed. The first team of four-to-seven-year-olds, who had only recently learnt to walk, gave us their interpretation of '*Dil ye baichain ve… aa ja saanvariya, aa, aa, aa… tal se taal mila…*' ('My heart is restless, come my lover, match your beat with mine'). Next came the eight-to-twelve-year-olds with their little feet pattering busily under looks of aching romance. Suddenly, a roar of applause broke out. The *lehenga*, the long Indian skirt, of one of the little girls had slipped, and she had caught it just in time, and to the beat.

I was trying to tell myself that these kids were all born British, as we moved up the years to more serious dancers. Someone was announced in as 'Hrithik Roshan in the making'. Brave promise, to be mentioned in the same breath as Bollywood's dancing dream of a hero. The spotlight picked up a plump little fellow, 12 or 13, who strolled very slowly onto the stage, in crimson trousers and a silver-coloured shirt, black glasses, black gloves and a baseball cap reversed into cool black American. At centre stage he stood still. So casual, see? Then, with all the flourish he could unleash, he flung the cap dramatically downstage and began his dance. He lived up to the announcement, and was unexpectedly quick for someone so obviously overfed. Another kid about the same age came next, announced as another Hrithik Roshan on his way; he was no slower, and you didn't want their mums fighting.

A bunch of girls who had set up their own Bollywood group 'Envy' was announced in. Other such groups followed: King's Crew – a bunch of Indian students from King's College; the Sens-Asians, the Tempt-Asians. Bollywood must run a fair bit of their lives if at school and college it was Bollywood dancing they ganged up for. Dancers from Ilford announced themselves: 'Let the battle begin…' This was Honey's home ground, and they had a thing to prove. In ones and twos and more, they danced to the likes of 'I am a disco dancer', *'Keh do na, keh do na, you are my Sonia'*, *'Choli ke peechay…'* One after another, Bollywood was taking them from Britain, or reclaiming them as Indian, depending how you looked at it.

In the end there were prizes for almost everyone. A great many went to Harrow, where India's first prime minister Jawaharlal Nehru had come once for another kind of education. For Honey's dancers this was the discovery of another India.

Up in that studio at Honey's dance academy with a mirror for a wall at the far end, these were not just Bollywood dancers. They'd come to learn Bollywood acting, they could be stars one day. 'Remember what Honey told you about Tom Hanks?' the teacher was telling the class of about twenty, sitting on chairs along the walls, with the space in the middle of the studio meaningfully vacant for the performances to come. 'He spent a year meeting AIDS patients before shooting for *Philadelphia*. You see, that is acting. It's not something you just go and do out there just like that.'

A chap in the class who'd made it as an extra in a Bollywood film thanks to Honey had known otherwise. 'We were only told five minutes before what to do,' he said. 'That was last year,' the teacher replied. 'Things will be different now.' It wasn't the best answer, but what could she do?

The class was waiting for Honey at her flagship centre in Seven Kings in Ilford. For the glamour it was out to generate, the centre on Farnham Road at the end of a row of houses was unexpectedly unpretentious. Some East London neighbourhoods have the feeling of barracks about them, and Seven Kings is particularly barrack-like. It must be the smallness of the houses along wide roads, and the near absence of anything green. A board outside only called the place the Supplementary Education Centre. That was the boring adult education stuff. Honey Kalaria had taken a couple of rooms there for her office and dance lessons. Whatever went on in her rooms, it wouldn't be boring. This room with the mirror must see more movement, and hold more colour than any other for miles here, east of east London.

Honey walked in, as usual faster than necessary, and after some rapid hellos, turned to the class, and to Hanks.

'When he was asked to do that role he spent a year going to all the hospitals that had AIDS victims. He saw their problems, their challenges, he saw how they behaved, how frail they were. He is such a great actor, and still he had to do all this. And which was the film with Brad Pitt? Yes, *Troy*. You think he went in and said I'm an actor, what do you want me to do?'

She waited for a reply. A white student in the class replied, 'No, he became more muscular to play the part.'

'Yes. He didn't just go and start doing something because oh, I'm so good.' And then she made her point. They must not leave at the end of a three-month term, they must stay the full three-year acting course. In that determination lay their hope, and her fee. Message given, some instructions handed out, Honey made her way out, just as fast as she'd come.

A teacher in blue denims and black shirt set the class on the acting course. She was the picture of confidence, the sound of eloquence, she had to be. She divided the class into groups. One group of two chaps and three girls went first, they were going to act out an idea Honey had given them to work on.

'What was the idea Honey gave you?' the teacher asked.

'It was like all her other ideas,' one of the chaps said. 'Pretend we've seen a UFO.' So everyone in the group stared at a blank wall, swayed about in horror, and fell on the floor one by one as they were overawed by what they were supposed to be seeing. Other such acts followed. The budding stars didn't look hugely enthused, but this was the best they could find in Britain for now to make something Bollywood-like come true.

Class over, some of us sat talking. A very Sikh-looking girl saved me asking that rude question, just what kind of actress she hoped to become. 'I qualified as a pharmacist, I work near Tower Bridge, and I'm bored out of my brains,' she said before I could say much to her. She didn't want to give her name, but since she was Sikh, it was a likely toss-up between Dolly and Pinky. Her bright eyes were in search of something more than pharmacy could offer.

'Why isn't pharmacy good enough?' I asked.

'It's good, but it's not creative.'

'Have you worked at more creative things before?'

'I did music when I was younger. My dad's very creative, he's a musician, and I used to sing *shabads*, sing in gurdwaras.'

'Now Bollywood's more interesting?'

'Oh yeah, I see all the films, stay up to date. I had an Indian channel, now I go to Upton Park to get my DVDs.'

'What do you like about Bollywood?'

'What I really like, whatever anyone says about Bollywood, is a degree of comfort in these films. They're melodic, they're colourful, they're about some ideal. You can't translate that into everyday life. But you do get transported into a different world. Films can be realistic and social and all that but there is a sector of arts that caters to all that.'

'What do you like best in this non-realistic sort of otherness?'

'The dancing, the choreography, the superb, superb dancing.'

'And what do you want to do with yourself in Bollywood?'

'Tell you the truth, I'm not looking for fame and fortune, but I'm so bored with pharmacy, I just want to build my confidence, learn to perform to a level.'

Others from the class were hanging around. I tried to guess which faces I might see on the film posters that come up so quickly one above the other on every spare wall in Wembley and Southall. Maybe that girl in black, probably older than the rest, very actress-like in that curving style so outdated now but waiting to make a comeback, who knows. She was Pakistani, as I had guessed.

'I'm studying biomedical science, I'm taking a year off studies,' she said. Biomedical science sounded like it was to her what pharmacy was to the other.

'Is this your first go at acting?'

'No, I've always been into the performing arts. I've done stage plays, school plays, fashion shows.'

'Are others in your family into the performing arts?'

'No, my dad's a teacher. He's from Pakistan.'

'So what language do you speak at home?'

'Punjabi, Urdu.'

'It's fine with your parents for you to learn Bollywood acting?'

'Oh yes.'

'Where do you want to take this?'

'I'd like a career in acting. I've done Bollywood dancing in the past.'

'You want to act in Bollywood films?'

'Yes, and also Pakistani TV plays. My uncle's in Pakistani TV plays.'

The white guy was of course the least likely figure in that room. 'Maybe not today, maybe not tomorrow, but I'll be one of the first guys here to break into Bollywood,' Wayne, as he was introduced, had announced earlier.

'What do you do otherwise?' I asked him.

'I work in a factory in Walthamstow making installation tubes.'

'So how did Bollywood come into it?'

'This chap at work said to me, you should go to Bollywood.'

'Indian guy?'

'Muslim, to be honest.'

'You're keen on this sort of thing?'

'I've been acting since the age of ten. And I said to myself I like Bollywood, I'd like to learn Asian culture.'

'What actually brought you to this?'

'There was the sixtieth birthday of this Trinidadian Indian, and they were dancing. I copied them. And they said where did you learn to dance like that? I said I just copied you.'

'So that was the inspiration.'

'Yes, then I just entered Bollywood dance in a search, and the first thing that came up was Honey. It was almost as if I was being led into something. And I said why not Bollywood. Why not be the white man that breaks through into Bollywood?'

'Do you see a lot of the films?'

'I don't know that many Bollywood films, I don't know Hindi, but I can mime to songs.'

'You seem to enjoy this.'

'It's the biggest stress relief for me. I just have to do Bollywood dancing on Friday, Saturday and Bollywood acting Sunday.'

'But it's more than stress relief, isn't it?'

'It's very important to me. This is my last chance. Because I don't think I'll make it in the Western thing. But Bollywood, I feel it will come.' I couldn't share his confidence, but still, it was not as mushy a bunch as I'd expected.

Shaban had more than an exaggerated swagger for age 15, for any age really.

'I've been doing Bollywood acting for a year,' he said. 'I've acted in a Bollywood show in Newcastle for a week.'

'Doing what?'

'I was a bus driver. A Jamaican bus driver. I had to speak in that accent.'

Shaban was a bit portly for 15, but he didn't think that would come between him and Bollywood heroism. He was cool, and that would make up.

'You speak Indian languages?'

'Yeah, I can speak Urdu and Gujarati. My dad's from Turkey, mum's from Gujarat. And I've picked up Hindi.'

'Through the films?'

'Been seeing films since I was five, six. Picked up the language there.'

'Who's your favourite?'

'Salman Khan. I see all his films. I like his style and his acting.'

'What's it been like, a year of Bollywood acting?'

'It's boosted my confidence. Earlier I was shy, not outgoing.'

'What brought you here to learn acting?'

'Earlier I was only doing Bollywood dancing, I used to be like every other guy, just copying what I saw on TV. Then I said to my mum I got this feeling that I want to be in Bollywood. So she found me these classes.'

'What now?'

'I'll be doing my acting and dancing classes for three years.'

'And then?'

'Hopefully I'll get into a Bollywood film. My two brothers, they also watch Bollywood films. But I'm much more into it. My brother also wants to join, but he's doing engineering. If I move into Bollywood, I'll just pull him into one of my films.'

Sheetal was waiting to talk to me, a little restlessly. She couldn't seem to stand still from the moment she'd walked in. And she didn't walk a regular walk either. Every step seemed a dancing step. Maybe it was those precarious heels; she had to move quickly from one to the other all the time to avoid falling. She was a party girl; every minute she wasn't at a party was that much life unlived.

'I just finished a job in a bank,' she said. 'Royal Bank of Scotland.'

'So, to dance, then?'

'No, I'm also studying accounts and financing for my banking skills. I'm also doing the beauty business, I do henna, aromatherapy, massage. Beauty is my side business, something to fall back on.'

'Going well?'

'Yes, that's going well.'

'Your first time acting?'

'Yes, been doing Bollywood dancing. But had to stop because I have to go to aromatherapy classes. I'm also doing reflexology.'

'Always been interested in Bollywood?'

'I started singing since I was thirteen. Didn't keep it up, don't have the time.'

'What brought you to acting?'

'You see, I was this extra in a film *I: Proud to be an Indian*. And, you know Sohail Khan, he was running for the love of his life. And we were all running behind him.'

'Why?'

'We were cheering him on. Because he was so happy.'

'You liked that?'

'Loved it. We were there nine hours, we had to do it again and again. And I knew that this Bollywood is the only thing I really wanted to do.'

'That brought you to Honey…'

'Yes, but I have these other things.'

'Think you'll stay the three-year acting course?'

'Of course.'

No, this wasn't a bunch that didn't know what they were up to. Maybe just the idea of Bollywood had done something the real Bollywood, or the real Britain around them, would never offer.

Yash Blush

The little play the two girls had put on for Yash Chopra was almost done before he realised they were playing lesbians. In fact, I had to tell him.

I hadn't managed to translate every word of their East Midlands Leicester English into the Punjab-processed sounds of English I'd grown up with, and I was in natural sympathy with Yashji's fellow Punjabi accent and lack of success attuning to Indian teenager sounds in Leicester. He'd been watching the skit expressionless and, I thought, a bit bored. It would have been a pity for the producer of Bollywood's biggest successes to watch a show and miss it for the small matter of an accent. That the rest of the world could make little sense of his own wholesome Punjabi accent did not matter, because he was Yash Chopra himself, that film producer from days long before someone coined the word 'Bollywood', a more phonetic than meaningful blend of Hollywood and Bombay cinema.

'They're lesbians, you know, and one is getting jealous because she thinks the other girl is seeing a guy,' I whispered to him. It felt like snitching. Yashji continued to look on woodenly. Unless he was meaningfully impassive; with these film chaps you never know.

Yashji was chief audience among about thirty of us in a large upstairs room the local council had taken in the Leicester city centre for this meeting. A fairly good turnout for little enough Leicester. The council had invited singers, dancers and actors to show Yashji local talent and what Bollywood meant to British Asians. The city council was hosting Yashji under a British Film Council tour of a picture-postcard selection of England and Scotland, and Leicester was the Indian flavour along the way. Yashji's *Dilwale Dulhaniya Le Jayenge* (*DDLJ*) as rapid legend had made it, had showed Britain off to millions at no cost because so much of it was filmed in London, and wouldn't it be nice if he came back with cameras for more? I once had to conduct an Indian tourist around the locales shown in the film; St Pancras railway station was of more interest to her than Madame Tussaud's or Windsor Castle because the railway station was where the *DDLJ* hero's predictably romantic journey began.

Yashji's last couple of films had featured Indians abroad, and think how much money he would spend in Leicester if just some of his next big film (or blockbuster, as every one of them is called) was to be set in Leicester. And think how many rich Indian tourists would head for Leicester once they saw it in a Yash film. If Yashji smiled on Leicester, there was money in it for the town. The council was gambling in the hope it was investing.

And who knows who Yashji might spot as just the one for his next film. One flick of his heavily ringed finger could mean a one-way ticket from a Leicester suburb to Bollywood fame. And that, too, would mean fame for Leicester.

I'd come to the Yashji meeting with a friend and her two teenaged daughters, and their friend, a neighbour's daughter. This one was being sent out under watch because her mother had found out she was seeing a taxi driver. 'Her mum thinks it will take her mind off that guy,' my friend said. 'Stupid.' But if Yashji were to spot her, it would solve a lot of problems. Mum would pack the girl's bags happily for that Bombay flight. You never knew with Bollywood, but at least she'd stop seeing the taxi driver. Serve him right if he got to see her one day only in a film at the end of 14 trips to the bus terminal.

The lesbian skit was nearing its end. The girl in orange was the jealous one. She just knew that the other girl in the black shirt was seeing someone else, and a guy at that. No, said black shirt, they were just friends. No, no, orange knew better. And so it went on until confession. Not a performance that would lead either girl to speak of this hall in an interview one day as the place where Yash Chopra spotted her. The girls vacated the middle of the room for the next to appear in the hope of getting spotted, and not just seen. Yashji did not join in the polite clapping. It was my fault.

A lightly built girl, too light for Bollywood, walked up to do a dance. Her blue sari would never fool Yashji's eyes, but then she'd never been taught that when you wear a sari you don't walk like you're wearing jeans. A friend switched on a tape for her. She swayed into some willowy movements, then faded from the floor to join that vast population that once tried Bollywood. Another girl stepped up to deliver a dialogue in intended Hindi, and Yashji heard her out, more kind than interested.

Not everyone had to perform; you could sit there and hope to get seen as the face of the next film. A chap next to me was shifting about every now and then to catch Yashji's eye. He was the lad of the times in every detail – single earring, gelled hair and baggy jeans with pockets by the knees that are always empty and still manage to bulge. 'Going to do something?' I asked. 'No, I'm here just, ya know, just…' Just to be seen.

Finally it was time for Yashji to say something, and he had something to say.

'We believe in family,' he said. 'For us family is very important. We do not believe in showing sick emotions.' He did not look at either orange or black, but looked like he was looking away particularly from them. Then he turned to the dancer who'd disguised her jeans as a sari. 'You know, for dance, you need more light. Lot of lights.' His sets were coming back to his mind. 'For my dance I can have hundred lights, more than hundred.' He glanced up at the one or two lights on the ceiling and turned his eyes away. It was their most lowly moment since someone put them up there. But he wasn't going to leave without encouraging words. 'Very good, very good,' he said into the air generally as he got up to leave.

Good thing the Bollywood dreamers couldn't hear what Yashji said to me as he left. 'These people, you know, very important. Look at the difference in price. Here one cinema ticket easy five hundred rupees. This market has become whole territory. Like Delhi-UP this NRI market has become whole territory.' So Indians abroad were now as big a market as a hundred million Indians in all of Delhi and the state of Uttar Pradesh, UP. Yashji wasn't here talent spotting, or even location hunting. He was looking at where that easy 500 rupees a ticket comes from, and in hard currency. Ten times the price of most tickets in India, and three to four times as much as the most expensive of the lot. Non-resident Indian ticket prices multiplied nicely, and Yashji was making his calculations.

The unspotted had begun to move towards the door; it was time to say goodbye to Bollywood. But wait, Yashji had something hot from Bollywood for them, a proper Bollywood script to work their acting skills on. 'It has English translation,' he said near the door, and handed out some copies. See what that meant? Young actors could take that script and act out a whole Bollywood film. A Bollywood script given to them personally by Yash Chopra, you know, the guy who made *DDLJ*.

I picked up a copy of the thick A4-sized script. The copies on offer were quickly grabbed away. But still, it was a script, not a contract. You spend years dreaming, hours grooming, then you're before that someone who could make those dreams come true. Then he's off, and it's all gone. Not the kind of ending Yashji would ever have liked for one of his stories.

I had left the room something of a hero for the three teenagers, my friend's two daughters, and their friend. They'd seen me talking to Yash Chopra himself, what's more, they'd seen him talk to me, and they saw as we got into the car that I had a script in my hands that had come straight from Yash Chopra.

'Can I see the script?' the youngest said.

'Let's wait till we get home,' I said. 'Then let's act it out.' Their squeals – on a pitch that only girls aged 14 to 17 can produce – told me they could hardly believe this. We were going to do a Yash Chopra film of our own. In their exclamations I heard also some surprise that I was not entirely boring after all. I rose in their esteem by the minute on our drive home.

We were home soon enough. My friend disappeared predictably into the kitchen, which left us a cast of three girls and myself as hero in the sitting room. I placed Yashji's gift on the sofa where everyone could see it. The girls crowded around the script reverentially, like it was scripture.

'Yash Raj Films', it said on top. Then, *Darr*. That was our film. Produced and directed: Yash Chopra. Music: Shiv Hari. Below were the contents – written as reel number and footage, nothing as dull as chapter and page.

I leafed through some pages. The Hindi script was on the left column on every page, its English translation on the right. Whether Yashji had the translation done for the visit to London or whether this is standard Bollywood practice for a script, I do not know. Maybe the lines in English were intended to double as subtitles. I glanced through the lines with a rare thrill. They were in a language as yet undiscovered by much of the world

– Indian English. Much of that Indian English comes from Punjab. Plain English took a long soaking in every one of those five rivers before it could emerge into this language. This story was going to be a thriller even if nothing happened in it. But first we had an act to perform.

'Why don't you read it loud?' I said to Bijal, the younger one. Like all 15-year-olds these days, she talked like she was 25.

'OK, here goes,' she said, and began reading.

'Kiran is lying and reading the letter.' She paused.

'Silly, read the thing on the right,' said sister Rupa.

Bijal read the opening lines of the script, the lines that Kiran, who promised to be the heroine of the film, was reading from a letter: '"My heart, I am far away from you but you are still in front of me. I feel as if I am looking at you."'

'Boyfriend's letter, wow,' said sister Rupa. She was always one to get straightaway into the sentiment of anything.

'Guys are never like that,' said the third one, the teenage neighbour in the wrong kind of love, because her mum didn't think the object of it ought to be a cab driver. 'Bet no one writes letters like that.'

'What's he say?' said Rupa.

Bijal read further. '"You are reading this letter sitting on a stone and all the things around you are coloured by your colour."'

Again she stopped. 'That's weird, what's he mean "coloured by your colour"?'

'It's because he's in love,' Rupa said matter-of-factly. She knew these things, and she had seen enough Bollywood films by now.

Bijal continued to read out the letter Kiran was reading in the script. '"The clouds must have spread like the *kajal* of your eyes."' *Kajal*, eyeliner. Bijal wasn't impressed. 'Oh yeah? She must have put it on and washed her face.'

Bijal wasn't getting into the romance of it, and she was spoiling it for Rupa.

'Shut up Bijal, just read.'

'"You must be looking around and the entire earth is looking at your face. And I have become the sun and am kissing you."'

Now Bijal had to stop. 'So he's the sun, right? And so he's snogging her, right?'

'Come on, it's only a love letter,' said Rupa.

Bijal read on. The script column had gone blank but there were directions.

'"Kiran looks up. Kiran gets up. Kiran comes. Kiran comes. Kiran standing. Opens her buttons. Kiran opens the buttons. Kiran opens her dress. Kiran turns while removing her clothes."' Bijal finished reading, her voice rising with Kiran's every action. The room was filled with the high-pitched giggles I'd heard earlier in the car, that teenaged girls produce from nowhere for moments like this.

'What's that?' mum's voice demanded from the kitchen.

'It's OK, mom,' Bijal shouted back.

Bollywood was supposed to be safe, family entertainment, and here we'd run into steam on page one.

'Let's skip this,' I said. But the script had steered to safety anyway. Kiran was interrupted before she could remove any more clothes. She appeared now with female friends.

'Wait, there's a song,' I said. '*Jadu teri nazar.*'

'I know that one,' neighbour girl said, and began to sing it, really badly. Bijal stopped her with a 'shut up', exactly what I'd been relying on her to do. She read on but she'd begun to lose her way a little. This wasn't English as she knew it. She read the next lines from Kiran.

'"I know, Sunil he here somewhere. But he is not coming in front of me."'

'"Second girl: What is the reason for him to hide?"'

'"Kiran: He gets enjoyment in worrying me."'

"'Third girl: I know where Sunil is.'"

"'Kiran: If you know, why don't you tell me? Tell me where he is.'"

"'Girl: 'Here in the mirror of heart is his photograph.''"

"'Kiran: 'Oh, oh'.'"

Bijal gave me the next bit to read, presented at the start of the film by way of a deep and meaningful voice in the background. "'When love crosses the limit then it becomes a devotion and then when devotion is hurt then it becomes a madness. This is the story of such a madness which has the truthness of Laila Majnu's love and the pain of Romeo Juliet's love. It also has the suffering of Heer Ranjha's songs. It has something else also, which is not seen in today's love stories… Fright…'"

'That's why this film is called *Darr*,' I explained. 'See, *Darr* means fear.'

We were almost at the end of Reel 1, and Sunil had come into the story. I read on.

Sunil: 'May I come in, sir?'

O.S.: 'Come in.'

Officer: 'Sunil, the terrorist have kidnapped my niece's daughter. They have kept a clause that they will leave the child only if we release their leader or they will shoot the child. We must save the child and only you can do this work.'

Sunil: 'Where is the child?'

Officer: 'In the middle of the sea, in their boat. All the best… all the best'.

End of Reel no. 1 at 738.10 feet. End, also, of our Bollywood adventure; the girls had other things to do.

They vanished upstairs for something or other but really to talk about the this-and-that of the day, what's the point of sharing happenings if you can't talk about them. The Yash spell hadn't lasted long. I realised then that I'd never actually heard the girls discuss a Bollywood story; it was always only the dances or the clothes.

Between the usual household interruptions, I leafed through the script.

Getting the film into the fear mood, Sunil decides to give his fiancé Kiran a scare by stepping out of a cupboard.

Kiran: 'Sunil, idiot, shameless, always frightening me. I thought a dead body fell from the cupboard.'
Sunil: 'Are you a fool, you don't know this much, that from girls' cupboards only old letters, old lovers and new *sarees* are found?'
Kiran: 'You old lover… what if my heart had to fail'
Sunil: 'How is that possible, your heart is with me?'
Kiran: 'Get lost! I am not talking to you. You are very bad. See how my heart is beating hard.'
Sunil: 'It is beating hard. Yes, yes.'

Love proceeds but never far from the stalking Rahul who's obsessed with Kiran. Sunil manages to get Kiran to a quiet house, she knows why.

Kiran: Mr Sunil Malhotra, the shine in your eyes and the smile on your lips state that your intentions are not noble.
Sunil: Intentions are good but morals have changed.

But Rahul calls just then to stalk her on the phone. 'Don't cut the line. I have to tell you a important thing. This Sunil is not capable for you.' He threatens to turn up on Holi, cloaked in disguise perhaps under the colours of the day. But when the day comes and he doesn't for some time, Sunil is free to flirt.

Kiran: From where are you coming behind me?
Sunil: To take bath.
Kiran: Have you gone mad?
Sunil: It is great fun to take bath together after playing Holi.
Kiran: You shameless creature.

Sunil thinks he and Kiran need to go away somewhere. But her sister-in-law Punam warns her of the pitfalls of love and courtship. 'Kiran, you remember one thing. Until the fruit is on the tree it looks nice but when it came in hand then it is in mouth. The lovers also become like this after marriage.'

But go away they must. Clever Sunil lets on that they are going to Goa, but he has a plan, as Kiran discovers at the airport.

Kiran: Well you tell me…
Sunil: Yes…
Kiran: That we came here but could not go to Goa. Why?
Sunil: We are going to Switzerland and not to Goa.
Kiran: Switzerland… really. Then why you have taken the ticket of the Goa?
Sunil: Because of that bastard we have to do like this. Till now he will come to know that we are going to Goa. He will be preparing for Goa and we will go to Switzerland.
Kiran: You are wise.

Stalking Rahul takes the flight to Goa. The woman at the hotel reception tells him they aren't there: 'Here no Malhotra is staying. From where such people are coming?'

In Goa Rahul runs into an old and by now alcoholic friend Vicky, just when Vicky is being warned by a waiter that he is about to spill his drink. Vicky says 'If it is falling then let it fall down. This is my wine. What you have to do?' Vicky is dying: 'It is difficult,' he tells Rahul. 'My lever has totally gone. The condition of the heart is also like this. The battle of the rat and cat is started in my life. When the cat will eat the rat that God only knows.'

Vicky dies and Rahul gets word out that he died instead. Kiran's family call her on their honeymoon in Switzerland to give her the good news, that the stalker can stalk no more. And she tells Sunil.

But the death story was a trick to discover from her brother, whom Rahul knows, where Kiran is. Rahul heads for Switzerland and runs into Sunil, who does not know Rahul is the stalker.

But in the end Rahul too dies, even though he had promised his long dead mother that he will marry Kiran.

Rahul speaks his last: 'Kiran, what reply I will give to the mummy? My life was started with your love and finished in your love only. I know that I am guilty... but you don't hate to me. I love you Kiran...'

The last of the script reads: '733.11 to 808.11. Different silent shots of the Rahul lying. Kiran is weeping including Sunil. Rolling titles starts. "The End". Reel no: 19 ends at 816.00 feet.'

Our hopes that Yashji's script would inspire us had ended a little earlier.

Pee Price

The four chaps who stepped out of their white vans one by one to pee in a lay-by on the road from Leicester to Nottingham were a sign that an idea for the British economy had failed. They were opening up a matter far beyond them and their bladders, or even between a man's needs on the one hand and countryside niceties on the other.

Locating the vans had been a small triumph after I set out in search of them from Leicester. Dipesh was not sure I'd find them when I called him on his mobile. 'Basically we are filming all around Leicester, you won't be able to find us,' he said. Like all good Gujaratis in Britain, Dipesh did things either basically or literally. He sounded like he had very little time to talk, and hung up quickly.

I was looking for Dipesh because Ather Mirza at the University of Leicester had told me that Dipesh was de facto location producer for a new Bollywood film being shot in Leicester. Mirza had persuaded Dipesh to do some filming on campus so that Leicester University would figure in a Bollywood film. This mattered enough to the university for Her Majesty's government to circulate a press release to mark the success.

'A new Bollywood blockbuster is being shot at the University of Leicester and in the city and county. *Raakh*, which means Ashes, is being described as a "sophisticated gangster movie" and stars Sohail Khan, the brother of Bollywood megastar Salman Khan.' Mirza added his own views in the press note. 'The University of Leicester is pleased to be playing host again to a Bollywood movie. India is the biggest film producer in the world – the potential to reach out to a global audience and showcase the university is huge.'

The university was naturally an eager extra. Leicester University, where DNA was discovered, needs students from India for it to keep going and growing. Every Indian student who watched *Raakh*, liked the look of the Leicester campus and came to join the university would bring a useful £8,000 or so a year in fees, besides feeding the local economy through their living expenses. A thousand or more would bring millions in income. Who knows what undiscovered DNAs wait out there that Indian fees could pay to research? What better advertising at no cost than to get seen in a Bollywood film?

Dipesh and the film crew had done with the university campus and moved on. 'We are on Melton Road now, we are heading out on the road to Nottingham,' Dipesh had told me on the mobile. 'Basically we are in four white vans.' That had set me off on the white van chase.

I had followed the signs to Nottingham, through the very Indian Melton Road and on to the countryside where England had begun to reclaim itself. A ten-minute drive, and I spotted the white vans – the film crew of *Raakh*. I parked behind the last of the vans.

Its rear doors were held wide open. A camera faced out, set to shoot someone following. Half a dozen very Mumbai chaps sat around the camera, looking silently out. I was a little taken aback by their motionlessness. They looked straight past me. Like that camera, they looked programmed to focus on something else. I stepped out of the car and walked on past them towards the three vans in front. Even for parked vans, they seemed still in an odd sort of way, like everything within was not as still as it seemed. Or was it the gangster movie mood getting to me?

Some chaps in the next van looked blankly into the countryside past me. I guessed they'd been warned about a pursuing journalist and told they must give nothing away about the film. You didn't want the producer whining over whisky two years later that no one would have guessed the end if it wasn't for some journalist chap near Leicester. Or that another blockbuster had stolen their story.

I moved on to the front two vans like some peeping prowler. I couldn't have looked inside them if I'd tried. Shirts, jackets, saris on hangers had made purdahs of windows. By now I was almost enjoying a spooky sense that there was someone inside and that they had seen me, and that I was not meant to see them, not even for a moment, to know they were there.

I waited, and they waited. Then a youngish fellow came out of the camera van. He had shoulder-length hair and trousers that looked like pyjamas, more or less the uniform of the creative in the cinema business. He walked up to me, and stood waiting to be spoken to. In my now suspicious mode, I thought a mobile or two had got busy, and he had been sent out as official spokesman.

'So what's this film about?' I asked.

'It's underworld and love story mixed.' I must have nodded in a so-what's-new way, because he added, 'But it's not the usual mix.'

'So what is it?'

'You know, a different kind of gangster movie.' In short, ask no more. He was doing his PR job well.

'And what are you shooting here?'

'The don, the gangster boss, you see he is from Leicester.'

'And will the film say he is in Leicester?'

'Yes, the story will show he is from Leicester.'

I asked because the Bollywood hit *Hum Dil De Chuke Sanam* had been filmed in Hungary and the story pretended it was Italy. Hungary offered the Europe look cheaper, and Italy was a better name. I had attended a screening of the film in Budapest to which the Hungarian President was invited. The Indian hosts had no idea either that the story would make Italy out of Hungary; they saw the film the first time with the President. From the look of the President after the screening, I saw he was not amused. But presidents and the diplomatic service have a way of getting past such embarrassments.

'And what are you shooting on this road?'

'This girl, you see, is getting to know this chap, so they are out on a drive.'

'The girl is going out with the don?'

'No, with this other chap.'

'Villain or hero?'

'No, not like that.'

I was asking the usual simplistic questions of a complex film. The hero might prove villainous, or the villain could emerge as a hero. Bollywood separates them nicely, but this film was getting it all mixed up.

The spokesman was not keen to speak any further. Couldn't blame him. He asked me to wait for Dipesh and the director; they had gone for a recce of the Nottingham road for some driving shots and to set the scene for some roadside action.

They drove up shortly in a silver-coloured Mercedes, old enough by now to have become one of the poor non-gleaming cousins from that family. Dipesh was every bit what I thought he would be; young, just short of bulky, smart leather jacket, smart accent, the man who knows how to play the role of the man in charge. He introduced me to director Hansal Mehta, a wide and amiable chap, pushy in a more laidback style. There was barely time for a hello; they had things to do.

Their arrival brought the still white vans to life. The two in front opened up like a Trojan horse. The first yielded the heroine, in a lemon-yellow sari around the facial paint mandatory for a star. A woman dresser carrying a little mirror followed her like a shadow. Just beyond intrusion, just within reach. She had a job to do. Perfecting is always a process; besides, new light and the outside air must call for new measures. Breeze is known to be disrespectful of hairstyles, and on a set there's always room for more paint.

'The heroine?' I asked one of the crew who had found a surprisingly idle moment by my side.

'Yes, yes. Isha Koppikar.'

'Is she famous?' I asked, suspecting it could be a rude question.

'Yes, very famous. She has done items.' The item is, of course, that spectacular and revealing dance that the rest of the film was only an excuse to present.

The hero-like chap, or part-villain because this film was different, stepped out of Van Two, shadowed by his own dresser with mirror in hand. Hero and heroine stood on the roadside, each accepting final touches from respective dressers. The hero was not satisfied with his hair, he never would be. He tossed it around, the dresser brushed it, then he tossed it some more. This went on for some time.

Dipesh and Hansal squeezed into the camera van, back doors tied wide open so the camera could see. The van eased slowly out from the lay-by onto the two-lane highway. Girl and boy followed in Mercedes, under the gaze of the camera looking back at them. Girl liked boy but I gathered she wasn't so sure. Gangster with a heart fights hero with a dark side over a woman who loves one but not entirely, cares for another but not that much, and in the end nothing is concluded. The off-beat genre perhaps.

Their departure left me with three white vans for company. And a very relieved and, as it turned out, relieving crew. This is when the four men emerged from the vans to pee by the roadside and raise those crucial matters between India and Britain.

Britain was not promoting itself as a location for filming for nothing. This then was the reason to invite Yash Chopra to Leicester, to send a British minister to a Bollywood promotional event in Mumbai. By UK Film Council standards, a respectable production unit convoy should hire mobile make-up studios, generators, cars for the stars, catering vans, lights, the works, and yes, mobile toilets. It should have meant hiring a film crew here, not flying everyone in, hiring equipment from production companies in Britain, not making cargo of it in Mumbai. But the crew had brought just about everything with them, and the countryside was providing the toilets. On screen, it wouldn't matter what kind of van the paint was applied in before the camera was switched on.

Filming here should also have meant hotels for the crew so that some money was spent on local economy. The stars had them, but the rest clearly hadn't woken up in a hotel room that morning. If nothing else, the crew could have eaten out at local places to feed that business a bit, but I gathered through some chatting among the film crew that the *Raakh* unit had brought its own cook, so they were saving on that too. And it seemed a safe guess that the crew were not on a per diem they would go shopping-crazy on.

The van the men had stepped out of announced it was from Rolfe St Garage in Birmingham. So some van dealer had found customers for a couple of weeks. A couple of drivers too had found work. But it could hardly be what the UK Film Council had in mind when it chose to promote Britain as a destination for Bollywood filming. UK Plc was not doing remotely near the business it might have expected. That roadside pee meant something was working for India but not enough for Britain. And no one has a count yet how many Indian students arouse from the Ashes.

He'd earlier wanted to film *Raakh* in Prague, director Hansal told me. 'It's a gangster film, you know. Prague has a very desolate, gloomy atmosphere.' The pleasant-looking clock tower in the Leicester city centre by the pavement where we stood talking was gone for the moment from his mind's eye, as he measured British gloom against that offered by the Czech Republic.

Prague won on gloom, but at a price. 'And there were so many logistical problems in Prague. Language barrier, big thing there. And you know they have no experience in dealing with Bollywood kind of shooting, the kind of budgets we work on. The cost for shooting in Prague was working out to four to five crore [40 to 50 million] rupees. They are used to Hollywood films, like Bond and all that. They talk in those terms.' The cheerful bit about the Leicester gloom was the lower costs compared to Prague. 'Here our total cost for three weeks of production will be under a crore, which is reasonable.'

Happily, Hansalbhai found Leicester at least partly as grim as Prague had promised to be. He offered a director's analysis of Leicester: 'The outskirts of Leicester are quite charming, they have this desolate, gloomy feel, it is overcast all the time, grey skies, but also there is good landscape, and a certain kind of isolated urbanisation. Feels right for a film like this, a gangster film with a focus on relationships. A very complex matrix of relationships.'

But a crore of rupees still seemed like a lot to middle-class me. Hansalbhai offered more director's philosophy. 'No, I do not make expensive films, only expensive-looking films. I do not cut corners, I cut costs. Money should be spent in front of the camera, not behind. Behind, we will have comfort, not luxury.' He sounded just the man for villainous heroes and heroic villains.

Maybe a crore wasn't bad for half of a feature film. The first half would be filmed in India. And Leicester brought other advantages. 'I have the stars captive here, they only go back to a hotel, not home.' Most of the remaining crew wouldn't go back to a hotel, but to a couple of houses rented for the shoot. Cheaper captives. 'The unit is not rushed, and it functions more efficiently this way.'

Hansal now wandered off to one of those what-next meetings with the crew, and I searched again for an opportunity to talk to Dipesh.

Everyone was hanging around the clock tower except the stars who could never be so commonly seen. A white chap who too obviously hadn't showered for weeks rode up on a bicycle unwashed in years. 'Spare some pennies,' he said, circling the crew that he imagined were rich tourists just off the bus. This lot had few pennies to spare. The bicycle man was finally cornered into a conversation by a policeman, and the crew was spared any further contribution to the British economy.

Dipesh was standing near the clock tower, busy on the mobile. He signalled that he was on his way to the bench I'd found nearby. On the way to me he spoke to chaps from the crew, to the director, to the driver, but finally he was there.

'Busy?' I said.

'Oh, really busy. I'm the line producer.'

'Line? How line?'

'I do locations, management. I'm the producer of this film outside India.'

'So that's a line producer.'

'Yes.' He'd begun to look away from me already. He really didn't have time to educate me about these things.

'You a Leicesterwallah?'

'Yes I'm based here. Promoting East Midlands. I have an independent company, Siddhi Entertainments and Productions UK. I've got a lot of Bollywood films to the UK for filming. Four to Leicester in the last three years. *Is Pyaar Ko Kya Naam Doon, Aa Ja Re, Kyon Ho Gaya Na*. Now *Raakh*. I also do a lot of Bollywood shows here. I brought Hrithik Roshan and Aishwarya Rai here, to East Midlands.'

'Do the East Midlands authorities pay you for this?'

'No, but they should. Those people, they do nothing. They just talk. But they should pay me. Just kidding. But I do it because I live here. The producers pay me.'

'So you offered the location here to the *Raakh* people.'

'Oh no, they approached me.'

'What is it you offer?'

'It is a very good deal that we offer. Main thing is getting here. Once they are here we can arrange basic needs easy, and get public locations free of cost. They spend a little bit on staying and eating but it's not much because you get everything here and they get the cook from India. You can have full crew at very little cost.'

'Is that a lot of crew?'

'Yes, cameraman, his assistants, assistant directors, art directors, make-up people, dance people, production controllers, spot boys, everybody. You've had about forty-five people or so come in for this film from Mumbai.'

'And what's in it for Leicester?'

'It comes on the world map. People come to know where Leicester is. People abroad say this film was shot in Leicester, tourist interest increases. I'm getting three more films in the next three months. Hotels here get business. It's good.'

Dipesh was looking away firmly now, he had to go. It was action time and he was done with his giving me something. He headed off to one of the vans I'd encountered on the road to Nottingham. The ones that *Raakh* did spend some money on.

Brideless

Near Mrs

I can't remember another evening when I was turned down by hundreds of women.

The two marriage melas, or *saathi sammelans* I went to were crowded in just the right way. Hundreds of Indian women had turned up at these fairs in search of husbands, many more than men in search of a wife. There'd never be a better chance to end that never-ending search for someone somewhere. For too long now I'd been to weddings as a guest. It was time to turn up for my own.

The two *saathi sammelans* were being held in Wembley. White Brits know of Wembley for all the wrong reasons. They visit the stadium, now very big and smart, to empty out their lungs over beefy chaps kicking a ball around to make their millions. They know almost nothing of the real Wembley, the land of *dandia* and *garba*, those unmatched Gujarati dances, and of *chevdo* and *gaathia*, those deeply satisfying accompaniments to tea yet undiscovered by Brits who just pass Wembley on their way to the stadium. To a football fan at his politest – if there is such a thing – Indian Wembley is just something ethnic on way to the stadium. To the Gujarati Londoner, this is Gujarat that somehow moved to within half an hour's drive from London from the usual eight-hour flight.

There would be some non-Gujaratis too, I'd been told, at these two conjugal bazaars, from London and outside. I picked my smartest shirt and jeans for my crowded date with multitudes of single women.

It wasn't easy to find parking space for my ancient banger amid those Mercedes Benzes and BMWs at the school by the Alperton tube station that had been hired for the first *sammelan*. The schoolchildren had long gone home, to make way for a different species of girls and boys. A kindness of Indian tradition, that: as long as you're trying to be husband, you're a 'boy'.

'You candidate?' a Gujarati chap at the door asked when he could find time for me through the many others around his desk just outside the hall. I found the courage to say yes, and he let me in on a £5 ticket. I walked into the school hall, with no way to go but forward. On rows of chairs along each wall, watching everyone come in, were the girls, the boys, the parents – hundreds I saw at a glance. By the time I saw what I'd walked into, it was too late to turn back and run, and I had to keep going down the catwalk. To the extent I dared look, I saw unexcited looks all around the room; I had never been sized up and written off by so many so soon.

'You from Southall?' a woman behind the desk at the far end asked. My straight trajectory had brought me right before her. It was not a polite question. From Southall they come Punjabi, big and loud. Wembley is for Gujaratis, gentle and traditional. There must have been something Punjab-born about the way I walked.

'What your specifications?' she asked, matter-of-fact, like a woman behind a railway counter asking where I want a ticket for. 'What year you want?' I didn't know immediately what she was saying, so I just stood there trying to guess. She had all sorts of lists and forms spread out before her. I looked at them, a little intimidated. But I didn't have to answer. She'd figured me out. I wouldn't be looking on the lists for the twenty-somethings.

Others had walked in behind me, and I had to step aside to place myself before the lady at the second desk. She wasn't wasting time either. 'What is your caste?' 'I don't know,' I replied. My £5 ticket had only said this was a social gathering 'for all single Asians to meet prospective partners.' But I now understood the little caution a friend had sounded. This was a *saathi sammelan* for Gujarati Lohannas, that caste that has descended from the god Ram himself. I'd decided to go anyway because I was Indian, and in need, and because the standard wisdom in advance of such meetings is that you never know.

But now I felt an outsider. 'You are Hindu Punjabi?' the lady asked. Nobody had ever called me that in India. Among Indians in Britain you get used to sub-Indian flags, and this was mine. HPs, we're sometimes called in Wembley.

The lady was looking through her lists. 'We have one Hindu Punjabi girl here, but she's too young for you.'

'I was thinking of the Gujaratis,' I said.

'It is very difficult but I will try,' said the plain-speaking lady. I'd made it through the gate, but I wasn't getting past the reception. I could of course go and sit and watch others walk in.

I did, next to a very expectant-looking family. 'Smile, for God's sake, smile,' the mother was telling her near-bridally dressed daughter in the front row. She failed to produce the commanded smile. I felt one with her – in spirit only of course, because the lady at the desk would no doubt have said she was too young for me as well. We were far too inspected to smile, and when we did our own inspecting there did not seem a lot to smile about either. We sat there pretending we were not under watch, and trying not to be seen looking.

A volunteer who had been busy for a bit with a ghetto blaster on stage decided to get us all into the mood with some music for the occasion. '*Aaj main upar, aasmaan neeche...*' ('I am soaring above the sky...'). Soaring above the sky was not how I was feeling, or others I guessed, but she must have figured we needed some optimism.

Another young lady volunteer, very pert and pink, took the mike when the song was over. 'All you boys and girls please come up to the desk and register. Please stand up, and mingle. Don't just sit there. Make the most of your time here. Parents, will you please sit down, encourage your children!'

My neighbour, the mother, again leaned towards the semi-bride. She nudged again but the girl wouldn't budge. A few other prodding mothers had been more successful. And so, a little more than before, the eligible abandoned the sides to brave the catwalk ground in the middle. It seemed to take the courage of a gladiator. A little more than before, boy began to meet girl. Some had even begun to talk.

Finally the mother had persuaded her daughter to leave her seat. With a sickening feeling that I would need to summon valour, I too entered this no man's land. With a show of a stroll, I headed for pink-and-pert lady. 'Can you help me find a wife here?' I said. 'I am Punjabi,' I added apologetically.

'Doesn't matter,' she said. 'Some girls won't mind, tell me who you like and I'll introduce you.' As every Indian male knows, this is the moment to slink away. I was going to be brave.

'You see that lady in the black sari. I think she's wearing it really well.'

'Oh, she has three little children, she's just helping. She's ever-so-nice, you know. Anyone else?'

A lady in a darker shade of pink than hers passed by. 'She's graceful,' I said.

'Oh don't be silly, she's my aunt.' This was going to be my evening of near Mrs.

'But it's good that you're asking,' she said. 'Now you're getting into the spirit of it. But what is your caste?' I was lost for an answer, and she quickly lost interest.

I wasn't the only one getting nowhere. I ran into someone I knew who was from the south of India. He too must have accepted that in Britain no kind of Indian can keep away from Gujaratis for long, they are everywhere. 'I am looking, for my son,' he said. He too wasn't going to find a Gujarati daughter-in-law easily, his family too had spent generations getting born in the wrong place.

Another looking-man joined our corner. 'All this is just moneymaking,' he said. '£5 per head, take away a bit for hiring the hall and for snacks, and they make a packet. I am going to the other *sammelan*.'

So were most others after some time. We were running out of time and faces here. A reverse flow began along the catwalk. Outside, we were now a colourful procession along Ealing Road, and then right down Stanley Avenue to the other school hall, to see and be seen, in search of that someone who would change our lives for ever. And the traffic thought we were just pedestrians.

This second gathering was announced in a leaflet I picked up at the gate of this school as the 'Lohanna and All Hindu Gujarati Youth Sammelan, An Event Of Get-Together & Introduction Programme'. It was organised, the gossip on way from one school to the other had told me, by Jethalal Hindocha, a Lohanna matchmaking rival to Madhuben Rabheru who had organised the first marriage mela.

A woman at a desk outside the hall was collecting £7 from every candidate (I'd become used to thinking myself a candidate) and handing out badges. 'Match Your Heart' a placard on her desk advised. Match colours to match age, that is. Bright orange badge for age 20 to 24, green for 25 to 29, blue for 30 to 34, white for 35 to 39, and a very red for 40 plus. On the badge we wrote our name, educational qualification and ticked either of two boxes 'Single' or 'Divorced'.

She handed me a list of 'Girls 30–34'. I read some entries: date of birth followed by 'GMD 034 4.9 Chunilal Acc assistant OA level Middx'; 'GLF 449 5.0 Raja Office Secretary course Middx' and so on.

The legend below explained.

GLD = Girls Lohanna Divorced
GLE = Girls Lohanna Engagement Broken

GLF=Girls Lohanna First Time
GMD=Girls Mixed Divorced
GME=Girls Mixed Engagement Broken
GMF=Girls Mixed First Time

'Mixed' meant anyone not Lohanna. This most useful lettering was followed by identity number, height, surname, job, education and location. Someone was an accounts assistant, another an office secretary, someone had done O Levels at school and then A Levels.

I bought a list with about 250 female entries. 'Refunds are not available for lists purchased,' the top page announced. The list offered 250 potential wives for £2; I couldn't possibly haggle over that. In any case by the time I hit the stage where I'd want my money back, it would probably be too late to reclaim those £2. And what would I be saying about myself if I did?

The girl put me down on another list, the one that the girls would pay their £2 for. 'You are a BMD,' she told me. 'You go look inside, and if you don't find anyone I'll introduce you to someone. But she's like this,' she said, and stuck her elbows outwards.

This *sammelan*, I heard someone outside say, was more organised. I saw, as I stepped into the hall, that that the organisational skill lay in one simple act. A rope had been stretched halfway across to separate parents from the boys and girls. The cordoned-off parents could do no more than sit on chairs and look into the eligible half of the hall. As one of the boys, I walked past the parents, crossed the rope, smartly I thought, just as I caught that frightening word over the mike here too – someone was asking us to go 'mingle'.

For once someone approached me – a man. 'I'm looking,' he said, 'for my sister. She's over there.' He pointed to her. The sister looked dark and bright and very attractive in her sea-green salwar-kameez, or Punjabi suit as Gujarati women call it. 'Oh yes, I'd love to meet her,' I said. But, wait. 'Tell me about yourself,' the businesslike brother said. 'Are you Hindu Punjabi?' 'Yes.'

'Actually my sister wants to marry a Lohanna. He must have seen disappointment on my face. 'I don't mind as long as you're Hindu, you know. But it's her choice.' He walked back to her. A potential wife lost.

Now a woman walked up, looking interested. She was more radiant than lovely, and had all the confidence I lacked. She was coming up to talk to me, and I felt a quick surge of hope, I was getting more mingled with than mingling. After a rapid hello, she started to tell me about the next *saathi sammelan* she was organising. She'd walked up to advertise her own *sammelan*; she must have been confident that I'd leave this hall single.

'I have a boyfriend and I told him I'm coming here just to advertise,' she said. 'But I'm also looking.' So she could replace her boyfriend, but the new one would have to prove himself better. We chatted a bit, then she left, saying 'I'll go chat up someone else now.' Two steps on, she looked back. 'I'm honest, you see.'

Her efficiency left me floored, and I stood a while doing nothing. A suited Lohanna took the mike on stage. 'Hey guys and girls! It's stupendous to see you mingling out there! Great, great! Just carry on!' OK for him to say. He didn't have to mingle like his life depended on it.

An announcement followed for someone sought. 'Yogesh, will you please come to the stage. A really lovely girl wants to meet you.' Good for you, Yogesh, and damn you. That was from me and I'm sure others around. There must have been plenty of disappointed Lohannas around as well. Being Lohanna is a help, not a guarantee. After the Yogesh announcement, came that song again, '*Aaj main oopar...*' You had to be Yogesh this evening to like it.

A queue was gradually forming to a side for the snacks and I headed straight there. It promised samosas and escape, and I wanted both. In the queue, someone father-like behind me was offering his views on the evening to another like him. Too many were looking, Lohanna, this, that, the other, too many others who were not Lohanna. But there was an edge to his remark. So many others had come here in search of single Lohannas, when Lohannas could not find enough of their own.

Picking up a white plastic plate with cold Gujarati eats on it – I found no samosas at the table – I finally walked up to the very elderly and very wise-looking Hindocha who had organised this *sammelan*, and who seemed at last to be enjoying a free moment. He knew just what to say to sad faces. 'It took me four years to find a match for my daughter,' he said. It can take many *sammelans* for one *saathi*. 'What to do, there are no opportunities to meet others who are like you. Results usually take two to three months after a *sammelan*. But every week I get one or two calls from people marrying who met through my gatherings.' He was in the business of marriage for some, hope for the rest.

'Don't worry, we have your name,' he said. 'You will hear from someone.' I never did.

Right after he'd finished singing a Bollywood song very badly, the chap in the black shirt covered at least half in pink print asked our table at the *mochi* bar in Leicester if anyone was going to the marriage mela in Birmingham. Only I was interested, and this started some beer-fuelled digs that I'd walk away with a *mochi* girl. That girl, like this bar, was really meant for a Gujarati male of shoemaker ancestry.

The singer gave me a number to call, and I was invited to attend after polite agreement that it would not be as a prospective groom.

A late start from London made me among the last arrivals at the smart new Shree Krishna Mandir on Henley Street in Birmingham. A young fellow was also walking towards the mandir hall through a crowded corridor as I headed in. I asked him if he was a *mochi*.

'We are all *mochis*, you know, shoemakers.'

'And what do you do?'

'I'm a computer systems analyst up in Manchester.' He stopped to talk to someone, and I pushed through to the hall.

It was a bright morning, made brighter by the weekend buzz around the temple. The weekend is when the business of life gets done. It's when the English rest or shop, go fishing or repaint the fence, do up an attic, do a roast, the rare one even goes to church. A good Indian moves from England to India on weekends; to those halls where everyone meets by way of one event after another, to one another's houses, to Indian shopping. It's the time to be with your own, or to look amongst your own so you could marry and multiply and go on being with your own.

A few hundred eligible *mochis*, expensively dressed, had crowded into the large hall under the white bud-like dome of the temple. The suits and silks in the hall, the shining cars outside, were far from the picture of the *mochi* in India as I knew him to be – the man with his workshop on his shoulder who miraculously never seemed to notice the heat. These were well-heeled *mochis*.

By the side of the hall, some people had taken their shoes off to enter the shrine. Shoes had brought everyone to this temple, outside this shrine they were a little more meaningful than outside others.

Past that shrine, eligible *mochis* had the hall to themselves; parents were kept back in the corridor. That naturally didn't stop those closest to the door from seeing, just happening to, whatever was going on within.

By now 262 single *mochis* had entered the hall already, a male volunteer said at the entrance. Someone was keeping watchful count. For a silly moment I was pleased at the even number, like everyone would necessarily leave the hall half of a pair. But it was not in any case a gender-balanced gathering. There were clearly many more women than men, and in their colourful best. Everyone wore an off-white badge with a number on it that would lead back to the candidate's CV for this most important of all jobs.

A man on stage was calling out numbers. 'One hundred and forty nine. Eighty-eight.' The numbers were singles who'd appeared interesting to someone. 'Nobody give your phone numbers, please.' This would have to be processed pairing.

Had I been eligible *mochi* number 263 this morning, I'd have taken the number maybe of that woman taller than almost all the numbered men, the one therefore made for a Punjabi. Or others. The more women I looked at, the more I wanted an off-white piece of paper with a number on it. But I'd been let in only as witness to supervised flirtation. If my forefathers were shoemakers, I could have become a husband. Here I was badgeless, hopeless.

But I still felt the need for fantasy search. My sly survey rested on a light-eyed girl in a peach *chania-choli*, that Indian translation of skirt and blouse much extended by way of folds and colour, on that bright-eyed woman in the yellow and red sari. As *mochi*, I'd have wandered past each one casually, made a note of the number when no one was looking, and gone straight to a volunteer. I'd have given my number, given hers. Her number would be called out and, who knows, she would have mine called out, and we would live happily ever after.

I spotted the chap I'd met in the corridor outside. He was slim, and his jet-black hair combed remorselessly back matched his moustache, the one thing so many Indian men have and the British don't. That with the blue blazer and striped tie made the complete smart man. He looked a good catch for a sensible woman.

'What do you think of all this?' I asked. Not a clever question, but all I could think of.

'Mixed feelings, really.'

'How, mixed?'

'Well, it's a good idea if people can meet, nothing wrong with that.'

'But you're not very sure.'

'Well, yeah, it's this caste thing, you see. I mean by now we should be moving further and further away from it, right, but this kind of thing is only promoting that.'

'You said you're from the shoemaker caste.'

'Yes, shoemaker. Mochi.'

'But you're a computer analyst.'

'Yeah, but that's my work.'

'So in what sense do you think of yourself as a shoemaker?' I was hesitating as I asked, but he seemed a lot more comfortable talking about his shoemaking origins than I was.

'It's the parents. It's the whole community.'

'Are you here because you want to be here or because your parents want you here?'

'Well, it's for the parents, really. But there's no harm if you can meet somebody.'

'If you like a girl from another caste, would you marry her?'

'Well I don't know but if I marry within the community, right, my parents would be happy and I'd be happy.'

'Met anyone here?'

'Yes, I have, actually.' He led me with his eye to the girl facing us in the group to the left. The one in the peach who I'd considered for myself only minutes back in my *mochi* dream world. 'She's just the kind of person I've been looking for.' He couldn't hold back his smile when he spoke of her. A blush appeared in the neighbourhood of his moustache, and a light brightened his eyes 'I'll invite you to our wedding,' he said. He didn't have my address, and didn't ask for it, just wanted to share his joy with someone, and I happened to be around.

Things had moved quickly. He'd given her number to his parents. They had spoken to hers, and apparently heard approving words. He looked impatient to announce the wedding. 'She's just finished college,' he said, looking again towards her, staring almost. An arranged marriage can sometimes be the same thing as love at first sight. But he looked a little worried too. I had heard her number called out three or four times, and that may not have been all. He must have heard it far louder than I did every time. I left him in desire short of certainty, that awful space to occupy.

I was looking at one half of a *mochi* love story. Not that there was anything peculiarly *mochi* in his desire – shoes didn't come into that, the emotion wasn't informed by leather – but they couldn't have met without sharing family memories of shoemaker origins.

For Dinesh Chauhan, who was managing the event and had invited me to it, theirs would be another happy story of shoemaker weds shoemaker, but he'd be just as happy if either was replaced by another *mochi*. He was more keen on the *mochi*-ness of love in that room. Chauhan, young for a community leader and very proper in his grey suit, was off-stage now, and I sought him out in a corner past some girly groups and male conferences. In the given style of important people, he spoke to the point.

'We have a Mahasabha [central association] UK with nine constituent associations in Birmingham, London, Leicester, Bradford, Leeds, Preston, Wellingborough, Coventry, Greater Manchester. But our boys and girls in Birmingham will not know if someone from the community is available for marriage in London. Now introduction is available. So this is a *sammelan* for the candidates to come into contact.'

'Or they might never meet.'

'Yes, finding a suitable partner is a big problem because the people are scattered. In your area you may not meet person with right age and qualification.'

'You think this is a good way?'

'Oh yes, we cannot just have arranged marriages. Here they see each other first hand, they can talk and exchange views and hope to find a partner.' He surveyed the hall with much satisfaction. 'You see, they are mingling. Given the situation in this country this is a very viable way.'

'But is it necessary to call out someone's number on the mike?'

'Yes that is the way they have to contact a volunteer.'

'But then everybody knows that someone is interested in a particular person.'

'No, but we are not calling candidates on top of the stage. If somebody finds somebody likeable to talk to they have to go only to the volunteer. There are no obligations on anyone.' After a pause he said, 'You see the parents want to carry on the tradition. So we have this new temple. It is the central focal point for everybody to get together.'

'But what about other Gujaratis, other Hindus? Wouldn't they do?'

'We are doing this for the community but there are no restrictions with Gujaratis or Hindus.'

'But if you're doing this for the community, why not invite other Hindus?' I was making a daring suggestion – why not arrange for one Hindu to marry another Hindu?

'Hindus are most welcome. We can do that, but the Hindu community is so vast it is difficult to organise.' Chauhan had drawn the *mochi* circle, at least partly, he was suggesting, for logistical reasons.

An elderly Gujarati in a suit walked up to call Chauhan away for some matter that couldn't wait. Chauhan made his way to the stage and announced, 'You have been intermingling for two hours. Now the parents are coming in, as you can see. We will break for lunch now but after lunch you will get some further intermingling with each other.'

The parents were pouring into the hall fast, a 'what happened?' look on every face. The future of the family could depend on those last two hours. On numbers called and heard, or the numbers not called. Some numbers I heard again and again, many I never did.

Some of the women in near bridal best were leaving the floor like the bridegroom had failed to turn up. They'd stood two hours waiting to be liked, minute after undesired minute, number after another's number. All those days of preparing for this day – this sari, no, that salwar-kameez, those bangles, these earrings, the nails just right, the hair… no, that's never absolutely right but still – and after all that, this silence.

Would this day ever end if your number didn't make it to the mike? Quite an avalanche of undesire that would be to live with. And other *mochis* would talk. You were there, and you're still single? Want to think of marrying someone that 150 men rejected straightaway? Over lunch I began to not miss a number of my own.

I decided to skip the post-lunch intermingling, but sought out my near bridegroom friend to say bye. Coincidentally, as we had arrived together, he was heading out to the parking lot, not staying for the post-lunch intermingling. He looked defeated and now rather white around his dark moustache.

'All well?' I asked.

'They said no. She said no.' He turned away and was gone.

Fast Work

'You will have three minutes each with twenty ladies,' Ann Little said when I called her. She must have wanted to answer my silence over this. 'When you come to think of it, three minutes is quite a long time in which to get to know someone.' She was right, of course.

I had turned to the agency called A Little Creation. I was running out of time and Indian women, and a friend persuaded me it was time to try my luck with English women. In any case, Indian women in England weren't Indian, really, they were first Gujarati or Sikh. I wasn't quite either, but being either would not be enough. The Chha-gam Patels would not invite me for their matchmaking parties if I wasn't one of them, the other Patels would leave me out of theirs. Jat Sikhs sought Jat Sikhs, Ramgarhia Sikhs searched out and found their own. As none of the above, I found no one among them. There's nothing quite like the desire to marry to teach an Indian how much an outsider he can be to other Indians.

I had slipped into the Lohanna bazaar twice, but where could I hide my un-lohannaness? Maybe it was me, not the Hindu Punjabi in me that turned all those faces away. But mostly I never got far enough to be turned away, I just bumped into one closed door after another. I was dismissed before I'd had a chance to prove myself unworthy.

It was time for A Little Creation. A friend showed me the way at the very suburban-yuppy David Lloyd's club in Sudbury. We found the posters pasted just above the Internet access points by the pool and bar. 'A Little Creation presents fun-dating', the poster read in many colours. A joyous couple, with a clock on the side to remind you that time was running out, were silhouetted as logo. The couple and the clock worked, I called Ann Little, and before I knew exactly what I was letting myself into, I was speed-dating.

I went in my coolest blue shirt and casual-smart black trousers; you can't let the wrong clothes come in the way of 20 such possibilities. Twenty was a lot less than the hundreds at the Gujarati *saathi sammelans*, but here I would get to talk to every one of the 20, which was about twenty more than at the Indian marriage melas.

Ann Little was easy enough to find at a table by the Internet point. 'And you are…?' she asked, with the distant ease of a receptionist. She peeled off a sticker with my name on it under the 'Fun-Dating' imprint and I stuck it on my shirt as instructed.

'Let me explain what happens,' she said briskly. 'You see these twenty tables, each has a number. The ladies will just sit at their table. We think it is more appropriate for the men to rotate. Every three minutes someone will blow a whistle, and you move to the lady at the next table. You start at table seven. Take this coupon. It will get you your first drink at the bar free. We find that people usually need it.'

Ann handed me also a little eight-page booklet, some blank post-it notes and a pencil. 'Those blank ones are in case you want to make some notes about a lady. On the form, you enter the name of every lady you meet. If you would like to see her later, tick the box to the side. The form will tell you more. And have a great evening.'

Ann was right about the drink. My beer at the bar went down at speed as I waited for the rotation to begin. I saw others with 'Fun-Dating' stickers at the bar making rapid progress with theirs. We all looked away from one another. The men were all alone, the women all in groups. The agony of waiting was relieved a little by the knowledge that I didn't have to approach the women at the bar, I'd be moved past every one of them like the needle of the clock that A Little Creation seemed so fond of. For the first time, I was at a crowded bar knowing I would talk to every woman there. Going up to Ann Little had taken courage; going up to the women would be pre-arranged routine. I sat urgently arguing its advantages to myself, to work myself into an upbeat state I didn't feel.

As the beer disappeared from the glass, I turned to a snapshot account of speed-dating in the booklet Ann Little had provided.

HELLO AND WELCOME TO FUN-DATING!

The aim of the evening is to ensure that we all have a great time. You will be meeting like-minded people in a relaxed atmosphere and the emphasis of tonight is to have fun.

Fun-dating at speed is a great way of meeting and chatting to people that you might never get the opportunity to talk to in normal circumstances. You would have three minutes to decide whether or not you would like to get to know a person better and then move on.

Fun-dating at speed also gives you a fairly quick escape route if you need it! I wonder how many of you have been on a blind date and within three minutes you have wanted to leave? Well at Fun-dating you can! You just move on to your next date.

Thank you for coming along tonight and who knows it could be the first three minutes of the rest of your life!'

Too soon, a whistle started my first three-minute date. I walked up and sat down across from a lady at table seven. She was sharp and elegant in that chiselled English way. I wish I could say she'd been waiting for me.

She spoke first, thankfully. 'Have you done this before?'

'No. And you?'

'A couple of times. It's not so bad. OK, now let's see where we start.' She glanced at a printed green sheet placed on the table to guide women on what they could talk about over three minutes.

'You go to a gym?' she asked. She spoke like someone who did not know life outside a socially pleasant plateau.

'Sort of, sometimes.' I could see that she did.

'And what do you do?' she asked.

'I'm a journalist.'

'Who for?'

'Just write articles here and there, in India, in some other countries.' So I was not BBC. I felt my score drop. I wasn't giving her anything that would make me respectably introduceable to her friends.

'And you?'

'I'm a nurse. Up at Clementine Churchill.'

'Yes, that's just round the corner isn't it?' I'd been given only a few seconds to be scintillating, and was failing badly.

'Yes, and there's lots of us from there around today. We're all friends, we all came here together.'

'Lots of nurses here, is it?' I had no idea why that should make me nervous, but it did.

'Oh yes, lots. But that's your whistle.' I thought she'd been a bit quick to point my attention to it. The man ahead of me had moved on already, and I replaced him across from the lady at table eight.

I was now opposite another nurse, the first 'Hi, I'm so-and-so' confirmed. Everyone had a name tag, but it was still polite to engage in unassisted introductions. I decided to be brave, and looked straight at her. She was pretty and bright in her turquoise blue dress. Streaks of grey in the sheer drop of her hair to the shoulders added anchor to her good looks. She was a woman fighting off experience with spirit.

I found myself talking Clementine Churchill again.

'That hospital's more like a hotel,' I said.

'Oh yeah, it is really very nice. But, you know, when you work somewhere, it's just work.'

'Of course,' I said, and went blank.

She didn't. 'Do you think there's something really very sad about all this, the way we are meeting. You know, meeting like this just because we couldn't find anyone otherwise?'

'Yes, it is sad. It means, I suppose, that the magic didn't work for us, chance didn't sort of deliver anything. So you play a numbers game, and hope something happens this way.'

'How long have you been on your own?' she asked.

'Oh, long.'

'Which means?'

'Years, many years. And you?'

'I broke up with my boyfriend last month.' She needed someone faster than I did, but she didn't need me, and it didn't take much perception to tell.

This time I heard the whistle. The whistle-blower was walking right by our table, a twenty-something given charge of moving 20 men every three minutes.

I left table eight with a feeling of some indignity. I was leaving tables, and would leave another 18 because someone would blow a whistle in my ears. I wished Ann Little had found other ways to mark the passage of time.

I would never recall everything said at every one of those 20 tables. I never did make notes on those blank slips of paper – couldn't, in those three minutes of throwing up some talk, write anything, and couldn't in between. And after the first couple of conversations, I really stopped listening. There was nothing to note, nothing to say. OK, you have three minutes to make an impression in, 90 seconds to talk, 90 to listen, and your time begins now. Under such pressure, I developed even more cramps between my ears than usual.

But through those three-minute multiplications, what got said didn't really matter. It was the expressions I found myself remembering, and wishing I didn't have to. Looks say enough, and every three minutes a new one was saying 'no'. Ann was right, three minutes really is quite a long time. The real choices had been made already in those quick glances at the bar. This business is so fast it's over before it begins.

So I knew the Cypriot girl was from Cyprus only because we had to say something for three minutes. But a shutter had dropped over her grey eyes before I could sit down. Before those eyes three minutes was a very long time. I had no idea what to say to her, and no particular desire to say anything. I found myself longing for the whistle, because this time it would bring escape.

We found no room for those social rituals that hide the hard decisions, or for those playful nothings that could really bring two people that one step closer. We met with raw purpose, and when we saw we were getting nowhere, no one cared if it showed. I began to feel like a train passing through stations; I stopped at platforms to stare at faces, exchanged a word or two, then moved on to the guard's whistle. I went past the Greek lady who said she had a store selling designer stuff, past the school teacher from Ireland, the management consultant handling male resistance to her at an office in Newcastle, the Essex-like girl who so, so, loves to travel and has been almost everywhere and couldn't wait to go everywhere else.

One table I remember well; here I met a Gujarati girl. Most reassuringly, she told me her caste even though I wasn't it. 'I'm a Prajapati, you know, from the north of Gujarat. Saurashtra. But that is my family. I'm from Kenya. But to tell you the truth, I do not want to meet a man from my community. I would like to go out with a white guy. But I did not really come for myself. My friend, he is just going through a divorce. So I brought him here to meet girls, then I said why not join myself also?'

I'd found no time to look at the men in the circle and had no idea who he was. But about halfway through my table tour I figured who was behind me. He spoke to me after a quick whistle to draw my attention, in obviously Pakistani Punjabi, 'So which one are you going to screw?' I must of course have been just as obviously Punjabi to him. I only had time to say that I thought neither of us would get anywhere with anyone this evening.

Towards the end of the circle, I began to notice also the guy in front of me. Everyone did. I'd seen him at the bar. He was the picture of the tough English football fan, sort of bulky but with a sporty manner, he probably had the cross of St George on his car outside. But through his progress along the circle he had become more and more unsteady. He'd been speed drinking longer and at greater speed than anyone else, and he was now getting slower and slower off each table. I have never before felt more sympathetic towards someone who had had more than he could handle.

And never before did I think it would be such a relief to sit at a table only because it was called table six. The round was done, and fast enough, perhaps, the evening was over. I was on my own at the end, as I was at the beginning. Only now I felt my ineligibility wasn't Indian any more, it had gone, as they say, mainstream.

The first woman I saw on my big evening out caught me admiring my moustache in the ladies toilet. I apologised rapidly and walked out fast, lucky not to run into another walking in. But the club was seriously dark, and she could have excused the intrusion.

Everything from the black facade was dark about the Turnmills Club on Clerkenwell Road. Just right for a nightclub, which it would become again after our all-Asian speed-dating event ended.

I half-guessed my way towards the party hall downstairs. The stairs were lit in a shade between diffused and disappeared. But it was all helpful. The dimness would fade out our imperfections and create 'atmosphere'. We could wear disguises over our expressions more promisingly, and our mistakes wouldn't be spotlighted under a glare.

It had promised to be a particularly rewarding evening because Apna Speed-dating was going to put me on a circuit created especially for Hindu Punjabis. After the misadventures with Gujarati Lohannas and white English nurses, this was going to be home turf.

The Apna website had announced the event would be for 'H/ P & Separate Muslim'. Hindu Punjabi and a separate Muslim event, that is, at the same place, at the same time. Tricky, at the least. Nothing gets the Hindu parent more worried than the fear of a daughter taking off with a Pakistani, since at an event like this Muslim would really mean Pakistani. And what if circuits got mixed up somehow?

I joined a queue headed downstairs to a desk where a chap and a girl were ticking arrivals. The bare shoulders and glance-stopping forms descending before me looked good. The girl at the desk marked what she thought was my name on what I guessed was a register, and gave me a coupon for the first free drink at the cellar bar. Everyone knows the need for that one.

I said hello to the chap beside her, he was the one I'd spoken to on the phone earlier. In that darkness of the Turnmills basement, it was still clear he was Pakistani. I thought again what parents of Hindu Punjabi girls might have to say to daughters descending into a dark basement for a group date being managed by a Pakistani, and with lots of other Pakistani males around at a simultaneous event at the same place. I guess it wouldn't be 'have a great night out, darling'. I groped my way towards the bar, mainly to work myself out of vicarious parental mode.

Beer in hand, I entered the dating room. Tables were set and numbered. This is where Apna would rotate us in three-minute slots. The clock on the Apna website, quite the favoured emblem of speed-dating managers, had suggested what minute by minute progress might mean. 'It's time', the clock with only three, two and one etched on it declared. Three, a couple appeared sitting opposite one another. Two, they got closer. One, they were holding hands. All of us knew we would fail against that clock.

A lot of us had begun to hang around the paired chairs. That was the idea. 'It's the ice-breaking time,' a girl with papers and lists in her hand announced a few times through a quick tour of the room. The website had announced this as a new feature. 'New: Ice-breakers are being introduced at all our events from May onwards, these will help you get relaxed and put you in a positive frame of mind before the dating gets underway, please ensure you arrive at the specified time to take part in these activities.'

There was no separate breaking of ice for Muslims and for Hindu Punjabis. I joined a group at a table by the side of the dating tables, and I saw eventually that I'd joined two chaps with Muslim names, Pakistanis clearly, breaking ice with two girls with Hindu names. The two Pakistanis looked everywhere but at me, they wanted me to be anywhere but there. We chatted a while, and then I got up and strolled towards the lady with the lists.

'Are the Hindu and Muslim events separate?' I asked.

'Yes they are, but we are going to have some Muslim tables in the Hindu room. Excuse me.' She was off, this was not something she wanted to talk about. After breaking ice, some Pakistanis and

Hindu Punjabis would speed-date in the same room.

I looked around the room at the guys, and walked up to a chap with a Hindu name on his sticker. 'Where are you from?' I asked, which could mean something as usual as where in London, a fairly dull opener of a question. He looked past me and walked towards the bar. I followed. 'What's your drink?' I asked. Now he walked away from the bar. He wouldn't say a word, not to me.

In the dark, I tried to read stickers on the women without appearing like I was staring at their breasts. Couldn't find a Muslim name immediately; maybe they were in some other room. A religious mix should be something to be pleased about, and maybe this one had the innocence of a cross-religious togetherness we could all smile upon. Togetherness in itself seems such an ideal, separation such a shame. But the method here seemed dubious, and certainly at variance with the announcement. The Hindu–Muslim divide in matters sexual is issue enough; between Indians and Pakistanis it can be the stuff of family devastation.

The dating began. I began at table one. I had a scorecard in my hand from the front desk, so had all the girls. My curiosity had taken over my need for a woman in my life. I just wanted to see who these Indian girls were at this event.

I began with a nursery school teacher, light and pretty, whose parents she said had come to Britain from Mauritius. She was renting a flat in smart Notting Hill with a friend. But Notting Hill was not a good place to meet others ethnically like her. 'It's always nice to meet Asians,' she said. 'There's just so much more you can share, it's not the same with the whites, is it?' Her parents weren't in London, so how would she ever meet anyone if not this way? She'd seen an ad for the event in *Metro*.

'Well, you've been looking around for an hour,' I said. 'Seen anyone interesting?'

'No, not really, but let's see how it goes.'

The girl at table two had invested in a strikingly short dress.

The dress code that evening was minimal, but I could see a sales catalogue class this one micro-minimal. Only one girl wore Indian, a *churidar-kurta*, and that long dress over leggings was here almost a mistake; dressing conservatively was hardly the flavour of the evening. Table two was a personal assistant to a manager at an IT firm, and she looked most relieved that she did not have to put up with my Indian accent for more than three minutes.

The next girl was Gujarati. And why was she here? 'I really like Hindu Punjabi boys. I think they're so sexy. But there seem to be hardly any around today.' The ice-breaking hour had dashed her hopes already. In the rush, I had no time to feel pained that she seemed to exclude me.

Table four was also Gujarati, and a speed-dating veteran. 'Been to many of these, you know, speed-dater and some others.'

'Didn't find someone?'

'No, not really. It's not easy, you know. Guys, you know.' She held her scorecard with a practised hand. After I moved to table five she'd mark me in the 'No' box, if she cared to do that. She must have crossed a hundred speed-dating 'NOs' by now. At least she could never say she'd been short of choice.

I was not doing a very good job with my scorecard. I had forgotten tip number four on the website: 'Try and keep notes of your dates, adding comments in the space provided on your scorecard for people that have impressed you. This will remind you later of who they were.'

Table ten was unforgettable, though, and not because she wore something from the plunging pages of that sales catalogue. I only had to say 'Hi' before she said, 'You're from India.'

'Yes. The accent, is it?'

'When did you arrive?'

'Been here ten to fifteen years.'

'What? Ten years? And you talk like an Indian?'

'What else?'

'But... ten years? You didn't change?'

I said this was one failing that didn't embarrass me.

'But you must be from India,' I said.

'Yes, I only came here three weeks back.' Already she sounded far less Indian than me.

'And how long are you here for?'

'Only another three weeks.' I did not ask the rude question: what was she doing speed-dating here then?

She sounded Delhi to me, and I was right. 'Why don't you go back and start speed-dating in Delhi.'

'It would never work there.'

'Maybe not if people just pay over the phone and walk in like here, but if you pre-select a group and put them together, it might.'

But she was here thinking London, not Delhi.

'What brought you to London?'

'I'm a fashion designer, here for a course.' She looked like a woman with other designs. For three minutes that was a lot. I moved on, and so did she, whether in Delhi or London I don't know.

The transfers came to an abrupt end at table 17. Someone suddenly announced an invitation to the Anexo bar next door, with offers of coupons for two drinks for the price of one. It was a relief. We were now headed for a free-for-all party, no one was pretending that Hindus and Muslims would be separate there.

'Maybe they should have just parties instead,' the private secretary, table number whatever, said as I walked upstairs with her. Apna had beaten her to the thought. They had announced parties coming up, and the next speed dating event was not promising to be Muslim only, or H. P. only. 'Summer Bonanza All Asian Mixed Speed-Dating Event, Tickets on sale below... Meet and Date up to 30 People, From Only £15...' The usual promise had been tagged on: 'Imagine a room full of between 15–25 eligible singles who want to meet someone like you... No pressure, it's fast it's fun and you could meet the one!' Apna was also offering 'limited spectator/chill-out zone tickets (£15.00 each)' in case you wanted to observe the dating and not join in.

Almost none of the Hindu girls walked into the bar next door, all of them just seemed to be leaving. That should have reassured their parents, if they ever knew enough to need such reassurance. The girls could have been waiting for the one-to-ones resulting from the scorecards we'd handed in before leaving. But my guess was there wouldn't be much of that.

That left four of us Indian males at Anexo to brood over the evening, and I exchanged names with them more happily than I had with the girls. About the quietest-looking was a chap to my side, Rakesh. He was 24, he said, and he'd been pushed by friends to attend the event because he was still a virgin. 'I've always been shy of talking to girls.'

'So how did you get on this evening?'

'How can you talk to these girls? They all wear, like that.' He made a horizontal move of his hand at chest level in line with the low-cuts of the evening.

'That's good man, that's good.' This was Jaz, the lone Sikh. It's hard to find a young Sikh in London who's not called Jaz. Jasminder, Jaspal, Jasbir – they're all Jaz.

Jaz was taking Rakesh under his wing. 'You know I was shy like you once. And look at me now. It's a phase, man. It's just a phase.'

'I'll tell you what,' said the fourth, Mukul, 'You come with me to Sports Cafe at Piccadilly. Polish, Hungarian, Chinese girls. I'll make any one of them shag you.' We were all getting quite concerned about poor Rakesh's virginity. He listened quietly and looked like he just wanted to go home and wished he hadn't left it at all.

Mukul was resigned to a wasted evening. 'I won't get anyone tonight,' he said, in a loud funky-punky kind of accent that belonged nowhere. He'd come from Bangalore three years back. 'You just came from India,' he told me. 'I can tell.'

I delivered the shock to him now. 'You been here ten to twelve years? You still not managed to change? I can't believe it.'

'Why do you think you won't get anyone?' I asked him.

'I can tell, I can tell.'

'How many girls did you tick?'

'Just four, five. You have to be selective.'

'I ticked everyone,' said Jaz. 'If I give seventeen girls the chance to have me, I have a better chance. Mark just three, four, less chance. But you,' he said, turning to me. 'You should not look so Indian, man. I have a Pakistani friend, he couldn't get no girls. Then I told him to shave off his moustache and he got plenty girls. You should shave off your moosch.'

He didn't make the connection that his own moustache was probably bigger than mine. With a beard like his for company, a moustache is probably not a moustache. I hadn't expected the evening to begin and end with my moustache.

Lucky Ducky

We'd meet, we Indians, some Pakistanis maybe, at a place as white English as you could get. Ask a tourism consultant in London which part of England is most England-like if you had just a day, and Henley is what you'll hear.

It's the kind of place nature custom-designs for tourism boards, a picture postcard waiting to be walked into. Wooded hillside descending into a meadow right down to the clear waters of the Thames, the rafters by the pretty white boats under the ancient stone bridge which you must cross to enter the village street for the tea houses with the hot scones, the ones right by the old clock tower in the square… There was nothing they could call cobbled, but even Henley can't have it all.

I was there in less than an hour, after what the tourism chaps would no doubt have called a 'scenic drive from London'. I put aside the map that would tell me where to go from the parking lot, because a more interesting possibility arose by way of an Indian girl who emerged from the passenger door of a red Renault two cars away. She must be headed for the party – why else would an Indian be in Henley, and in that high black skirt and little yellow number (not what an Indian tourist is likely to wear)? She'd come looking for a someone, as I had, though she didn't look half as tentative as I felt. She looked, in fact, assured in a defiant sort of way. She surveyed the surroundings and dared Henley to be good enough for her.

I was going to pay £35 to meet single women in Henley this afternoon, and I could get my money's worth starting now.

'Hi, do you know where we have to go?' I asked.

'No, I don't come here every day.'

I had to be clumsy, and she had to be clever. It's the way it is with women like her – you can tell. And it must be something about chaps like me too, and no doubt she could tell. I've often wished it was only my Indian accent that puts off Indian girls in Britain so quickly; that I can't help where I'm from is a little better than I can't help who I am.

By now the girl who'd been driving the Renault had stepped round, too. She held out her hand straight to me in a warm handshake. 'Hi, I'm Neera.' My spirits were restored a little. She must know that any male her companion spoke to needed instant restoration. The power women can have, one way and another.

'Let me look at the map,' she said. I stood so I could be seen to be looking at her map while I could also have a good look at her, the usual sly male thing to do. She was wearing a black blouse made of the kind of see-through cloth a proper Indian tailor would use only for a *dupatta*. The blouse ended its descent some distance above a blue skirt streaked with yellow, which left room for plenty of midriff and more in between. I thought it proper to move vision to her hair, which was woven into a bunch of rather complicated curls that began black, and turned blonde.

They looked like they'd taken some doing, even if the boring female explanation was plain highlighting.

'That way,' she said, and placed the map back in her bag. She pointed to a path along the river. I felt momentarily awkward that I hadn't looked at the map at all. The three of us walked on together, and I was much comforted that I would arrive in what must at least appear to be a group.

Another picture postcard presented itself. We passed toy-town boats enlarged to life-size, with names like Sundown Lady and River Lark. A couple of them sailed by carrying men in hats. Two women went past on a polished wooden deck, inviting the afternoon sun to brown their legs just a little. Trees stood above tipsy reflections on the banks until a boat came along and bust it all. Ducks and swans rode the wake to complete the picture.

We were paying for the prettiness of the place. The Patel couple who had arranged the singles party presumably factored in a 20 per cent romantic-setting surcharge.

The map had led us to a point across from the chalet on Rod Eye Islands where Mr Patel had told me on the phone the singles party was happening. He said chalet like he'd like me particularly to notice the 'ay', and that he was sophisticated enough not to pronounce the 't'. We joined five or six others who were waiting for a boat to take us over to the shall-ay.

A slim Sikh in a light jacket and a turban equivalent of a rakish hat had taken over this little pre-party.

'Why don't I grab a duck and ride over?' he said.

'They took one look at you and swam away,' a plump girl with her back to us replied.

'Let's all jump into the water,' he said.

'Yeah, like that would get rid of the ducks, right?'

I got the sick feeling that these and the like would be the clever lines of the day, and that they'd fail me all afternoon. This was going to be the slim Sikh's day, not mine. I settled into the sinking feeling that his £35 was going to work a lot better.

He was splashing out the GSOH I'd seen advertised in those Asian matrimonial and dating ads: Good Sense of Humour. White seekers in *The Guardian* and *The Sunday Times* struggled to write clever things about themselves. Indians simply wrote GSOH, and left it to you to discover in person how clever they really were.

The Sikh with dash introduced himself as Lucky. Lakhvinder, I presumed. This afternoon you had to strike the cool mode rapidly, and Lucky was on target before we'd even got to the dream island. He had put us all under pressure to produce GSOH, and soon.

Our voyage lasted only a few yards. The arrival of the boat at the chalet lifted the pressure. The white boatman led every girl into the boat by hand. 'C'mon, darling', 'Come, love', he went. Girls like a show of protection at moments like this.

Over on the island a woman, the female Patel host, clearly, marked us off on a list and collected the money. A lovely girl with straight black hair, but I was looking at her because I couldn't bear to look in the direction of the 70 or 80 Indians, or Asians, already out there on the lawn watching new boat people like us come up. They were sizing up everyone who came off the boat. We were late, and the later you arrived, the more scrutinised you'd be. We're quite an inspecting culture.

I crossed the lawn and walked into the chalet kitchen because it was frightening to just walk into one of those groups on the lawn. A good decision, because it was a friendly lot in there. Everyone introduced themselves cheerfully as some Patel or other. One was serving, someone was setting up the barbecue, one was in charge of the bar. The Patels had come together to take care of everything between them. Who's better than Gujaratis as exterminators of overheads?

Some quick beers later I ventured into the lawn, like a batsman stepping out on a difficult wicket. About fifty women stood around I could say hello to.

I walked to the nearest group, and into instant hostility. I said 'hi' to a chap in the group with crew cut hair in a long creased shirt drooping low over his trousers, very deliberately casual for a day like this. He did not reply. 'Go pick up someone somewhere else,' his body language said. There were girls in the group, and he had been talking happily to them.

'Ever been to the Regatta around here?' I said generally to everyone. Anything to get started.

'Woz that?' said a less unfriendly chap in a sleeveless shirt.

'You get lots of boats and there are races and things,' said a round sort of girl. Lucky, had he been around, might have suggested a race on ducks' backs. But he must have thought up new clever lines by now.

Our group broke up quickly. The rounded girl had no further interest in muscled chaps getting into boats to out-row one another. I moved over to the barbecue, as pleased to leave as long shirt must have been to see me go. The barbecue was by a high-ish wall, right below the gaze of two girls sitting on it, one of them Sikh, she couldn't be anything but. She wore a skirt, which on that wall was more or less eye-level height to anyone standing before her, as I was. Another of those challenges males are presented to put mind above gut.

'I teach in some colleges,' she was telling her friend, and some of us who'd gathered round. 'Been doing some seminars with business people. Really planning to set up my own consultancy.'

'Do you find a lot of the usual, you know, all family businesses?' I asked. I was painfully aware how dull this was after Lucky.

'Oh yeah, but that's also the strength. Because you can have compact management, you can save costs, be more competitive.' Her toes were right there before me. The paint had begun to chip off the nails.

'But doesn't it mean that if you do things that way your business will stay small?' We were reproducing every bit of stock wisdom on Asian businesses.

'No… well, yes. Corner shops and stuff but you have big ones also in family business. But they've got to get more professional. Can't go on and on like that.'

'But do they want to change?'

'That's the thing. There's always resistance to change. But when you tell them there are efficiency models, and that's gonna make you more productive and you're gonna get more profit, then they listen.'

'Sounds good for your consultancy.'

'Yeah, I'm getting like really good response.'

The others in the group had not joined this split-level seminar. It was not the stuff dates are made of. Soon, this group too scattered.

'You picked your spot,' the chap in the long shirt said to me as I ran into him again around the barbecue. Now that no girls were around him, he was a lot friendlier. He lowered his voice. 'Look what I got.' He produced a piece of paper with six female names, with phone numbers. 'Guess I'm sorted for the next six months,' he said. I was having a listless day.

I guessed that everyone thought everyone else was having a great time, but that no one really was. Even Lucky was now eating quietly. Through that afternoon we had wandered from group to group. You clocked some reasonable minutes saying just anything, then asked for a number. Things – if anything – would happen only later depending on who you called, whether it was a real number, and what you heard back.

The groups had almost all broken up, because organised flirtation hadn't worked. Over barbecued chicken, pulao rice and salad we were now divided into male groups separate from female groups. The chaps were drinking beer; the girls were engrossed in conversations, presumably about how vague the guys were.

It wasn't much later that the boat chap began to get the first Asian singles off the island. Everyone wanted to go; we needed to lose ourselves in London again.

www.summersdale.com